KENFIG FOLK:

KENFIG IN TUDOR AND STUART TIMES
1485 – 1699

Barrie Griffiths

THE KENFIG SOCIETY

Published in the UK by the Kenfig Society
3 Cwm Cadno, Margam, Wales SA13 2TP, UK

Registered Charity no. 702279

Website: www.kenfigsociety.org

ISBN: 978-0-9567701-2-7

A CIP catalogue record for this book is available from the British Library

Printed by ImprintDigital.net, Exeter EX5 5HY, UK

Barrie Griffiths 1942—2009

Barrie was that best of amateur historians — enthusiastic, knowledgeable yet sceptical about what he read and saw. As a retired police-sergeant it came naturally to him to question the evidence, especially the earlier writings of those prone to mystic fantasy. Nor would Barrie accept the confident assertions of 'experts'; only by weighing the evidence would he come to a conclusion.

In this series of books Barrie lays out the depth of his knowledge and understanding of Kenfig over a period of 700 years, from the coming of the Anglo-Normans to the mid-Victorian era. Barrie, a colourful character in life, wanted to explain Kenfig and its story, but also what was going on in the wider world and how it affected the town. He does this in his own inimitable style, and has produced a highly readable account, which should please both the general reader and the historical specialist alike.

Never one to shrink from controversy, after 20 years or more of close examination and reflection on the evidence, Barrie was able to form many new insights and interpretations, which will be found in these pages. But this is not done in a rancorous way — reasonableness and good humour shine out from Barrie's account of the life of Kenfig Folk.

A Note from the editing committee:

We have retained Barrie's text in full, but in this volume some major changes to the structure have been made. Barrie was justifiably proud of his original research into 'the folk of Kenfig', and included in the text much detail about individuals and their houses. Much can be learned by studying individual histories, but it was felt that this obscured the bigger picture – what was going on in the Borough of Kenfig, and how national events like the Reformation, Catholic recusancy and the rise of Non-conformism impacted locally.

So the first half of this book is the story of Kenfig, how it survived in the times of the Tudor and Stuart dynasties of England. The people and their homes have not been forgotten – their stories can be found in the second half of the book. If you are a family historian with an interest in the area, this will have obvious uses. But even those with a general interest in the area will find it rewarding to 'dip in' to these family stories.

Of course any changes, especially ones as drastic as outlined above would normally be checked and approved by the author. I hope we have held true to the spirit of Barrie's history, and produced something which might appeal more to the general reader.

In editing this volume I have been greatly helped by an ad-hoc committee consisting of Terry Robbins, Ken Williams, Brian James, Keith & Janis Edger and Dennis Jones. But as the person in overall charge mine is the final responsibility for any errors or omissions.

In producing this series of books we have been assisted by a generous donation from the Trustees of Kenfig Corporation Trust.

Conall Boyle,
Publications Secretary,
Kenfig Society
June 2012

The front cover shows 'The Prince of Wales', now an Inn, but originally built as the Town Hall for the re-constituted Borough of Kenfig.

Contents

MAPS

INTRODUCTION to Part Two

It is said that history is "made by people", but far too often 'the people' in publications relating to our past are drawn from the ranks of the 'great and good' whilst those who formed the massed ranks of the 'general public' of their day barely rate a mention.

Archaeologists have already woken up to this fact so that today, excavations in Egypt are as likely to be concerned with the homes and tombs of the people who built the pyramids as the palaces and temples of the pharaohs buried in them. Those who delve into the past by means of documentary material have been quick to follow suit. The problem here however is that whereas members of the rich and titled class often left diaries and letters revealing something about themselves and the times in which they lived, few if any such records exist created by those from society's lower echelons. The vast majority would never have dreamed of setting pen to paper to record something about their lives (even if they were literate), so as a class they consequently remain largely unheard.

I particularly became aware of this when, between 1978 and 1988 I carried out a project on the former manors of Stormy and Horgrove to the south of Cefn Cribwr. It also slowly dawned upon me that I had the means to discover more about the ordinary citizens of the area beyond the fact that they lived, had children, and died. The method of research I used then (and subsequently employed at Kenfig) is one I call 'the Hoover system'. I collected and noted every scrap of material I came across relating to the area no matter how insignificant or trivial it might seem at the time. To collate these I then created two indexes, one for the farms, cottages and land; the other for the people who lived and worked there.

My patience brought its own reward as slowly but surely individuals gradually emerged from the dry lists of names on manorial rentals, suit rolls, and such like. At Stormy and Horgrove I eventually collected information on some 750 people. Although in most cases this was quite brief and not particularly informative, in others I was able to chart something of the ups and downs of their lives as they battled their way through their slice of history.

That research was never published other than in the form of a manuscript lodged with the local library (We hope to publish Barrie Griffith's *Sturmi's Land* at some future date (ed.)). Nevertheless I thoroughly enjoyed the experience, and when the Kenfig Society came into being I cheerfully launched into a similar project aimed at telling the story of the people of Kenfig Borough. It wasn't long however before I realised that I now had a far larger tiger by the tail! Information literally poured in to the extent that I was initially overwhelmed by the sheer mass of material.

It was clear that the old pen-and-paper approach which had served so well at Stormy was now totally inadequate, so very reluctantly I entered the computer age. Initially it was a battered and (as it subsequently transpired) totally inadequate second-hand Amstrad. That was followed by an 'all singing; all dancing' Compaq which loyally struggles with unfamiliar spelling and grammar – my own as well as that from documentary sources! Fifteen years on, and the well-spring of Kenfig material shows no sign of drying up, but common sense dictates that the time has now come to put what I have collected to work.

It was not practicable when following the story of the First Borough of Kenfig (Part I in this series of Kenfig Folk) to see the life of the Borough through the lives of its people. In this account of the subsequent history of Kenfig, after the abandonment in about 1439 A.D., I have tried, as far as possible, to do so, though there are certain limitations. In fact there is practically no documentary material covering the end of the medieval town and the century that followed (1439-1600). What we know is only what can be surmised from a few written references and the evidence on the ground.

From the early Tudor period onward, documents steadily become more plentiful, and my trusted computer now holds files on over 3,500 individuals who had some connection with the district during the three centuries between 1550 and 1850. The increasing interest in family history has had many benefits for local historians, not least greater accessibility to source material. Over the years I have been happy to offer assistance to any family historians whose ancestors have a Kenfig connection, and in return they have kindly responded by making available any material they themselves have collected. This generosity has sometimes saved me hours of work and provided me with information I would probably never have discovered by myself. Even quite small snippets, tendered almost apologetically, have proved invaluable in building up the 'bigger picture'. It seemed only right therefore that I should include a special section that lists these family historians by name. To them and to the staff of the various libraries and record offices that I have haunted over the years, I offer my sincere thanks. Hopefully I have done justice to the material they provided.

One characteristic of this history that should perhaps be pointed out is that the spellings of personal names has been standardised. I make no apologies for doing this for, even in their own lifetimes, the spelling of the names of the Kenfig folk often changed several times — it was simply a question of how they, or the writer, thought it should be spelled. Jean Evans, who claims descent from the Yorwerths, has listed over a dozen different variation of that name, and despite the fact that they all derive from the same stock, some of these variation were adopted by descendants and thus become permanent. I have taken the version 'Yorwerth' and stuck with it, and similarly 'Katherine' is always 'Catherine'; 'Anne' remains as 'Ann', and so on. Hopefully this will make individuals easier to trace, particularly for any who are descended from Kenfig families.

As in the main introduction to this work, my thanks are again due to Jean Evans and Dennis Jones for the many hours they have spent poring over my work, correcting my mistakes and offering suggestions.

In the centuries covered by Parts II to V there is little or nothing that happened here in Kenfig that was of any importance in the larger scheme of things. For we ordinary mortals, births, marriages and deaths are the greatest and most important events in our lives, but normally of little consequence in the history of our nation. This book will, I hope, reduce history to the scale of a normal human life — occasionally dramatic, sometimes humorous, but normally a simple story of ordinary folk coping with life's highs and lows as best they can.

As I stroll amongst the memorials in the old graveyard at Mawdlam church I mentally nod a greeting to those I know from my research. High and low; hero or villain; they all now lie peacefully in their graves, and it is to them — the past inhabitants of Kenfig Borough — that the next four sections of this history is dedicated.

Barrie Griffiths

Chapter 1

Starting Again: the 'second' Borough of Kenfig

As related at the end of Part I, in or about the year 1439 the first Borough of Kenfig came to an end. Driven out by an irresistible combination of advancing sand dunes and persistent flooding, the burgesses finally abandoned their town on the south bank of the Kenfig and sought temporary refuge on adjoining high ground both north and south of the river.

Because of the lack of documents relating to this period, the circumstances of this momentous event and its aftermath are largely conjectural, but it seems that by 1460 what might fairly be termed 'The Second Borough of Kenfig' had come into being.

The original borough, as set out in the town's charter of 1397, occupied a relatively small piece of territory. Only whilst they lived within those boundaries could the Kenfig burgesses claim the status and privileges of their Borough and Charter. When they abandoned their town and settled in the land beyond its boundaries they effectively disenfranchised themselves. By extending the borders to include these adjoining areas it meant that they could still claim the rights due to them as "in-dwelling burgesses".

The expansion of the new and enlarged Borough into the Abbey lands north of the river was therefore mirrored by a similar expansion on the south. This included not only the land about Heol Las but also the common at Kenfig Down that had been given to the town by charter in 1397. All this land was the property of Henry Beauchamp, Earl of Warwick. He was the Lord of the manor of Kenfig the boundaries of which at this time roughly coincided with those of the parish of Pyle & Kenfig today

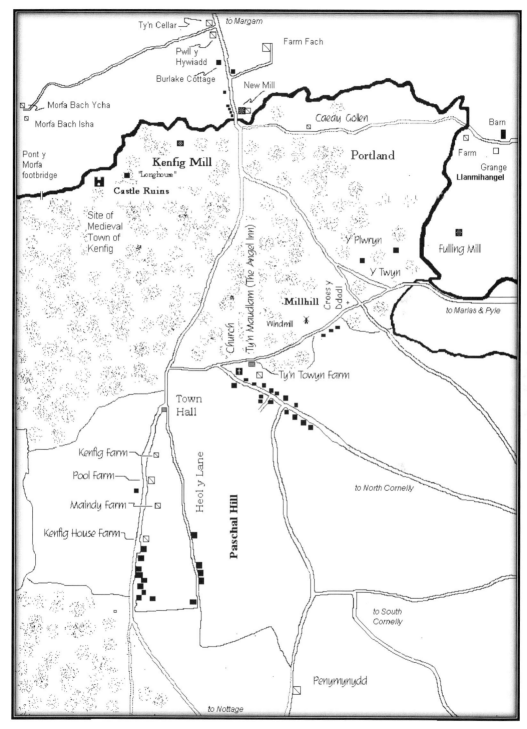

KENFIG IN THE 16TH AND 17TH CENTURIES

There were however, within this parish two existing centres of population that could not be included. These were the villages of North and South Cornelly, each of which was the centre of a small manor held by lords who paid a fixed rent to the Lord of Kenfig. Starting on the river Kenfig at a point near Pyle Church, the new borough boundary therefore headed more or less due south skirting the western borders of these two manors, then turned westwards along a boundary it shared with Neath Abbey's Grange at Sker on Kenfig Common to reach the sea. The western boundary was the seashore itself.

We have already seen (in Kenfig Folk Part I, p.172) how Richard Neville became earl of Warwick when Henry Beauchamp died aged 21. Having secured possession of Glamorgan (and thereby Kenfig) in 1449 he seems to have determined upon moving the site of the Borough from Kenfig up to Pyle. It may be that travellers along the Portway (the main highway from Cardiff to Neath) had already started pioneering a 'short cut' from Stormy Down to Margam along the route of the present A48 even before the abandonment of 'old' Kenfig to the sands. Once the town was abandoned there was little reason for them to follow the old road known as Heol-y-Sheet to North Cornelly, Kenfig, and onwards to Water Street.

Documentary evidence shows that fords had existed in earlier centuries at Pyle across both the Afon Fach on the south and the Kenfig river to the north, but it seems that there was never a direct connection between the two, nor is any settlement ever mentioned there. Once a connection between these fords was made (whether informally through travellers seeking to shorten their journey or by direct order of the Earl) the slightly longer coastal route via Mawdlam inevitably fell out of favour. What the Earl now proposed to do was to re-establish a new town of Kenfig on this highway between the fords. It would be centred on the crossroads where it met an ancient track-way from Mawdlam to Cefn Cribwr ridge. That this was his plan is, like much else in this opening chapter, just conjecture, but is nevertheless supported by certain facts.

As a first step, a new parish church was built here to replace the one abandoned to the sand at Kenfig. This was the church dedicated to St James, as had been its predecessor in the old town. Much of the fabric from the abandoned building was re-used in its construction. This has long been recognised from the 'up-side-down' walls of Pyle church where, contrary to common practice, the stones in the upper portion are considerably larger than those in the lower courses. The logical explanation for this is that it was the result of the masons who built it re-using materials from the old church as it arrived on site. Since the walls of the former parish church would have been dismantled from the top down, the smaller stones arrived first.

It has always been my understanding that the blocked-up priest's door in the south wall and the fine timber roof of the nave were also items that had been salvaged from the former church. In 2004, however, I had occasion to visit the church in the company of Dr Max Horton of Bristol University. He is an archaeologist specialising in the Medieval Period. Although greatly struck by the beauty of the church roof he nevertheless had no hesitation in describing it as fairly standard 15th century work. Whilst the priest's door itself could be of an earlier design he pointed out that the decoration over the arch matched those of the two adjoining windows and the east window. Again this is characteristic 15th century work. Although the materials incorporated into the south wall had clearly been re-used from an earlier building he found no architectural details which contradict the documentary reference that describes Pyle church as "newly built" in 1485.

The location of Pyle church itself is yet another clue to the intentions at the time it was erected. It stands on the road to Margam. It predates the erection of the inn known as *The Tap* (*Ye Olde Wine House*) which was built in the 1680s. So the church was for many years the only building on the main highway north of the crossroads. This oddity seems to be explained by the fact that in most medieval **towns** which have a key road junction at their heart they normally reserved the adjoining land for the market place, town hall, and premises owned by the leading burgesses. In a **village** on the other hand, the church was the most important building, and it usually occupied a key location at its heart.

ST. JAMES CHURCH, PYLE: NORTH FACE

NOTE THE SMALL STONES AT THE BOTTOM,

LARGER AT THE TOP

It is a matter of record that the Kenfig burgesses bitterly opposed the construction of this parish church. They subsequently accorded this status to the Church within their own borders at Mawdlam. As I explained in Part I of *Kenfig Folk*, this was the former chapel of the Malederia (leper hospice). It was in ruins when the burgesses created the adjoining village in the 15th century, but had been rebuilt as their own centre of worship by 1541. The Burgesses maintained this view for centuries, but it now seems that their dislike of the one at Pyle actually stemmed initially from their opposition to the proposed re-location of their borough, of which the construction of a new church dedicated to St James was supposed to have been the first step.

Although some sort of community was established at Pyle almost immediately, the proposed new borough and town never materialised. The most obvious explanation for this is that Earl Richard Neville, having changed sides once too often during the Wars of the Roses, was captured and executed at the battle of Barnet in 1471. His Earldom was then conferred upon the future King Richard III who would have had little time for the aspirations of his predecessor's supporters amongst whom the prospective burgesses of Pyle were probably included. High in the darkness of the nave at Pyle church the date '*1471*' has been carefully carved on one of the wooden shields that decorate the roof. Was this perhaps a clandestine tribute by the people of Pyle to their dead benefactor for whom they could not erect a more obvious memorial, since he was now officially a traitor?

With the death of the Earl any plans for the transfer of the borough came to an abrupt halt. Even so, the inhabitants of Pyle continued to foster hopes for many years that they might be supported. In this they were of course opposed by the Kenfig burgesses. In 1485 the "townsfolk of Pyle" (as they insisted on calling themselves) obtained a ruling from a Consistory court held at Margam ordering the burgesses to accept Pyle as their parish church (PM 2812; Gray, 1909: 94). This was a mere three weeks before the battle of Bosworth which ushered in the Welsh Tudor dynasty, but it was not until the 1660s however that the Pyle inhabitants finally ceased appointing Aletasters at their manorial court in preparation for the great day that never arrived.

Improbable as it might seem the anonymous burgesses who successfully campaigned against the removal of their borough to Pyle probably spoke English as their first language even though they would, most likely, also have been fluent in Welsh. The original medieval town had been an Anglo-Norman transplant into a district. The native population from the hill territory to the north may have been welcome to visit for the purpose of trade, but they were not allowed to settle and live. For centuries therefore English continued to be the every-day language here, and in the 16th and early 17th centuries many of the fields and landscape features were still known by English names. There is a rather absurd claim that Pyle originates from the Welsh word '*Pil*' (Fortress). As there are no traces of such a structure in the vicinity of the village, this it is claimed, must be a reference to the prehistoric camp at Pencastell on Cefn Cribwr ridge – over a mile distant and in a different parish! One might as well relate it to Kenfig castle which is about the same distance but in the opposite direction! Pyle is an English word meaning 'mansion' or 'big house' and perhaps originated as a derogatory term applied by the Kenfig burgesses to the detested new parish church.

Two other, and potentially more significant fieldnames are Winters Hill and Winters Mead in Mawdlam. In earliest records "Winters" is rendered "Whitters", an old English word that apparently means something like 'Belonging to the Community'. This is particularly relevant as both fields were originally very large enclosures containing acre plots belonging to various individuals some of which still survived in the rump of Winters Hill as late as 1847. There seems to have been no settlement at Mawdlam prior to the abandonment of Kenfig town, so these fields would most likely have been created and the names given by the burgesses who settled here as refugees making it their new home.

The survival of English as the language of the local population so late in their history also begs the question as to how many of those we can subsequently identify in the 17th century were descendants of burgesses who had lived and worked in the old town. Some, like the Aylwards could trace such a connection back to the early 13th century, but again the lack of material relating to the century that immediately follows the end of the first borough hampers any positive conclusions being drawn.

As the 16th century progressed and surviving documents become more numerous the picture they paint is of a community where Welsh was rapidly supplanting English as the first language, and even people with English surnames were adopting the native practice of using patronyms. How far this latter process had advanced in the preceding years is impossible to say, but in theory a case can be made that many of the 'Welsh' families then resident in the Borough were actually descendants of English burgesses who had made a permanent transition to the use of native patronyms The occurrence of the names such as Thomas ap Thomas Gethin, Maurice Meurig, Gwenllian Montfort and Iowan Wilkyn in 1450 (D/D Ty) shows that Welsh names were already current in Kenfig at this early period.

Another tantalising suggestion showing a certain continuity between the people of the medieval town and this second Borough of Kenfig is found in the manner some of these later burgesses made their living. Almost the entire population of the second borough were engaged in agriculture either as farmers or labourers, but there were also quite a few craftsmen. These included (as might be expected) carpenters, masons, smiths and suchlike but there were a small number of 'cordwainers' or shoemakers as well. Since leatherworking had been a major industry in the medieval borough it would be nice to see this as continuing that tradition, but since they only become apparent in the records of the latter part of the 17th century, we can only conjecture that such continuity may indeed have existed.

Chapter 2

The Lay of Kenfig's Lands

If I had to describe the landscape of the borough to a stranger I would ask them to picture a coastal plain largely covered by sand and marsh in which the lake at Kenfig Pool is the most conspicuous feature. Behind this plain and parallel to the coast lies a low ridge broken only where the river Kenfig has forced a tortuous path through it to the sea. South of the river this ridge was formerly known as 'Paschal Hill'.

North of the river this ridge is separated from more high ground further east by a shallow valley, which follows the line of Water Street. The stream that formed it enters the Kenfig river near the castle and is now called Nant Maelwg. Formerly it was known as the Burlake (Bwrlac in Welsh) , an interesting name that combines the Old English word 'laak' (meaning water) with 'bwr' — an archaic Welsh word meaning 'stronghold'. Originally it is thought to have derived from the English word 'Borough', so I suppose an acceptable translation of the whole name would be "The Borough Stream".

On the south side of the river the main ridge (known formerly as Paschal Hill) projects a spur inland towards Llanmihangel. Today we call it Mont Mawr, but this in fact is a name of fairly modern origin and previously it was called "Windmill Hill" or, more usually, "Millhill" — the name I shall stick to in these notes.

Millhill forces the river to make a great loop around at its north-eastern end and above this it negotiates a little gorge known as The Collwyn where Llanmihangel mill is situated. On the south it is bounded by the spur of high ground upon which Marlas Farm stands. In the 13th century this was the home of the Grammas family, and for centuries afterwards the spur was known as Grammes Hill.

On the south side of Grammes Hill runs a stream called the "Afon Fach" which separates it from the 'back' slope of Paschal Hill. Again this is a name of recent origin; earlier documents always refer to it as "the Goylake". Its headwaters lie in the vicinity of Stormy and Pen-castell and it defines the southern side of Grammes Hill from its confluence with the river Kenfig upstream to the point where it is crossed by the main road through Pyle. On the opposite side of the Afon Fach there is a 'dry valley' in which stand the villages of North and South Cornelly. It runs south towards Porthcawl and divides Paschal Hill from Stormy Down.

The Early Settlements: In this area to the north and south of the river Kenfig, the refugee burgesses settled following the abandonment of their town. Since theirs was now an agricultural community, many of them lived in scattered farmhouses and labourers' cottages dotted carelessly across the map, but from the outset there were three small but identifiable communities. Along Water Street in Higher Kenfig there was a scattered ribbon development on the road to Margam. Most of the houses were towards the southern end near the bridge across the Kenfig known as New Mill Bridge (Pont Felin Newydd).

Millhill, which was on the road from Mawdlam church to Marlas, was a hamlet of perhaps six to eight cottages that had been there since at least the latter part of the 14th century; then it had been known as Millhamme. Each cottage had an acre of land attached to it, and in the mid 17th century they seem to have been considered desirable residences for some of the slightly better off in local society.

But the principal community in the area was a village that bore the name of Kenfig, but which we today know as Mawdlam. To avoid confusion I shall stick to this more modern name, though it does not occur in records until the latter part of the 17th century. Mawdlam was a ribbon development along Heol Las to the east of the church dedicated to St Mary Magdalene and its origins are something of an enigma.

Some 150 years after the abandonment of Kenfig old town, the burgesses claimed that this village and its church had been constructed by their forebears as their new home. Rees Merrick in his *Morganiae Archaiographia* (written about the year 1578) states unequivocally that "the church was newly builded upon the hill".

Thomas Wyseman in 1592 is even more specific (PM 9616).

> The burgesses hath been dryven of late tyme to buylde them selfes many new dwellynges and a new church further from the sea sand toward the lande.

Yet the church of St Mary Magdalene is specifically mentioned in a Margam charter dating from circa 1255 and south of Heol Las, particularly on Paschal Hill. The field patterns apparent on old maps strongly suggest a medieval origin. There are even some stray references to them in documents of that time.

On the face of it therefore we have two irreconcilable statements but there is, I believe, at least one plausible explanation. Recent research (see Part I, Appendix VII) suggests that Mawdlam church, together with the nearby Angel Inn, were originally elements in a medieval hospital or leper house ('malederia') known to have existed outside the Mawdlam Church boundaries of Kenfig in 1202. It was not therefore built as the heart of a small community. In this connection it is perhaps significant that the documentary reference from fifty years later talks of Heol Las leading to the chapel rather than a named village.

The agricultural development in the immediate vicinity may therefore have been in the nature of 'assarts'[1] created by some enterprising Kenfig burgesses, and later expanded as the sand encroachment began affecting their common fields inside the borough. Further developments such as the common fields at Whitter's Hill and Whitter's Mead followed when the refugee burgesses created the village. The continuance of "acre plots" within these fields is also interesting as this practice (as opposed to the more common division into strips) seems to have been used in the common fields of the first borough.

Taking the claims echoed by Merrick and Wyseman at face value, it therefore seems that the Malederia and its chapel fell into decay as Kenfig town declined. When the burgesses abandoned the medieval town and literally 'took to the high ground' in and about Mawdlam they repaired and refurbished this former chapel so that it could be the centre of their new community. One possible indication of this is the magnificent font which dominates the entrance of the church today. Several writers in the past have commented that it looks rather out of place, so much so that it seems obvious it was brought here from elsewhere. The derelict (and abandoned) church of St James is the prime candidate. As part of a former leper hospice built to serve the needs of the sick and dying the former chapel is unlikely to have required a font to baptise infants!

Once again my account has become full of 'ifs' and 'maybes', but some of the people of Kenfig from whom Merrick and Wyseman ob-

---

[1] A piece of land cleared of trees and bushes, and fitted for cultivation; a clearing.

tained their information were the descendants (perhaps even the great-grandchildren) of the burgesses that had made the move from the old town. Writing over four centuries after their day I am certainly not of a mind to challenge their claim!

Highways and Byways: Also important to our understanding of the later Borough of Kenfig are the roads and tracks that bound together its farms and small communities. Most are still in use today, but several have vanished with scarcely a trace. (see Map in Chapter 1))

In the heyday of the first borough of Kenfig, the main highway along the South Wales coast had approached it from the west along the road known as Water Street as far as Ty'n Cellar Farm. Here it veered slightly westwards to enter the town of Kenfig across the river, then continued due south to Mawdlam church and, as The Greenway (now Heol Las), it headed off in an easterly direction towards Cardiff. At some stage, and certainly by the middle of the 13th century (when a bridge is mentioned at what is now New Mill Bridge) a by-pass road was created from Ty'n Cellar. After crossing the bridge it continued as "The Cartway" (now Heol Fach) to join Heol Las at Cornelly Cross in North Cornelly. When the route through Kenfig became blocked by sand and the main road diverted through Pyle this road lost its former importance but it remained, and still remains today, the principal highway in the locality (B4283).

Although now abandoned to the sand, another road branched off this highway a little south of New Mill Bridge and ran through the dunes up onto Paschal Hill where it continues today as the one from Mawdlam to Nottage. Just west of Mawdlam church it formed a T-junction with the road from Pyle (formerly known as Heol Millhill) as it passes The Angel public house. The existence of this former junction explains the acute right-angled bend at this point that has caught out many a motorist in the past, especially when there is frost and ice about. It is actually still possible to make out the beginning of the former continuation of this road towards New Mill Bridge for a short distance from this spot until it becomes lost in the sand.

Heol Las, a relic of the former main medieval highway, joins Heol Millhill in front of the church's western end. It connected Mawdlam to Cornelly Cross and North Cornelly. Heol Broom, which leaves this road a little east of the church also gave the village a direct link with neighbouring South Cornelly and also, I suspect, with Pen-y-mynydd and the common at Kenfig Down along a now abandoned track that today exists only as a footpath.

One other former track that is probably worth mentioning started at the south end of New Mill Bridge and ran from there to the ford at Llanmihangel farm and thence to Pyle church. Some portions are still open to wheeled transport, whilst the remainder exist only as foot-paths. It was probably along this route that the materials from the de-molished church of St James at Kenfig were hauled to be recycled in the construction of its successor.

These were the little highways and byways that bound the scat-tered farms and communities of the new Borough of Kenfig to the vil-lage of Mawdlam at its heart and each other, and they figure frequently (if unspectacularly) in the story of its history that follows.

Chapter 3

The New Borough – Built from the Old

It was the continued existence of the Borough itself that gave the community an organisation not only of self-government, but something in which everyone (even non-burgesses) shared a common interest. Surprisingly perhaps it continued to function with very little change after the great upheaval following the flight from the old medieval town. The man in charge was the Portreeve, assisted by the Council.

To have any say in this organisation one had to be a burgess: in the medieval town this meant that one had to be a male over the age of 21, and owner of a burgage plot. Such plots, it will be recalled, were strips of land adjoining the main streets of Kenfig upon which stood the houses and business premises of the inhabitants. They could be bought, inherited or gifted, and once acquired the new owner presented himself before the Portreeve and the Corporation to obtain their approval.

This largely centred upon his willingness to accept the provisions of the burgesses' oath that he was required to take. The actual details for Kenfig are unknown[2] but undoubtedly involved acceptance both of the authority of the Portreeve as the chief officer of the Borough and Council and the provisions of the town's charter.

To enjoy to the full the privileges of their position, burgesses had to live inside the borough itself. Those who did not (the 'out-burgesses') earned only the right to trade within the town, and my guess is that in medieval times that they were burgesses from other Glamorgan towns who had set up a branch of their business at Kenfig.

---

[2] The Oath required from a Burgess at Cowbridge in 1610 was:
"Yee shall sweare that ye shall be true unto [our King/Queen]; ye shal be obeysante and obediente to the Maior, Baiiffes and other officers and Ministers of this Towne; the liberties, aunciante and laudable Ordenaunce and Custome thereof, shall uphoulde, mantayne and keepe to the uttermoste of your power, and this Towne keepe harmeles in all that, that in yow now is or hereafter shalbe. Ye shalbe Contributors to all maner of Charges within this Towne as Somons watches, Contributions, Taskes, Scott and lott, and all other Charges bearinge your parte in your abilitie and power as every other Freeman shall doe".

Recycling –
16th Century Style!

Once abandoned the former town of Kenfig and its castle became a quarry for those burgesses seeking to build new homes in the expanded borough. At Ty'n y Cellar Farm on Water Street the barn adjoining the house contains many such fragments of masonry such as in this light slit in the west wall. The bottom stone on the left is clearly part of an arrow slit as is the stone with the carved circular feature amidst orange algae on the opposite side. Known as an "oillet" the latter were placed at the terminals of arrow slits to improve the archer's range of vision. Both were presumably removed from the ruins of nearby Kenfig castle.

Burgesses were exempt from many of the taxes and duties imposed upon the mass of the general population at the time. They were, for example, exempt from military service; their Lord was not entitled to seize a 'heriot' — a levy from their property when they died. He could not force them to buy or sell goods as he might wish. They were in truth free men, which was a status enjoyed by even the town's lowliest citizens once they had lived within the borough for a year and a day. Inevitably there were some small alterations to this order when the new borough was created, but they were surprisingly few.

Initially it is likely that the burgesses retained possession of their ruined burgages within the old town to legitimise their position. This seems to be the significance of a curious document (D/D Ty 1) in the

3: THE NEW BOROUGH – BUILT FROM THE OLD

collection of Tythegston MSS at the Glamorgan Record office. It records the transfer, in 1450, of one such burgage from a burgess named Maurice Meurig to a Thomas ap Ievan Gethin. It is described as being in "Munkestrete" (Monk Street) between the tenements of Wenllyan Monfort and Iowan Wilkyn. No money apparently changed hands, and Maurice had himself received it as a gift from a John Marshall.

Had it not been for the fact that sand soon obliterated the ruins of many of the properties, perhaps the practice might have continued longer at Kenfig. As it was, when the dunes began marching across the site, obscuring the property boundaries, the burgesses (presumably with the connivance of their Lord at that time) developed new 'burgage plots' within the area of the enlarged borough.

Once abandoned, the former town of Kenfig and its castle became a quarry for those burgesses seeking to build new homes in the expanded borough. At Ty'n y Cellar Farm on Water Street the barn adjoining the house contains many such fragments of masonry in the west wall.

The bottom stone on the left is clearly part of an arrow slit as is the stone with the carved circular feature amidst orange algae on the opposite side. Known as an 'oillet' the latter were placed at the terminals of arrow slits to improve the archer's range of vision. Both were presumably removed from the ruins of nearby Kenfig castle.

In **Kenfig Lower** (south of the river) where the land fell directly under the jurisdiction of the Lord of Glamorgan, the former system was adapted and things continued pretty much as before — the cottages and farmhouses that the refugee burgesses built for themselves becoming the new burgages. Whilst the Lord retained about a hundred acres of land for himself ('The Demesne') the rest was freehold land and the houses and farms upon it were held at a fixed nominal rent. The occupants were free to dispose of them as and how they wished, so these houses now became the new burgage plots, and new occupants automatically became candidates for admission to the ranks of burgesses.

The basic unit seems to have been the cottage that invariably had an acre of land attached. All the dwellings in the hamlet of Millhill and several of those I have identified on Heol Las, for example, were of this type. Other burgesses created farms by buying up plots on Paschal Hill and 'assarting' or enclosing land from the manorial waste with the lord's permission. Their homes developed into farmhouses, some of which were quite substantial, but, large or small, these too enjoyed bur-gage status, and the occupants were free men.

North of the river, in Higher Kenfig, things were rather differ-ent. Here burgess status was accorded only to the tenants of farmhouses and not to the cottage dwellers of the manor who were mainly farm la-bourers. There was another very important difference too. The bur-gesses who lived here were not freemen.

The first refugee burgesses to set up a temporary camp on the high ground about Water Street probably did so expecting the tradi-tional charity of the Margam monks to help them in their distress, and no doubt this was the case. The abbot of the day, however, also saw them as a heaven-sent opportunity to aid his own community's flagging fortunes, for the monks were at this time going through a difficult pe-riod in their history.

The problem was not any hangover from the Glyndwr revolt or the damage caused to Abbey property by the floods that had helped drive the burgesses from their homes. Rather its root cause lay in a dearth of men entering the order as lay brethren to work the Abbey lands, for it was they who were backbone of the grange system.

Land in Higher Kenfig which was not 'unimproved waste' was (or had been) part of the Abbey Grange of St Michael's, or Llanmi-hangel as it came to be known. This Grange was probably already be-coming derelict, so the Abbot allowed the burgesses to create farms both from this land and on the waste, and it is these holdings that be-came the new burgage plots. They enabled them to become self-sufficient in the matter of food and earn a livelihood, rather than be-coming a drain upon the Abbey's finances.

As I explained in Part I, this generosity came with a price tag. In return for their plots the burgesses surrendered their status as free men. They became instead tenants of the Abbey paying a rent for their hold-ings and performing the customary services due to the Abbot as lord of the manor. Their corn could only be ground at his mill; they made him an annual 'gift' of poultry when required; provided men to help fetch in the harvest; and so on. Subject to the terms of their tenancy he could amend their rents as he wished, and eject them from their homes if they failed to agree. Once ejected, of course, they ceased to be burgesses and the right to that office would be taken over by their successor.

Initially, when the new arrangement was thought to be temporary, this may not have seemed to matter very much. Everything would change once the new borough was created. As time passed and the situation became permanent however, problems started to arise. Politically the Higher Kenfig burgesses were now completely at the mercy of their lord, and through them he not only had eyes and ears in the Borough council-chamber, he had the means to affect the decisions taken there as well.

Such then was the Borough of Kenfig as it entered the sixteenth century. It is at this juncture in our story that documents start to tell us something more about the people to whom it was home. This is usually nothing more than their names but just occasionally there is something more. We will meet them in increasing numbers as our story unfolds.

Chapter 4

The Mills of Kenfig[3]

At the time when the town of Kenfig was abandoned around 1439 there were four mills in the vicinity, three for grinding corn and the fourth a fulling mill for processing woollen cloth. The three corn mills have a particularly interesting story that will gradually unfurl in the succeeding chapters. In order that this can be properly appreciated it is nevertheless advisable that I include some background information about them at this early stage.

Bread is made with flour which is manufactured by grinding up the seeds of corn — wheat being the most popular form. Two thousand years ago it was milled by our ancestors in hand-operated querns — small grindstones between which the ears of corn were ground. Although the Romans in Britain are known to have used mills powered by donkeys or water-wheels to grind corn in larger quantities, the humble querns continued to be used in most households up until the arrival of the Normans. With them came the practice known as 'suit of mill'.

This was widely disliked (not to say hated) by the populace at large, but, like so many iniquitous practices, it had started life as a good idea that subsequently went wrong. Grinding corn by hand was a tedious and time-consuming practice, so access to a powered mill was much appreciated, and nobody begrudged paying a fair price for the service. Since money in the form of coin was a rare commodity millers during the medieval period traditionally charged a sixteenth of all corn brought to their mills for processing. Similarly, since the mill was built and maintained by the Lord of the manor, it was only right and proper that he too was entitled to make a small charge to cover the expense of maintenance and repair, and allow him a little profit as well.

So far, so good! The manorial lord, however, pointed out that unless all tenants of the manor made use of the facility then the mill would not be profitable either for him to build, or for the miller to oper-

---

[3] A more detailed account of the Kenfig mills was the subject of my booklet *The Five Mills of Kenfig* which was published by the Kenfig Society in 2002.

ate. When mills were few and far between it was a valid point, so an agreement was reached whereby his tenants undertook only to grind their corn at his mill. This was the iniquitous Suit of Mill which, whilst it never achieved true legal status, was rigorously imposed upon the peasantry and tenants. If charges were fair, and the miller was honest, there was little to complain about. Unfortunately (human nature being what it is!) landlords were often unscrupulous and the millers thieves, yet despite this the inhabitants could not simply take their business elsewhere. If they did they would be heavily fined in the manorial court.

Rightly or wrongly millers in general had an evil reputation during the medieval period and afterwards. The uncouth, self-serving and brutal character portrayed in Geoffrey Chaucer's *Canterbury Tales* may be a caricature, but it would have been one easily recognised by the people of the time. "In goes a bushel; out comes a peck" sneered one medieval jingle commenting on the way in which customers' corn mysteriously vanished in the dark recesses of many mills.

At Kenfig things may have been a little different. 'Suit of Mill' could not be imposed upon freemen or burgesses, so when William, Earl of Gloucester (d. 1183) provided the town with its first mill, there may only have been a handful of tenants in the manor that could actually be compelled to use it. These would not have included those living in the sub-manors of North and South Cornelly who, since their own lords never built a mill, were also free to grind as and where they pleased.

Discovering the location of this first mill at Kenfig proved something of a puzzle to the late Haydn Reynolds and myself. Haydn was one of the founders in 1989 of the Kenfig Society, and made the mills of Kenfig his particular project. I agreed to help with some of the 'book and paper' research. Although he sadly died before we completed the project we did eventually determine where, approximately, Kenfig mill would have been.

Right at the outset we realised that the Earl's mill must have stood on the left or south bank of the river Kenfig since all the land on the other side belonged to the Abbot of Margam. Similarly we anticipated that it would not be too far from the town it was designed to serve. At that point our investigation stalled. Haydn spent many fruitless hours searching the present and previous courses of the river for suitable locations, a task not made any easier by the fact that much of the land was covered by sand and a former railway marshalling yard.

It was Thomas Gray (1909) who eventually provided us with the breakthrough we needed. I had already discovered that there was a millpond attached to the mill, and water for this would obviously have been provided via a channel or leat from the river. In his book *The Buried City of Kenfig* Thomas Gray has left us a description of the old bridge at New Mill Bridge which carried Water Street across the Kenfig. Many believed it to be of Roman origin, so when the time came for it to be demolished and replaced by a new structure, Gray was on hand to see what turned up. He was interested to note that within the bridge structure, on the south or Kenfig side of the arch across the river, there had formerly been a culvert. Not knowing the location of the 'New Mill' from which the bridge takes its name, he believed it was a leat connected with this, but we now know that in fact New Mill stood on the opposite side of the river.

I also came across several references in the early 18th century to a weir on the upstream side of the bridge, sufficiently close to the structure as to apparently be considered part and parcel of it. At that point 'the penny dropped'! This weir had been intended to divert water from the river into a leat that had been carried through the bridge structure by the culvert *en route* to a millpond further downstream.

Shortly after Haydn's death contractors digging a pipeline through the dunes near the motorway viaduct at this point unearthed the remains of a stone structure. Kenfig Society members Graham John and Rennie Davies, who had been keeping an eye on the work, persuaded them to enlarge the trench sufficiently to allow a closer inspection. The depth of sand, and the crumbling ballast from the adjoining former marshalling yard made proper excavation impossible, and no dateable artefacts emerged that could be associated with the ruin.

What had been uncovered was a fragment of stone flagged floor and a wall in which clay was used as a bonding material rather than mortar. It was clearly old, and I have little doubt that it was part of the former mill.

The next mill to be built at Kenfig was another water-powered corn mill a little further upstream at Llanmihangel. The remains of this are still there today, along with some of its rusting and decaying machinery abandoned shortly before World War II. Built by the monks of

Margam to grind corn harvested on their adjoining granges it was not initially a manorial mill, though it may have accepted any 'free trade' the area had to offer in competition with Kenfig Mill.

As the monks withdrew from directly farming their own land they rented this mill out to lay tenants and its role changed, particularly after the creation of the manor of Higher Kenfig in which it stood. Suit of Mill was rigorously applied to all those burgesses and others who had made their home there and was extended to include any other

FRAGMENTS OF A BUILDING ON THE SITE OF LLANMIHANGEL FULLING MILL UNCOVERED DURING THE COURSE OF LAYING A PIPELINE IN THE 1990S.

Margam tenants in the manors of Pyle and Stormy.

Our third corn mill was a windmill. Its exact location has been lost but it stood somewhere on Mont Mawr, the old name for which was Windmill Hill or, more usually, Millhill. A "Millmotte" here in the late 14th century, an indication that it stood on a mound - a typical medieval 'post mill' in which the mill itself was built around a massive central post upon which it could be rotated so as to face the wind.

During the medieval period the land on Millhill was made up of a patchwork of plots owned by various burgesses and probably part of a common field. Erecting and operating this mill was therefore probably a piece of private enterprise on the part of a Kenfig burgess. As such it was in direct competition with Kenfig Mill for the free trade of the district, but would have been hit hard by the abandonment of the old town. Many of its former customers were those who had taken refuge in Higher Kenfig and who were now required to perform 'Suit of Mill' to Llanmihangel. Although still operational in the early Tudor period, its days were already numbered.

The fourth mill, as mentioned earlier, was a fulling or 'tucking' mill. After woollen cloth is woven it has to be cleaned to remove all dirt and grease before being dyed. This was done by soaking it in water with agents such as tallow, fuller's earth or burnt bracken and then giving it a really good pummelling. Fullers are mentioned in documents relating to the medieval town of Kenfig, and these would have done this by hand. A waterwheel at the mill powered giant hammers which performed this function mechanically, and the process pre-shrank the cloth, giving it a felted texture. The cloth was then hung out to dry on large frames thickly studded with sharp nails called tenterhooks (hence the expression 'on tenterhooks' for somebody pent up with nervous anticipation}.

Like Llanmihangel corn mill, the fulling mill was erected by the monks, and is probably the second of two mills mentioned as belonging to them here in a Papal Taxation document of 1291. By the time the monastery was dissolved it seems to have fallen derelict, but was revived and was probably back in production by the end of the 16th century.

Chapter 5

Reformation: Abbey dissolved: Granges sold

In its day St Michael's Grange (Llanmihangel) had been one of Margam Abbey's largest and most prestigious granges. Its area in 1336 was some 700 acres (modern measure) comprising arable and pasture with 55 acres of valuable meadowland. It had been home to a large staff of *conversii* or lay brethren. It was they who grew the corn that not only fed the community at the great Abbey but also the poor people of the district as well as travellers along the high road called The Portway that sought shelter within its gates.

The brethren also tended some of the Abbey's vast flock of sheep, the fleece of which found a ready market with weavers as far away as Flanders. Some the monks wove it up into cloth for their own use, and Llanmihangel was equipped with a fulling mill that stood a little further up the valley. Further upstream again, at the point where the lane from the Grange crossed the river to join the ancient highway we know as Marlas Road, was the gristmill. Powered by the river, it was here that the corn they grew, together with the harvests from other granges such as Stormy and Llangewydd was ground into flour.

Yet for all its apparent affluence by 1336 this Grange had already started to decay. A decline in religious fervour meant that fewer men were prepared to subject themselves to the rigours of life as a lay-brother. Many of those that did had ulterior motives. Far from being inspired by religious fervour they were often fugitives from justice eager to claim 'benefit of clergy'. If subsequently arrested this meant they would be tried under ecclesiastical law in which there was no death penalty.

Echoes of this unsavoury aspect of monastic life are apparent in a case involving staff from St Michael's Grange late in the 14th century. Two of its lay-brethren were brought before the Shire Court at Cardiff charged with a robbery committed on the adjoining sand dunes, and alongside them was the Grange Master who was charged with harbouring fugitives from justice. The sheriff over-ruled their attempts to claim benefit of clergy, but in the event he found there was insufficient evidence to support the charges. Nevertheless the incident illustrates a certain loss of respect for the Abbey at Margam in general and its community of lay-brothers in particular.

Eventually the Abbey realised the futility of continuing to farm its Granges in the traditional manner and the monks began letting out their land to tenants in return for rent. How much of the original 700 acres at Llanmihangel still remained within the Grange in 1528 I cannot say. As I noted in a previous chapter some of its land had probably gone to create the farms of refugee burgesses following the abandonment of the town of Kenfig circa 1439.

A 17th century document states quite categorically that one farm there known as Farm Fach had indeed been created out of former Grange land (PM 1280). It is nevertheless probably safe to say that in the dying years of the monastery, the lay tenants of the Grange and its outbuildings were probably paying rent on something between 2-300 acres of land which, in the context of the times, made it a very large farm indeed. Its size was so great in fact that most tenants chose to regard it as a small estate. They sub-let portions to local farmers and lived the life of gentlemen on the proceeds, farming little (if any) of the land themselves.

The development of most immediate concern would have been the dissolution of the monasteries by the Tudor King, Henry VIII. The last Abbot of Margam, Lewis Thomas, formally surrendered the Abbey and its extensive lands to the King's commissioners on February 27th, 1537. From that moment Llanmihangel became the property of the Crown. Meanwhile, the site of the dissolved Abbey of Margam, its church, and many of its former granges (Llanmihangel included) had been sold by the King to Sir Rees Mansel for the sum of £938. 6s. 8d.

Mansel's home lay at Penrice in the Gower, and this double change of ownership in just over three years must have been very unsettling. Equally unsettling would have been the religious changes of which the Dissolution itself was just one aspect. The people of Kenfig had been raised as a Roman Catholics, and had been taught that the Pope at Rome was God's representative on earth. This King Henry had altered with a few strokes of a quill pen, declaring himself to be the new head of the church in England and Wales.

The cult of the Virgin Mary was similarly swept aside and dismissed as 'superstitious nonsense'. At Margam, the nave of the former Abbey church was converted for use by the parishioners and the remainder sold off. But both here and at the humbler little church dedicated to St Mary Magdalene at Kenfig, the religious upheaval actually brought little outward change. Services were still conducted in Latin, and the order to destroy the images of the saints and cover the bright murals that adorned church walls was not passed by Parliament until 1546. Nevertheless, the old religious certainties had gone forever leaving committed Christians throughout Britain confused and concerned.

As a former Abbey Grange, Llanmihangel would almost certainly have been equipped with a chapel where the brethren who lived there observed the daily round of monastic services. Elsewhere the chapels of the former Margam granges seem to have quickly fallen into disuse. At Llanmihangel too, the days of its chapel were numbered. The Elizabethan historian Rice Merrick writing some forty years later, mentions that an Abbey Grange had existed here in the past and that "within it stood a chapel" implying that this was no longer the case in his day. Some fragments of window tracery incorporated into the garden wall of Llanmihangel Farm are probably all that now survives.

Chapter 6

English Law imposed on Wales

Important as the religious changes would have been, there was a second great and recent change which had also occurred Llanmihangel which also affected Kenfig. This was the introduction of the Act of Union between England and Wales in 1536. Consolidated by further Acts of Parliament, its effect was to bring the laws and administration of the Principality into line with those of its neighbour. What had been for centuries the Marcher Lordship of Glamorgan was now combined with the neighbouring Lordship of Gower to create a new County of Glamorgan. This would be administered along the lines of an English shire. Its sheriff, who had previously been answerable only to the Lord of Cardiff Castle, was now an officer of the Crown, and the former judiciary over which he had presided became part of the English Legal system. Hitherto the highest court for the residents of Kenfig had been the *Comitatus* or County Court held in the shire hall at Cardiff Castle.

This old familiar system was now swept away, and with it too went the ancient and eccentric Marcher laws that it had enforced. These were a curious mixture of English and Welsh legislation, to which had been added laws derived from customary practice or introduced at the whim of the Lord and his shire court. It did not even apply universally throughout Glamorgan: in the 'Welshries' such as Tir Iarll or the Lordship of Avan the predominately Welsh population retained the right to observe their own native laws and customs.

Kenfig Borough it will be recalled had made its own laws, and if the Portreeve and the Constable of the castle felt that a law current in Glamorgan was working to the detriment of the burgesses, they could declare it null and void within its borders. Now there was to be just one law, and it was the law of England.

Kenfig 'ordinances' were relegated to the status of local by-laws. The Welsh custom of 'gavelkind' by which a deceased's estate was partitioned amongst his sons was replaced by the rule of primogeniture favoured by the English, so that the eldest son was now the sole heir.

Although not catered for by the parliamentary legislation, this revolution in Glamorgan's administration seems to have been backed up by a major reorganisation at grass-roots level. I have noticed, for example, that it was about this time that the parishes of Laleston and Tythegston were created out of what had formerly been the parish of Newcastle. These, together with Pyle & Kenfig, Llangynwyd, Margam (the latter created from the former Abbey land) and other neighbouring parishes had been part of an administrative division called the Hundred of Kenfig for which the Constable of its castle was responsible to the Sheriff. Originally the courts that dealt with the legal and administrate business of the Hundred had undoubtedly been held at the castle. Once that fell into ruin they were probably conducted at some large house in the area. Perhaps the nave of Mawdlam church was utilised, but inns and alehouses were popular venues for such meetings, and if the present Angel Inn was operating as such at this time, then it is likely that it would have been used for this purpose.

As late as 1532 there is a record (Clark, 1910) that a man named Llewelyn ap Griffith "was hanged for felony at Kynfig". The same document also mentions that Lawrence William in his capacity as a Deputy Recorder and Clerk to the County Court had presided over another court held here at an unspecified date. This involved the trial of a man for breaking "a forbode" (binding order). For this he was liable to forfeit the sum of £3.0.1d to the King as Lord of Glamorgan, but the writer was aggrieved because Lawrence altered the charge to one of trespass. "Thereby", the writer complained, "the sum due to be forfeited by the offender was lost to the King". The account indicates, incidentally, that the jury sitting on the case numbered just six men as opposed to the 'twelve good men and true' later to became the norm.

.

Politics: Further legislation relating to the Act of Union emerged from the Parliament at London designed to give the people of Wales representation in the House of Commons. The new County of Glamorgan was to be allowed two Members, one to represent the people of the shire, the other the inhabitants of its Boroughs. Both were to be chosen by election, though of course at this time in our history the right to take part in such ballots was confined to a very small and select percentage of the population.

Election of the MP for the Shire was in the hands of the County's freeholders, who were dominated by the landed gentry. They tended to settle matters amongst themselves so that no actual election was held for this office until 1734. Not surprisingly therefore these early members invariably belonged to one or other of the leading families, and a similar situation affected the election of the MP for the Boroughs, of which Kenfig was one. Here too the gentry seem to have settled matters amicably amongst themselves up until 1734.

Nevertheless, technically the election of the Member for the Boroughs lay in the hands of the burgesses of Glamorgan, a fact that became more widely appreciated in the 17th century. In both County and Borough elections the 'Interests' of the great families of Glamorgan was the deciding factor. This 'interest' was the number of votes the major houses could command for their preferred candidate. Whilst every voter, be he a burgess or otherwise, was in principle free to vote for whom he wished, the ballot was not secret. At elections the landowners' agents would be present observing how their tenants cast their votes and were not above using bully-boy tactics to ensure that they voted as per instructions.

There were at most 58 in-dwelling Kenfig burgesses. They were free to enrol as many outsiders into their ranks as they wished. These 'out-dwelling' burgesses would enjoy none of the rights and privileges of the 'in-dwellers' save one — they could vote at the elections for their MP. The Mansel family of Margam united the whole of the Borough under their control with the purchase of the Manor of Kenfig Borough in 1668, and soon exploited the opportunities this presented. Not only could they now bring pressure to bear upon all the Borough's 'in-dwellers' to vote as directed, they could (and did) pay for people whom they could trust to be admitted as 'out-dwellers'. As contested elections became more common in the 18th century so this aspect of life in Kenfig began to assume an important element in the lives of its people.

The Language of the People: Amongst the documents in the Tythegston estate collection is a record of a 'Final Concord' at Cardiff Great Sessions in 1564 (D/D Ty 15). This formally concluded the transfer of some land at Kenfig from a John William Lawrence to Watkin Lougher who had succeeded John Turberville as lord of that manor. The property consisted of three 'messuages' or houses together with 23 acres of land. I believe that this relates to Penymynydd Farm on the eastern edge of

Kenfig Down. This farm, which grew to be one of the largest in Kenfig Lower, is later mentioned as the property of the Tythegston estate, although apart from this possible mention, its early history is obscure.

It is tempting to see John William Lawrence who sold this farm as a relation of the Lawrence William who had died at Llanmihangel in 1540 for the name 'Lawrence' was quite rare in this part of the world. At this time the Welsh custom of using patronyms (rather than surnames) was widely practised throughout the borough, though in most instances people dropped the connecting 'ap' (son of) or 'verch' (daughter of). The son of Lawrence William of Llanmihangel for example was known as John Lawrence and not John William. One of the features of this period is the transition from an area where English language and culture had predominated in the days of the old town to one which was now becoming thoroughly Welsh in outlook.

Perhaps the most dramatic demonstration of this change was the way in which families who were descended from the Anglo-Norman settlers around Kenfig had toyed with the idea of using patronyms. The family surnamed Bunz or Bunce had been burgesses of Kenfig in the early 1300s, and an Evan [ap] John Bunce is mentioned at Higher Kenfig in 1618. The Aylwards who had flourished in the area for some 400 years also provide several such examples. There was William [ap] Thomas Aylward (men 1560-71); his son Henry [ap] William [ap] Thomas Aylward (men 1592-1605); and his brother Watkin [ap] Thomas Aylward (men 1597). There are similar examples amongst the Waters family of South Cornelly. In all these cases the descendants eventually reverted to the use of standard surnames but it is interesting that so many were clearly flirting with such a radical change. It may indeed be that some of the inhabitants of this period who had Welsh names were actually descendants of Anglo-Norman families that had made a complete and permanent transfer to the use of patronyms.

We can also see another element of the increasing predominance of Welsh speech in the changes of local place names. The Cartway became "Heol Fach"; the Greenway became "Heol Las", and so on. Such alterations tend to be a slow process, but although many English place names survive at Kenfig even down to the present day, it was a change that was already well advanced by the middle of the 17th century.

Unfortunately, because the dearth of local documents for the century following the abandonment of the old town, there is too little evidence to prove these theories one way or the other. What is neverthe-less clear is that from being an area where English had been the first language, following the establishment of the Norman town in the mid 12th century, Kenfig was changing to Welsh. Perhaps the establishment of the Welsh Tudor dynasty on the throne of England stimulated local pride in one's nationality in spite of the fact that the Tudors themselves barely acknowledged this aspect of their ancestry. The Act of Union in-troduced by Henry VIII actually required all holders of public office in the Principality to be able to speak and write in English, yet the evi dence here on the ground at Kenfig suggests that speaking Welsh was now not only common, it was the fashion.

Chapter 7
The Grove Survey of Kenfig 1570

The Herbert's, Earls of Pembroke: As we have seen, the Abbots of Margam were succeeded by the Mansels as Lords of Higher Kenfig, but the reign of King Henry VIII also saw a change in the ownership of the Manor of Kenfig Borough. When the King's father, welsh-born Henry VII secured the English Crown by his victory at Bosworth in 1485, he gave the Lordship of Glamorgan (and thereby this manor) to his uncle, Jasper Tudor, the Earl of Pembroke. Jasper subsequently died without an heir, so the property reverted back to the Crown with whom it remained until 1546 when Henry VIII awarded it to a William Herbert.

Eleven years earlier this William had married Anne, the younger of the two daughters of Sir Thomas Parr, and his fortunes unexpectedly took off when, in July 1543 the King took her sister Catherine to be his sixth (and last!) wife. A Welsh family in origin, the Herberts had briefly held the title of Earls of Pembroke in the 15th century, but surrendered it for that of Huntingdon when King Edward IV wanted to bestow the title upon his son Edward. Their former adherence to the House of York did not initially enamour them to the Tudor sovereigns, and their view of William personally was scarcely advanced as a result of a scuffle he had with a Bristol tailor in 1527 which resulted in the death of the latter. Rather than face the consequences, William fled the city and after a brief return to Wales escaped to the continent. One presumes that subsequent enquiries cleared him of blame, which enabled him to return shortly before his marriage to Anne.

Amongst the gifts showered upon William by the ageing King was the dissolved nunnery at Wilton in Wiltshire, which thereafter became the family's principal residence. When Henry died in January 1547 it was Sir William who was appointed executor of his Will. In it he was bequeathed the sum of £300, and was also nominated as one of the twelve members of the Privy Council to the boy-king Edward VI. Further honours followed, and in 1551 he was created Earl of Pembroke for his part in the overthrow of the Duke of Somerset who had been the Lord Protector. He then skilfully negotiated the subsequent transfers of power, first to the Catholic Queen Mary, and then to her Protestant sister Elizabeth, retaining the confidence of both as a trusted ally, before dying at Hampton Court on 17th March 1570 (Lever, 1967).

The earliest surviving survey of the Manor of Kenfig Borough was drawn up on September 27th, 1570, probably as part of a wider enquiry by the new Earl Henry, William's son and successor, who commissioned the survey, to discover just how much his estate was worth. Such surveys were instituted from time to time for just this purpose and consequently tend to be a recitation of the rents due to the lord from his tenants; what duties they owed; and what rights the lord possessed within their boundaries. Taken at face value they are pretty dry fare, but with a little knowledge the facts they relate, they can also tell us quite a bit about the area at the time.

Usually such surveys were conducted by the steward of the manor with the aid of a questionnaire supplied by the Lord's estate office. These questions he put to a jury of tenants, noting their answers, and then drawing up the final document setting out their reply. This particular survey was carried out by a panel of five Commissioners headed by Sir George Penruddock and including a 'Robert Grove, gent'. The latter was probably the clerk who did the actual work, so fittingly, the manuscript in the Margam collection is known as 'The Grove Survey of Kenfigge'. (PM 9616)

The survey itself indicates that the agricultural land within the manor was divided: between the demesne lands that belonged specifically to the lord of the manor; freehold property owned by various individuals; and the lands of the sub-manors. These last are listed as South Cornelly for which William Herbert junior paid fourteen shillings and North Cornelly for which Christopher Turberville paid 9s 10d.

The vexed question of the status of Pyle manor was apparently ignored. It had probably been created out of the original manor of Kenfig as part of the preparations for the re-establishment of the new borough of Kenfig by Richard Neville. The Mansels of Margam, who then held this Manor, owed no rent or other duty to the Lord of Kenfig.

WILLIAM HERBERT, 1ST EARL OF PEMBROKE   HENRY HERBERT, 2ND EARL

(BOTH PORTRAITS FROM NATIONAL MUSEUM OF WALES, CARDIFF)

Given the antagonism between the Kenfig and Pyle, perhaps the jurors wanted to suggest by implication that it didn't exist and was really still part and parcel of their manor! The survey also implies that the former Neath Abbey Grange at Sker (another Turberville property) also came under Kenfig at this time, though no rent is indicated and it is not included in later returns.

The demesne land, which was the personal property of the lord, was rented out as a whole to a William Jenkin by virtue of a lease dating from the time of King Henry VII. The survey claims that, in all, it covered 268 acres, ninety-eight of which were rented out to various subtenants in parcels varying from two to thirty-two acres.

Later documents indicate that the area of enclosed demesne lands was just over 100 acres, so it would seem that the survey jurors had included some of the un-enclosed land or waste within the manor in their total. This would not presumably have included the burgesses' common about the old town or the one on Kenfig Down (which they referred to as Newton's Down) for which they paid a fixed annual rent of ten shillings. Indeed they specifically state in answer to one question that this Down was land "they, their ancestors and predecessors have had, occupied and enjoyed ... time out of mind, whereof the memory of man hath not runne to the contrary".

Other than the demesne, all remaining enclosed land within the lower borough was owned by freeholders, but because of the manner in which these are listed in the survey it is impossible to be certain of the actual quantity of land involved. Those for whom the area of their holding is indicated held over 160 acres, but the individual amount held by each person is not shown in every case, and some of those omitted may have been quite large. Richard Thomas, for example, is simply listed as the free tenant of Marlas Farm which later documents indicate encompassed eighty acres or more.

This same Richard is also shown as the owner of "15 ruined burgages in the old town of Kenfeage". What his motive was in acquiring these properties that were largely covered by sand I cannot hope to guess, for the survey indicates quite clearly that the dunes were still on the move. In answer to one question the jurors presented in evidence:

a place of a winde mill with certain lands, about one acre by
estimacion, now in ruine and decay . by reason of the sea sands.

This was the mill that had given its name to Mill Hill — the ridge extending from Mawdlam church towards Llanmihangel. The ridge was also the location of a small hamlet adjoining the road to Pyle that was also now presumably coming under threat from the dunes.

In later surveys, the manor's freeholders are divided into three distinct groups — the Free Tenants; the Paschal Hill Holders, and those who owed only a nominal rent. In this survey, the last named group is entirely absent, with land belonging to the first two groups only being shown. They were totally free of any manorial obligations in respect of their property other than Suit of Court.

In the case of the Free Tenants their duties were limited to attendance at the Courts Leet held twice a year, whilst Paschal Hill Holders were required to also put in an appearance at their lord's monthly Courts Baron. Other than the fixed annual rent from these freeholders, the only other payment required from any of them was a penny from a new tenant to the Borough Recorder for entering his name on the manor roll. This Suit Roll listing those owing 'suit of Court' was kept in the custody of the Portreeve or his Serjeant, and the survey describes how they were responsible for producing it annually at the first manorial court held after Michaelmas. Written on parchment it was an important document, and they received two shillings a year for ensuring its safe custody.

Chapter 8

A Land Grab at the Rugge (Cefn Cribwr) 1572

The enclosure of part of the burgesses' common at The Rugge, Cefn Cribwr, was an important (not to say controversial) step taken by the burgesses under their Portreeve Evan Griffith. Further information about this is contained in an important Borough Ordinance or bye law (No 52) (Gray, 1909: 167-71) that came into force in 1572. At this time in history enclosure of common land by landlords throughout Britain was causing considerable unrest. Consequently the burgesses went to great lengths to justify in writing their reasons for making this move, showing that it had been executed in proper form and only after due deliberation.

The idea for this enclosure was almost certainly the Portreeve's. The details given reveal that in one respect the manner in which the Borough was governed had significantly altered since the medieval period. Back in the 14th century, the Kenfig Portreeves were advised by a town council composed of Aldermen, but there are no clues to indicate how the latter were appointed to their office. In the early 19th century (when the rank of 'Alderman' was merely honorary) the title was awarded to those burgesses who had previously held the office of Portreeve, and perhaps this had always been the case. What can be said with certainty however is that by 1572 Aldermen had no automatic right to a place on the council.

The bye-law describes how the Portreeve, Evan Griffith, with the consent of his fellow burgesses, called twelve of their number before him. Then of these he selected eight "of the most substantial, honest and best freeholders" as his councillors. Whether this was the first occasion this method was adopted is a matter of conjecture, but certainly from this time onwards it was these panels of Eight Elected Burgesses that formed the town council.

I presume that the twelve from whom the Portreeve picked his councillors had been nominated by the burgesses themselves, but it is important to realise that the eight chosen by Evan were his Council for that meeting and that meeting only. If another Council was required, even a day later, then the same procedure would be gone through again, and a completely different eight could be selected. Also, those chosen were councillors in the purest sense of the word, for they possessed no real power. Their function was merely to advise the Portreeve, and any decisions made were his and his alone. From this we can therefore reasonably surmise that the initiative for enclosing Waun Cimla (as it became known) must have stemmed from Evan himself.

In the preamble to the bylaw empowering them to enclose part of the Common, the burgesses explained that they were taking this step so as to replace land they had lost to the sand. Even after five centuries something of their anger and frustration over their impotence in the face of the advancing dunes can still be heard in the text:

> Wee...have consulted ourselves together, and agreed within ourselves for because wee have, and yett doe yearly, fall in arrearages and losses … by reason of the overthrow, blowing and choaking up of sand in drowning of our town and church with a number of acres of free land, besides all the burgages of ground within the said libertys except for three[4].

The Cefn Cribwr common (which the burgesses referred to as The Rugge) lay on the north side of the western end of Cefn Cribwr ridge, extending from the road at the summit down to the stream at its foot. At the eastern end its limit was marked by a bank and ditch called Clawdd y Ffin, and in the west it extended to Prince Road and a boundary with the lands of Pwllygath Farm beyond.

The portion that the burgesses proposed enclosing lay along the centre of this slope, the un-enclosed land above and below continuing as common land. The enclosure itself became known as Waun Cimla — a name that is now often (incorrectly) applied to the whole. With the passage of time the portion between Waun Cimla and the river became overgrown and developed into scrub woodland which the burgesses referred to as 'Tir Garw' (rough land).

Having made the initial enclosure, the burgesses then parcelled up the interior, creating 29 three-acre plots which they distributed

---

[4] The Borough referred to here is quite evidently the one contained within the former medieval boundaries, and the three burgages were probably properties like Glasfryn and Y Twyn at its eastern end. The Grove survey made two years earlier makes no mention of any burgages still occupied within the town walls, nor of the 'longhouse' on the site of the castle which was evidently built later.

amongst themselves. Since there were more burgesses than plots (though it is interesting that this number, 29, is exactly one-half of 58, which was the maximum possible number of burgesses), the Ordinance claims they were distributed by "chances by lotts". This suggests a kind of 'prize draw', but if so then it was undoubtedly rigged, for the first nine names 'out of the hat' were those of the Portreeve and the Eight Elected Burgesses who had passed the by-law!

Each plot-holder was responsible for enclosing his or her land and subsequently maintaining its fences, including the perimeter boundary where it bordered their property. The plot remained the property of their descendants so long as they were resident within the Borough and could be inherited, sold or leased out, though only to another burgess. In a subsequent Ordinance (No.53) the burgesses allowed that widows of burgesses could inherit these plots unless their eldest son (being a sworn burgess) chose to claim it. Once a plot fell vacant it reverted to the Corporation who would then reallocate it to another burgess who was prepared to pay the entry fee of one pound per acre (Ordinance No. 56), and no burgess could hold more than a single plot.

So what did the burgesses use these lands for? There, I'm afraid, I have come up against a virtually blank wall. These plots are invariably referred to in the borough minutes as "parcels of hay", but this phrase is not quite what it seems. Formerly a 'hay' or 'haye' was simply an enclosed piece of land, which indeed these were. Such evidence as exists indicates that the burgesses were free to utilise their plots as they wished. The only two references that I can discover specifying the sort of uses to which they were put, show that in one case the holder was growing timber, and in the other had created a coal mine! Neither instance is presumably typical!

There was, however, just one small problem with this enclosure — the burgesses had 'forgotten' to ask the permission of the Lord of the Manor! As commoners they had certain rights on the surface of the land but, like it or lump it, the Earl was undoubtedly the actual owner. Maybe they hoped that their appropriation of his rights would not be noticed, but if so they reckoned without human nature being what it is.

Those who had been allocated plots were no doubt highly delighted with their windfall, but those who missed out in the 'lucky prize draw' were understandably less so. In 1582 there were fourteen of them (giving a total number of 43 burgesses at this time), and they were becoming increasingly vociferous, arguing that it would be but a small thing for some more of the common to be enclosed, so that they too, could have plots of land. In the end they 'blew the whistle' on their fellow burgesses by taking their complaint to the Earl of Pembroke himself.

At this point in 1582 a character named Thomas Wyseman enters our story for the first time. Wyseman was a surveyor employed by the Earl, probably based at Cardiff Castle. He was the one that the Earl had sent to investigate this and other problems in the district. This, of course, exposed the true extent of the Burgesses' cupidity. Rather surprisingly however he tended to take their part, suggesting to his master that in return for the burgesses paying a rent (9d per acre) on the land they had illegally enclosed, the Earl should pardon the offence (Bute MSS M 15/1) and allow the rest of the burgesses to "take the lyke quantity of the said waste ... suitable in proportion as the others have". He pointed out that other landlords with wastes adjoining this common, including Mr Gamage of Coity, and had already enclosed them. He went on to suggest that (subject to the rent due from the plot-holders at Waun Cimla) the common be given to the burgess "and their sonnes burgesses for ever".

There was too, he suggested, another possible benefit in return for such leniency towards the burgesses in that they could thereby be persuaded to grant or release to the Earl

> a warren upon the comon, p'cell of the said borrough wherein they claim ... a free comon called The Sands wch lieth between the said Borrough and the sea.

This, quite frankly, I find amazing! There had been a warren belonging to the Lords of Kenfig in the coastal dunes as far back as the 14th century! The Earl owned the land, so why should he need the consent of those who only enjoyed common rights upon it? Later in Kenfig's history we know that the rabbits here were a considerable nuisance; perhaps this was also the case in 1582. Maybe Wyseman was attempting to silence the opposition by forcing the burgesses to acknowledge the status quo and accept with good grace the nuisance it caused.

Either way the point is academic for, after the inimitable fashion of the Pembrokes, Wyseman's report seems to have been shelved and no further action taken. The burgesses were never required to pay rent on their plots of hay; the fourteen burgesses never received permission to make themselves enclosures of their own; and the whole thing sank into oblivion — so far forgotten in fact that in 1639 the burgesses again obtained permission from the then Earl of Pembroke to extend their enclosures at Waun Cimla (PM 9623) though again they never seem to have taken up the option. The Borough had not, however, seen the last of Thomas Wyseman!

Chapter 9

The Catholic Threat from Spain

In 1578, and with war against Spain in the offing, a review was made of the sort of force that could be put into the field locally should the enemy attempt a landing on the shores of Britain. A certificate (Higgins, 1968: 25) submitted in respect of the Hundred of Newcastle (of which Kenfig was part) states that there were in all about sixty men able to bear arms, though only fifty of them owned any sort of equipment. In the main these were swords and daggers (an eloquent testimony to the violence of the times) though some also had helmets and corslets. Between them they could muster 17 muskets and 14 longbows. More alarmingly just ten men (four of them mounted) had received any military training though these, it was claimed, could be available at an hour's notice.

The Spanish invasion of 1588 was attempted via the English Channel and their great Armada was defeated at sea, so our local gallants had no opportunity to demonstrate any of the fighting skills they may have possessed. Their only participation in the conflict would have been to man the beacon on Stormy Down which they would have lit when those across the channel in Devon proclaimed the invasion fleet's arrival in English waters. Nevertheless, this war with Spain was to touch the lives of many ordinary people at Kenfig both then and for a long time afterwards.

Following Henry VIII's break with Rome, religion in England and Wales had veered wildly between Protestantism (under the boy-king Edward VI) and a return to orthodox Roman Catholicism under his half-sister Mary. Religion mixed with politics is a heady brew and whichever side was in control utilised their political clout in an attempt to eradicate the 'heretical' beliefs of the other. Difficult as it is perhaps for us to understand today, each faction saw itself as the guardian of the true religion, whilst all other beliefs were inspired by the devil — perversions of the truth designed to ensnare the gullible and the ignorant in society. They saw themselves, therefore, as fighting for more than just the lives of their fellow citizens; their struggle was aimed at saving their immortal souls from hell and eternal damnation. Consequently all parties saw this conflict of beliefs as just another aspect of the age-old battle of good against evil, Satan, and all his works; an unremitting struggle in which one used any and every weapon that came to hand.

It was because of these very real and firmly held beliefs that a religion, in which love of mankind is at the very core, tore itself apart. Every sect and group claimed to posses the knowledge of the 'true way' revealed by Christ and saw others as misguided at best, or instruments of the devil at worst.

In a desperate effort to prevent the country itself being torn apart over this issue, Queen Elizabeth and her advisors forced through legislation in the teeth of strong opposition to introduce a 'middle way' for the official religion of England and Wales in 1559. The Queen remained the head of this new Anglican Church. The liturgy attempted to tread a delicate path between the extreme views of Roman Catholics and the Puritans. Although Protestant, the new church retained a structure and an administration that would have been familiar to the laity of medieval times. On most of the purely religious issues that divided the two sides it left some room in its services to accommodate an individual's personal beliefs, and by such methods it was hoped that it would become acceptable to the mass of the population. In this the new Anglican Church was largely successful. It might have been even more so had not events turned it into just another pawn in the political infighting of the day.

Many compromises had been made to get the Acts of Supremacy and Uniformity through Parliament, and in doing so the Queen had been obliged to remove laws directed specifically against Roman Catholics which had originally been included. It was not that she objected to their religious beliefs but rather, like her father, she did not want a Pope in Rome interfering in the government of her nation. Many of the Catholic clergy appointed in Queen Mary's reign fled abroad rather than accept these new reforms. Once there they began to actively engage in plotting to overthrow the government. Their objectives are starkly outlined in a statement by Morris Clynnog the exiled former bishop-elect of Bangor in North Wales.

He declared that he would rather see his countrymen "attain eternal blessedness under a foreign lord than to be cast into the nethermost hell"(Mayer, 1915: 241). Under pressure from such extremists, the Pope duly excommunicated Elizabeth in 1570, thereby relieving her Catholic subjects of any allegiance they owed her.

Despite this provocation, the government's initial response was

SKER HOUSE – *SKETCH BY LESLIE EVANS*

surprisingly moderate — an Act passed the following year merely made it high treason to import or publish any document originating with the Papacy. Nevertheless tension continued to rise. Queen Mary's former husband, King Phillip of Spain, saw himself as the champion of the Roman church, something that (in view of the Papal excommunication) coincided rather nicely with his own plans for the invasion of England. In the event it appears that most Catholics in England and Wales had no problem in squaring their religion with loyalty to the Crown. The authorities had no way of knowing if this was the case or not. Faced with an alliance between Phillip of Spain and the Papacy, they regarded the priests who slipped surreptitiously into this country as spies, servicing a fifth column of native Catholics eager for an opportunity to overthrow

the government. New laws were therefore passed imposing harsh pen-
alties upon Roman Catholics ('recusants') and their priests alike.

These events far beyond Kenfig and district began to have an
effect here in 1587 (the year before the Spanish Armada set sail) with the
prosecution of recusants in the adjoining parish of Margam. Nor did
this persecution end with the English victory. If anything it intensified.
By 1590 people in Pyle, Kenfig and Cornelly were amongst those being
arrested and imprisoned for their faith.

The "Recusancy Rolls" for Glamorgan are lists of people prosecuted for their adherence to the Roman Catholic faith, and for our purposes in this history cover the years 1587 to 1611 (Pugh, 1954: 52-61). In
the main, though, those listed are probably the 'obvious suspects' —
people who came to the notice of the authorities simply through their
refusal to attend the services of the Anglican Church. Many others undoubtedly avoided prosecution by attending such services, sitting
through what they considered a meaningless 'mumbo-jumbo', and then
continuing to worship in their own way. Occasionally, they too may
have been detected and prosecuted, but many more probably escaped
the notice of the authorities altogether.

Debate over the value of the recusancy rolls has gone on for
many years. Taken at face value, outbreaks of recusancy in many areas
seem to flare up, die down, then rise again. In the Kenfig district, for
example, there are persistent prosecutions from 1590 through to 1596;
after that there is a lull before things flare up yet again in 1605 (the year
of the Gunpowder Plot). Does this reflect the activities of a fugitive
priest in the area; or just that officials were concentrating their efforts
here during those periods? Together with the knowledge that many
cautious individuals probably escaped detection altogether, this tends
to throw doubt upon their value as an indicator of the true extent of
popular adherence to 'the old religion'.

Nevertheless, it seems that there was indeed a strong Roman
Catholic community within the parishes of Margam and Pyle & Kenfig,
for there is other evidence beyond the basic information contained in
the rolls. The ruined Capel Mair on the hillside behind Margam Abbey
was known locally as 'Capel y Papishod' (The Papist Chapel). Popular
belief held that it was used for such clandestine services. Then there is a
mention in the records of the Carmarthen Assize of a Catholic mass being celebrated in 1583 at the site of another such ruined chapel attached

to a former Grange in what is today the town of Port Talbot. The service was conducted by none other than Morris Clynnog himself, and over 160 people were said to have been present.

In recent years 'priest holes' have also been uncovered at two local houses. These were places where priests could be concealed should the authorities execute a raid upon these dwellings. The one at Ty Maen in South Cornelly was a small cramped space behind a false wall in an upstairs bedroom. A similarly cramped hiding place has been discovered alongside the living-room fireplace at Ballas cottage on Heol Sheet during recent renovations.

Events a century later suggest very strongly that another such hiding place also formerly existed at Sker House. Sker was the property of Jenkin Turberville of Penllyn, and the house we see today is more or less the one he created out of the former monastic Grange. Jenkin actually lived here for a time after 1561 when he married and his father, Christopher, settled the property upon him and his wife. When Christopher died shortly after 1575, the house continued to be the home of several lesser members of the family, and was undoubtedly the local centre for Roman Catholic dissent. Its great hall was the ideal venue for clandestine services, and its isolated location meant that a watcher in the upper stories could give ample warning of approaching strangers.

The Turbervilles of Glamorgan, of whom the Penllyn branch were the most important, were staunch Roman Catholics and over forty people of that name are listed in the Glamorgan recusancy rolls. From 1590 to 1596 Lewis Turberville (Jenkin's brother?) and his wife Mary are regularly listed, having been arrested either at Kenfig or Cornelly where they would have lived at Hall which the family also owned. Sker at this time was apparently in the hands of James Turberville who is also listed regularly from 1590 to 1611, initially with his wife Mary, and later with his daughter Alice. Almost invariably members of the Began family who resided mainly in the Cornelly area, are included with them.

I only regret that the lack of records covering this period means I am unable to say a great deal about these local people who suffered for their faith at this time. As seems to have been generally the case throughout the country, those arrested considered themselves to be loyal subjects of the Crown and wanted nothing to do with King Phillip and his planned invasions. Yet they were reviled as "malignants and traitors", imprisoned, fined, and even tortured just for worshipping

Christ in their own way. Although I do not share their religious persuasion, I cannot but help but feel considerably sympathy for the sufferings and sacrifices they made.

Chapter 10

Wyseman's survey 1592

The burgesses of Kenfig were, as a body, a hugely secretive group of individuals. As our story unfolds in subsequent chapters, we will see numerous instances of how, faced with a direct question from an outsider concerning their organisation, they almost invariably attempted to prevaricate. Sometimes they were merely (as the modern saying is) "economical with the truth"; on others they simply told out-and-out lies!

In part, this furtiveness was an inheritance from their forebears. In the medieval town it was written into the Ordinances (which in part served as their constitution) that

> It is ordained that noe burgess, chencer nor inhabitant of the said town doe not say against the royalties and libertys of the same, nor of the charter (No. 31).

> Noe burgess shall discover the councell of his brethren burgesses (No. 36).

Against such a background of secrecy, even amongst themselves, it is scarcely surprising that burgesses were reluctant to divulge their doings to outsiders, and every burgess would have been aware of these provisions. Although many of their byelaws were merely archaic relics of the first town, later records show that they nevertheless regularly met together "to establish & confirm our ancient laudable ordinances according to the custom".

A very early example of this secrecy occurs in 1592 when the Earl of Pembroke's surveyor, Thomas Wyseman, returned to Kenfig in relation to an on-going dispute between the burgesses and Jenkin Turberville of Sker. Wyseman's draft of his final report (PM 9616) is perhaps one of the most interesting and informative documents relating to Kenfig. It traces the history of the dispute right back to 1397 when Kenfig Down (the area now largely covered by the Pyle & Kenfig Golf Club course) was given to the medieval town by Thomas Le Despenser as a common.

He did this to compensate the burgesses for the amount of common land they had already lost to sand encroachment, but some time later he or his successors revised this original gift and gave a third of the down nearest Neath Abbey's Grange at Sker to its Abbot. At the same time he imposed freehold rents on the two occupants — five shillings on the Abbot; ten shillings on the burgesses.

Shortly after the dissolution of Neath Abbey, the Turbervilles of Penllyn secured ownership of the former Grange at Sker, and in 1561 Christopher Turberville installed his eldest son Jenkin there on the occasion of the latter's marriage. Although Jenkin and his new wife lived at the house, the majority of the land was let to Watkin Lougher of Tythegston who, sometime prior to 1571 obtained permission from Jenkin and his father to enclose part of Kenfig Down. The resultant 'New Close', however, extended into the Borough's part of the common to such an extent that it enclosed some three acres of their property.

The burgesses advised the steward of the Earl of Pembroke accordingly, and awaited results. When no action was taken they reported the matter again, and again, and again! They also spoke to Thomas Wyseman about it when he arrived in 1582 to report on their illegal enclosures at The Rugge (Waun Cimla). In fact they asked him to request the Earl of Pembroke for permission to fence part of their boundary with Sker, presumably to physically prevent Turberville from taking any more of their land. Like everything else in that report however their petition seems to have been quietly shelved and forgotten.

Kenfig Dunes: Not until twenty-one years had elapsed from their original complaint did the burgesses' persistent nagging at last achieve results, and Thomas Wyseman was despatched to report on the matter. In part, the Earl's indifference seems to have been that of the absentee landlord concerning a relatively minor matter in an obscure corner of his widespread estates. At the same time he may have felt that this was something over which the burgesses ought to take action for themselves, and if so then in fairness he had a point. The ten shillings rent they paid annually was a fixed amount that could not be varied, and in practice the burgesses were the owners of their two thirds of the common. Whilst technically ownership was vested in the Earl, he could not sell, dispose of, or develop it — those rights rested with the Corporation.

The boundary of the common was not the same as that between the two manors; Sker's portion actually lay within the manor of Kenfig Borough. The original document relating to the division was still extant in Wyseman's day, and either he saw it amongst the archives at Cardiff Castle, or the burgesses showed him their copy. This they would have expected him to ask to see, but what must have raised a few eyebrows was his demand to also view the borough charters setting out their boundaries. These they duly produced, but when the surveyor then asked them to recite the boundary as it currently existed, consternation set in!

KENFIG POOL AND THE FORMER DEMESNE LANDS

It is apparent from their ordinance relating to the enclosure of Waun Cimla that the burgesses of the day were fully aware that their borough had originally been much smaller than it was in 1592. As set out in their charter of 1397 (which they had gladly produced for Wyseman's inspection) it was simply confined to an area about the castle between Mawdlam and Kenfig River. They possessed in fact no charters relating to the enlarged boundary of the borough they now occupied; one of the reasons why, I believe, was that the expansion was originally intended only as a temporary arrangement. Wyseman's request now brought this deficiency to the fore, and with it came the awful realisation that they had no legal document with which to oppose any future possible claims concerning the true extent of their territory from either the Earls of Pembroke, the Mansels of Margam, or anyone else.

Wyseman does not name any of the burgesses who formed part of the delegation that met him to settle this dispute, but according to Leslie Evans (1960) the Portreeve in 1592 was a John Evan, probably the son of Evan Griffith whom we met earlier. Old Evan himself was actually still alive, although now an old man in his late sixties or early seventies; it is very likely that he was one of the witnesses from whom Wyseman took evidence in the course of his enquiry.

Presumably it was John Evan in his capacity as Portreeve, that came up with a none-too-cunning plan aimed at concealing from Wyseman the fact that the boundaries of the 1397 charter in front of him actually bore no relation whatsoever to the those in being at this time.

Since the borough boundaries were not an issue in this dispute, it rather seems to me that in noting these details, Wyseman was only 'going through the motions' to show his employer the diligence with which he had investigated the dispute. Consequently he probably wasn't taking too much notice of what was said on this point, which is perhaps why he failed to detect John Evan's rather unsubtle subterfuge.

To cover the obvious discrepancies between their boundary marks and those mentioned in the charter, John Evan simply re-located two of the latter and incorporated them into his description of the existing ones. He also 'neglected' to mention that the present boundary crossed the river Kenfig to include Higher Kenfig on the northern side. This would immediately have given the game away since the charter in front of Wyseman stated quite baldly that the river itself had been the northern boundary in 1397. Despite this, the description of the boundary is of considerable value to us today. Only one other detailed recitation of it made in 1661 survives from these early centuries (Gray, 1909: 240-). Despite the presence of the two interlopers in the 1592 description, the two agree very closely with each other, and Wyseman's description (PM 9616) is therefore worth including in full.

> The southe syde is from The Botehaven adioyning to the Seavern Sea alonge by lang[side a] p'cell of the buyldings of the grange or ffarme [of] the Skarre. And from thence along[side the]southesyde of certen bounds, p'cell of th[e] sayde grange or ffarme callyd Goutesfur[long] unto the waye

or lane leadynge to Newton Notasshe, unto a hepe of stones there.

Unfortunately the edge of the original document has worn away leaving gaps (indicated by brackets), but these do not unduly affect the interpretation. The name 'Botehaven' (Boat Haven) is interesting. My first thought was that, as we know the boundary commenced at Sker Point, this was an example of Elizabethan black humour for so many fine ships have made their last and final landfall on those treacherous rocks.

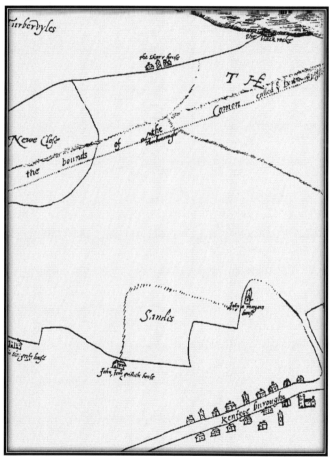

A PORTION OF THE WYSEMAN MAP.

THE HILLOCK CALLED THORBOROUGH IS THE TRIANGLE ON THE BOUNDARY BELOW SKER HOUSE WITH A MEAR STONE INDICATED ADJOINING IT ON THE LEFT (THE OTHER IS OFF THE PICTURE ON THE OTHER SIDE OF NEW CLOSE)

On Wyseman's map the location is called "The Black Rocks" and maps from the latter days of the borough indicate that the boundary started at an inlet in the heart of Sker Point known today as Pwll y Dyfan. This is a large pool with a sandy beach actually inside the rocks that form the reef, and is connected to the open sea by a narrow, almost ruler-straight cleft through them.

This undoubtedly is the 'Botehaven' of Wyseman's account, and it would just be possible, with favourable wind, tide and weather, for a small boat to slip in and out of this inlet. My next thought was why should anyone want to use it for this purpose when there are plenty of open beaches nearby where such a craft could be stored, simply by dragging them up above the high tide level? Is this perhaps a clue to the manner in which fugitive Roman Catholic priests slipped in and out of nearby Sker House undetected? Without local knowledge nobody would ever suspect that a small boat was sailing in and out of their midst next to this fearsome reef with its evil reputation as a graveyard of shipping!

The later 1661 account merely states that the boundary started at the sea and makes no mention of Goutesfurlong (The Furlong Gutter) simply stating that it skirted the end of the medieval barn at Sker known as Ty yr Ychen. By this time the "hepe of stones" on the road to Nottage had been replaced by a marker stone, though I hasten to add that this is not the one adjoining the gate of the track that until recently led to the house. This was spotted lying in the adjoining field by 'Albie' Evans, a local man with an interest in history. Realising that it was not of local material he deduced that it was presumably a former 'standing stone' and prevailed upon the farmer not to break it up, but to rescue and re-erect it at its present location.

John Evan, the Portreeve, on behalf of the burgesses, then gave his own interpretation of the next portion of the boundary from the cairn alongside the highway: -

> Then yt tornythe eastwards to a crosse callyd Crosse Green, & from thens to Howlotesford, & from thens to Taddelcrosse.

The corresponding account from the 1661 record confirms it; that since Wyseman's day the various twists and turns of the boundary here had been better delineated with marker stones. From one in 'Y Kae Issha' field (at the rear of the Pyle & Kenfig Golf Clubhouse) it ran to another stone on the south part of Heol y Broom, and from there to "a stone lyeing at Groes y gryn". This last is the 'Crosse Green' of Wyseman's account, and the crossroads we now call Cornelly Cross in North Cornelly.

From this point the two accounts differ. The 1661 boundary is described as running from Croes y Green to another stone lyeing in Kae Pwll y Kyffylau, and from that stone on the eastern side of Marlas House unto a cross called Croes Jenkin.

This is the same portion described in Wyseman's account, but here the standing stone on Marlas road (still known as Croes Seinkyn to this day) is called 'Taddelcrosse', a name plucked directly from the charter of 1397. The same is true of 'Howlotesford' which (given the topography of the location) must have been the point on the Afon Fach stream where it was formerly crossed by a lane known locally as Lon y Cariadon. This used to run through the fields from near Marlas Farm to the Hall in North Cornelly. The 1397 charter however indicates quite clearly that 'Howlotesford' was located on the river Kenfig, and is almost certainly the one adjoining Llanmihangel Farm.

The real 'Taddelcrosse' in its modern guise of 'Croes y Ddadl' still exists, as a Sutton stone base that formerly supported a wooden cross. It still lies almost hidden by sand and vegetation near the crossroads in the dunes between Marlas and Mawdlam.

Having made this statement John Evan and his burgesses must have silently prayed that Wyseman would not take it into his head to inspect the boundary himself! As it turned out, and as the investigation into the boundary of the common progressed they undoubtedly began to regret using this ploy which ultimately backfired. Their account of the boundary continues:

> The north syde thens comyth to a meade called Shocoke, nowe the possessyons of Thomas Mansell esquire; ffrom thens to the Morfa dyche; from thens to Halfewayestone; from thens to Grenewall, and so to the sea. And so alonges'd the sea syde, all the weste side thereof.

The description makes no mention of the fact that this boundary was actually north of the river Kenfig, though in fairness the same is true of the one made in 1661. By then the turn in the boundary at "Shocoke" (Shock-oak — an oak tree damaged by lightening) had been marked by a cross erected at "Kae Garw", and there is no mention of the Morfa Ditch. Instead it continued directly to "a stone by Notch Coarton" on the road from Margam to Kenfig which is presumably identical with the "Halfway Stone" mentioned in 1661.

Until the 1990s it was thought that this was a reference to the Pumpeius Stone near Eglwys Nunnydd. But a workman making a trench here uncovered what was undoubtedly the original Halfway Stone a few yards further south. This was a lot smaller, and engraved with a curious design of three adjoining crosses enclosed by squares. It is believed that originally it was part of a larger Christian monument dating from the Dark Ages from which this portion was cut and put to a more mundane use. When this marker was erected in the 15th century, the Pumpeius Stone would have been lying flat on the ground (it was later raised to a standing position by the Elizabethan historian Rice Merrick), so the latter would not have been suitable as a boundary marker at that time.

As to the remainder of the boundary, the two accounts agree, except that the later one makes no mention of the Greenwall which is nevertheless referred to in other documents of the time. So the burgesses managed to fool Thomas Wyseman that their existing boundary was the same as it had always been. But then, to again quote a modern idiom, 'it all went pear shaped'!

Eight years earlier Evan Griffith, the Portreeve, had apparently been able to confuse the status of the Earl's warren in the dunes sufficiently for Wyseman to believe that the Burgesses had a point regarding the status of the land given to the burgesses on Kenfig Down. But now that he had the charter of 1397 in front of him, he was able to point out that it specifically omitted the dune land nearest to the sea which the Lord had retained for himself as a rabbit warren.

The burgesses might have been able to make a convincing case if they had been able to point out that the borough boundary had been enlarged to include this land subsequent to the original charter. As they had already effectively denied any such alteration had ever been made, they could now only bite their tongues and say nothing!

It got worse. Their claim to the common land between Kenfig Down and the River Kenfig that they called "The Sands" at the time of Wyseman's 1584 enquiry, rested on the fact that the northern boundary was given as the demesne lands of the Earl. This, so they claimed, was Castle Meadow in the vicinity of the castle ruins, but Wyseman spotted that a block of demesne land occupied the land between Kenfig Pool and the road to Nottage. Logically, he pointed out, this would have been the land referred to since it lay immediately north (and closer to) the acknowledged southern boundary with Sker. Furthermore the document dividing the Down between the burgesses and the Abbot of

Neath had allocated him one third of the land, and the burgesses the remaining two thirds. Had their claim been true, then the Abbot's third would actually have been larger than the area of Sker Grange!

The burgesses were now in a flat spin, but there was even worse to come concerning certain rights they claimed in respect of Kenfig Pool. This, Wyseman pointed out, lay between the demesne and the rabbit warren so was part of the "lordes demesne or waste" rather than "the burgesys comon, beyinge not reppossed ['included'] in their chartre". This last he considered conclusive evidence, since, he added, any special rights enjoyed there by their predecessors would undoubtedly have been recorded in that document.

To realise the seriousness of this situation it has to be remembered that almost all the burgesses, even those living in cottages, kept at least one cow, and that other than the pool or the river there was hardly any other standing water in the area. The inhabitants of both Kenfig and Mawdlam relied on wells from which to draw water for domestic use. Fine for humans, but a cow drinks something like seventeen gallons of water a day! At several locations in the vicinity I have noted overgrown remains of former dew-ponds dug by farmers in an attempt to provide an additional water supply for their cattle, but most surely took their stock down to the pool once or twice a day for water.

So the burgesses duly reaped what they themselves had sown! The 1397 charter and the 1661 survey with its (true) recitation of their boundaries are carefully preserved amongst the treasured borough archives, but not so the copy of Wyseman's report. We know that they received a copy, because, strange to say, they preserved a version of his accompanying map that is now in the National Library at Aberystwyth. The latter, however, does not show the borough boundary, and one suspects that the 'loss' of the report with its incriminating evidence may not have been entirely accidental!

It may be too, that following this experience they also agreed to mutually 'forget' about the variation in the size of the borough, and to stand or fall by those outlined in the 1397 charter. Certainly the fact that the earlier first Borough was smaller is never again alluded to in their records and everyone seems to have come to accept that the boundaries then were the same as those when the borough was abolished in 1886. Only in recent times has the discrepancy been realised and the burgesses' fraud exposed.

Thanks to Wyseman's good nature the watering of cattle at Kenfig Pool did not subsequently become an issue. In fact in his report he
highlighted the lack of standing water in the district and specifically
suggested to the Earl that the tenants of Sker in particular be allowed to
bring their herds through the borough-common to drink there. So in the
end the burgesses got away with it, but it had been a near run thing!

The Turbervilles: They are often referred to as 'The Turbulent Turbervilles', and none were more deserving of that title than the Jenkin
Turberville with whom the burgesses found themselves in conflict over
his alleged encroachment on their common. Glamorgan during the
Elizabethan era was a violent, unruly place with a corrupt and unprin-
cipled legal system: Jenkin stands out as one of its most notorious citizens.

He was a member of one of the oldest Glamorgan families,
claiming descent from Pagan de Turberville of Coity who, if he was not
a contemporary of Robert FitzHamon, certainly arrived here not long
after the latter's conquest of the former Welsh kingdom. Their principal
seat at Coity passed out of the hands of the family in the fourteenth century, but other 'cadet' branches continued elsewhere throughout the
county. The one at Penllyn near Cowbridge was probably the most important of these, and the one to which Jenkin himself belonged. On his
marriage to Margaret Lougher in 1561 his father, Christopher, gave the
newly-weds the house and manor of Sker as their new home, and they
lived here until sometime after 1575, moving to Penllyn when Jenkin
inherited the family estates. It was about this time that he built the
house we see here today, created from the more modest monastic
Grange building he had inherited.

Throughout his life Jenkin and trouble walked hand in hand,
and in his 1956 book *Sker House* local historian Leslie Evans catalogued
just some of the many unsavoury incidents that punctuated his life.
During his time at Sker, in 1568, he and his cronies, the Carnes of
Ewenny Priory raised a small army and attacked the home of a John
Thomas at Brocastle near Crack Hill. When arrested for his part in the
affair Jenkin resisted violently, and was subsequently rescued by some
of his followers. So far as is known he was never in fact prosecuted for
his part in the affair, as those who formed the judiciary in Glamorgan
were often either members of his family or friends. Thomas Carne, the

instigator of the attack upon Brocastle, actually held the office of High Sheriff on three occasions between 1561 and 1580.

Seven years later Jenkin, together with members of the Lougher and Stradling families, accompanied by a mob of some one hundred armed retainers, descended on the annual fair held at Ewenny and caused total mayhem. John Kemys the Under-Steward for the Manor of Ogmore and his officers, who were responsible for policing the event, attempted to intervene. They were, he later deposed, "so pitifully hurt with shot arrows, beaten, maymed, and evil entreated that a great number of them did hardly escape with their lives". If the authorities did indeed succeed in calling Jenkin to account for this affray, then it had little impact. The following year he was almost certainly a member of a mob of Turbervilles and their supporters who fought a running battle through the streets of Cowbridge with the Bassets of Beaupre and their adherents.

Perhaps the most shocking example of the impotence or unwillingness of the authorities to curb the violence of Jenkin and his contemporaries is mentioned in the Acts of the Privy Council for 1591-2. Servants in the employ of Jenkin and Carne were arrested for the murder of a Lewis Rosser of Welsh St Donats, and it was strongly suspected at the time that in committing this crime they had merely been carrying out their employers' wishes. The culprits, having successfully escaped from custody, surrendered themselves back to the authorities convinced that they would escape conviction as the High Sheriff of the day was related to their masters.

Jenkin Turberville's Ploy: It was in the light of incidents such as these that Jenkin was implicated in the appropriation of three acres of the burgess's land pales into insignificance, but it is clearly obvious why the Corporation were so keen to get the Earl of Pembroke on their side. When Thomas Wyseman arrived at Kenfig they accompanied him to the location of New Close where he had arranged with Turberville to hold a site meeting to view the disputed boundary. When they arrived, there was no sign of the latter.

Having waited a reasonable amount of time for Jenkin or his representatives to arrive, Wyseman took such evidence as the burgesses produced which hinged upon the location of a hillock called "Thorborough" or "Tormel". This done he released them and their witnesses and

remained awaiting the arrival of Turberville or for some message to indicate why he had been detained.

The object of his vigil was probably comfortably ensconced in
Sker House, and we can imagine him sitting in an upstairs room sip-
ping wine and watching the proceedings on the border of his property
with some amusement. Eventually, however, Wyseman's stubborn refusal to simply pack up and go home brought its own reward. We can
only conjecture what Turberville's ploy was, but had Wyseman left he
could have claimed that he had been unavoidably detained and arrived
to discover that the meeting had finished and everyone gone home. As
the hours ticked by, however, this excuse became increasingly unten-
able. What explanation could he then offer for his failure to send a mes-
senger to notify Wyseman of his indisposition?

Six hours after the original time set for the meeting Jenkin and
his supporters finally made their way across the dunes to where Wyseman was still patiently awaiting them. The charade was now almost
played out, but Turberville led the surveyor to a location well inside the
borders of the borough's common. This, he declared, was the true location of Thorborough Hill. Hence all of the enclosure known as New
Close was therefore well within his bounds. Wyseman was not impressed. What Turberville showed him, he tells us, was not "one other
hill, but a good level parcel of ground" nor was he disposed to accept
Turberville's argument that "all the same was called Thorborough with
there many hills together". In fact, he had already collected indisputable
proof that the location of the hillock was where the burgesses claimed it
to be.

Wyseman's Judgement: I can't help liking old Thomas Wyseman. His report is a fair and masterly summing up of the grounds for the dispute,
and as indicated earlier, he had considerable compassion for the parties
involved. He was also no fool, and his wanderings about the dunes
whilst awaiting Turberville's arrival had not been aimless. During the
course of them he located two old 'mear stones' — boundary markers
erected sometime in the past. One lay on the eastern side of the hillock
the burgesses had identified as Thorborough, the other between New
Close and the Kenfig to Nottage road.

Both parties in the dispute agreed on the point at which the
boundary touched the coast and that it had run inland to a pool along-

side the road known as 'Goutesfurlong'. Wyseman had determined that these two fixed points, the two mear stones, and the hill identified by the burgesses all lay in a straight line beyond which the northern edge of New Close clearly protruded. It was game, set and match to the Corporation!

Faced with such incontrovertible evidence, Turberville appeared to cave in. Wyseman then suggested that the proper way to bring this dispute to a formal conclusion would be by a joint commission that would appoint an independent jury of parishioners to hear the evidence and give a verdict. "To w'ch the said Jenkyn Turbervyle (being thereunto advised by his friends then present ...) appointed and praid the said Thomas Wyseman to be a means that his L[ordship] maye like thereof, and assent thereunto".

But, somehow or other, the cunning old fox escaped his just deserts yet again! Take a walk through this part of the dunes today and there, just as is indicated on Wyseman's map accompanying his report, lies the disputed enclosure known as New Close, its boundary *still* projecting well into the Borough common.

Jenkin's violent and unruly existence was, however, now approaching its end, though it was not to come about in a manner one would wish even for their worst enemy. He and his wife, like almost all members of the Turberville family, were staunch Roman Catholics, and although they had formally 'submitted' in 1587, they continued to practice their faith in secret. In 1596 the authorities obtained information that they were harbouring Roman Catholic priests at Penllyn Castle, including the notorious Bishop-elect Morris Clynnog. A raid upon the castle produced the necessary evidence (but not the priests), and Jenkin and his two oldest sons were arrested and sent to the Tower of London. Here they would all have been tortured unmercifully to extract information concerning the present whereabouts of the priests and the organisation of clandestine Catholic worship in Glamorgan. Although eventually released, Jenkin's death followed almost immediately afterwards, so this vicious and unscrupulous man actually ended his life as a martyr for his faith.

The Wyseman Map: Now housed at the National Library of Wales, the map of Kenfig that Thomas Wyseman made to accompany his report is an interesting and valuable artefact from the Borough's past. At the same time it is important to realise that the (modern) description of it as 'A Map of Kenfig Borough' is in fact misleading.

For a start, it does not extend to the eastern boundary, nor does it show Higher Kenfig which lay north of the river. As we have seen, this last may well have been simply because Wyseman had been kept in ignorance about its very existence. At the same time, all he was actually interested in portraying was the area of common land that was the subject of the dispute, and only this element of the map is accurate. Elsewhere he simply indicated other features such as the castle and the village of Mawdlam ("Kenfege buroughe") that are mentioned in his report. Several important features that can be shown to have existed at this time beyond the boundary of Kenfig Down are not therefore shown. Whilst Wyseman showed the continuation of Heol Kenfig (the road to Nottage) from the Down through the sandhills to New Mill Bridge for example, he includes neither the road from that bridge to North Cornelly nor the one along Heol Millhill and its associated hamlet. Similarly we cannot place too much reliance upon his representation of any elements within this peripheral area of the map — the tower is shown at the wrong end of Mawdlam church for a start! So whilst the map indicates seventeen houses strung along Heol Las to form the village of Kenfig (alias Mawdlam), and whilst there are indications that this representation may indeed be fairly accurate, it is, at best, only an indication of its general form.

The Earl of Pembroke versus the Mansels of Margam: Jenkin Turberville was not the only one attempting to gain land at the expense of the burgesses' common. At about the same time the New Close affair was reaching its climax, in 1592 the burgesses' landlord, the Earl of Pembroke, was also getting embroiled in a similar dispute with Sir Edward Mansel of Margam (fl 1521-1585). Theirs was a wide ranging dispute covering alleged infractions at Avan and Llangynwyd as well as Kenfig, but it is tempting to see the belated and tardy action taken by the Earl against Turberville as an attempt to secure the support of the burgesses in this particular dispute. If any legal proceedings followed the initial skirmishing, then the evidence of the burgesses relating to these complaints affecting their borough would be crucial. Pembroke's despatch of Wyseman to sort out the vexed question of the encroachment on Kenfig Down may therefore have been taken in a spirit of 'you scratch my back, and I'll scratch yours'.

Unfortunately, the only details we have concerning this disagreement is a draft of Mansel's initial response to the allegations, which is undated (Clark, 1910). Having itemised the Earl's allegations in one column, he then set out his own response to each alongside. The notes are therefore very brief, and we do not know the eventual outcome of the matter.

Seven complaints in all were made against Mansel relating to his actions at Kenfig, two of which he flatly denied. To the accusation that he had 'abridged' (enclosed) part of Kenfig Common he stated quite baldly "I have never abbridged any bounds, nor ever enclosed one fote of comon of mine owne or other mens". He also denied that he (or more likely his tenants) had ever taken any "conies upon ye sands betwene the borough and ye sea", adding that he had never ever claimed such right on this land. This was the strip of land immediately adjoining the coast, which was the Earl's rabbit warren, so the latter had, in effect, accused Mansel of poaching.

Against a similar allegation, that Mansel had been illegally fishing in Kenfig Pool, the latter defended his actions by claiming the right to do so by "prescription". By this he meant that he had an ancient right to fish those waters, perhaps claiming it as a successor to the abbots of Margam. If so then he may have been on rather dangerous ground. In his archives at Margam he would have been in possession of a document (PM 231) dated 1365 regarding the prosecution of various parties by the Abbot of Margam for illegal fishing in Avan River and Kenfig Pool. What he might not have been so keen for others to see was another document in this collection regarding the subsequent proceedings at Kenfig church (PM 232). In it the charge relating to Kenfig Pool is not mentioned, suggesting that it was never proceeded with. Whilst other documents clearly indicate the Abbot enjoyed fishing rights in the river, none so far as I am aware relate to the pool. In fact these 14th century documents are the earliest known mention of it. The defence put forward by the accused challenged the monastic claim to own the fishing rights at Kenfig and Avan. Faced with the lack of documentary material to back his claim in respect of the pool, it seems the Abbot withdrew this charge before it came to court. The case would have been tried at the Court for the Hundred of Kenfig, and it is interesting to note that at this time this was held in the church rather than the castle. At the hearing the Abbot had no trouble proving that the right of fishery in the Avan River had been granted to the monks by previous Lords of Glamorgan, and the men were duly convicted. If Sir Edward was therefore relying on these documents to prove his "right of prescription", his case rested on a very flimsy foundation.

Two of the other allegations relate to alleged illegal enclosures. Forty acres of marshland at Kenfig was, Mansel claimed, part of his estate that had descended to him, and that the "three quarters of an acre of medowe grownde by ye castell" that he had enclosed lay on his side of the river, which formed their joint boundary at this point.

Wyseman in his report makes a confusing reference (the document is also damaged at this point) to "a medwe then near adioynynge to the said castle callyd the Lord's Meade". This implies that it belonged to the Earl, but it seems that the Mansels also held some property on the Kenfig side of the river at this point. A survey of the manor of Higher Kenfig made in 1633 (PM 1280) mentions ten (customary) acres of waste land described as being enclosed on three sides by the river, and on the fourth by "the ould church yarde". The jurors cited as their authority an earlier survey made in 1582 and certain other deeds, one of which was the original gift of this land to Margam Abbey which is still kept in the estate's archives (PM 105).

This had been made by Gilbert Grammus, and it is undated but probably belongs to the closing years of the 12th century since the grantor appears to have been dead by the year 1203. In it the property is described as "ten acres of land beginning from the water of Kenefeg and then along the ancient cemetery to the south until the whole area is made complete". (Birch, 1897: 157)

Where this land was is something of a puzzle. Thomas Gray (1909: 155) believed it to lie immediately on the east of Kenfig town and castle, presumably taking the graveyard to be the one at St James' church. This ignores the fact that this was still in use at the time of the original document, so would scarcely have been described as 'ancient'. Also, had the defences of the town and castle formed part of the boundary then this would certainly have been mentioned. In fact the lands belonging to the Grammus family at this time were centred upon their residence at Marlas, and contained within the isthmus between the Afon Fach and the Kenfig river on which it stands. Almost all the land

here seems to have been enclosed by 1633, and given the topography of
the land through which the river flows it is difficult to envisage a place
where ten acres of waste might have been situated.

Between the confluence with the Afon Fach and Kenfig Castle
the present configuration of the river today initially seems to offer several possible locations, but much of the land on the Kenfig bank was
utilised for other purposes in the medieval period. Besides Kenfig Mill
with its associated leat and millpond there were two large enclosures at
Portland and (below New Mill Bridge) 'Millermans Land'. Margam Estate did own land called Tir Ffin in the vicinity of Glasfryn, that had
probably formed part of the monastic estate, but this seems to be accounted for elsewhere in the 1633 survey.

Largely by process of elimination therefore, I have arrived at the
conclusion that these ten acres were downstream of the castle and may
even be the enclosure we know as Castle Meadow. The mention of the
graveyard particularly attracts me to this location. Any church or chapel
associated with it would surely have been mentioned so there was presumably none. This in turn suggests to me that it could have been one
created by the first burgesses at the time when their town was situated
within the fortifications of the castle. Church services then were most
likely held in the garrison chapel, (probably the one dedicated to St
Thomas mentioned at Kenfig during the medieval period.) but I cannot
imagine the Constable wanting burials inside his fortress. There is evidence that there was a gateway at the western end of the outer bailey in
which the town lay, and I would therefore have thought that their
cemetery would have been too far distant from it.

Castle Meadow, however, lies on the Margam side of an abandoned meander of the river created when it was diverted northwards to
allow the construction of the marshalling yards. The original grant and
the 1633 survey indicate quite clearly however that the ten acres lay on
the south side of the river. Estate records indicate that the course of the
river in these lower reaches has altered several times over the past 400
years, either deliberately or through some whim of its own. There is
therefore every likelihood that the river flowed northwards around
Castle Meadow and that the course suggested by the abandoned meander was created sometime after 1633 by one of these alterations in its
course. The evidence is not in itself conclusive, but it is a possibility that
has to be borne in mind. Indeed, these alterations of the course of the

river may have given rise to this complaint, if some change in its course had 'presented' Mansel with three-quarters of an acre on 'his' side.

With regard to an allegation that Mansel had been quarrying stone from the common, he responded with the statement that this was on a "peece of wast ground" belonging to him. There is a very fine distinction between 'common land' and 'waste land', for there are no commoners' rights in respect of the latter, and this was the point Mansel was making here. It was un-enclosed land belonging to him that formed no part of the burgesses' common.

Finally there was an allegation that Mansel or his agents had been threatening the Earl's tenants both here and in the Lordship of Avan. To this he responded testily "I threat'ned none but to take what advantage the lawe would give me". As the story of Jenkin Turberville has already illustrated, these were violent times in which might was right. In the absence of any effective law-enforcement agency the landlords, as Mansel was quite happy to admit, took matters into their own hands. With that final revealing insight into life at Kenfig under Good Queen Bess, we leave the Age of the Tudors and move on into the 17th century.

Chapter 11

A New Town – and Town Hall 1604

By 1605 Evan Griffith, the sometime Portreeve of the Borough of Kenfig, must have been a very old man. His name first appears in local records as early as the year 1557 when he acquired property in the lower borough. To do that he must have been at least twenty-one years of age, probably a little older, so as he lay on his bed "sick in body" and in the knowledge that his end was fast approaching, he would have been at least 70 years of age.

Earlier we saw how, under his direction and guidance, the burgesses had undertaken the momentous step of enclosing a portion of their common at Cefn Cribwr. Now, as the final grains trickled through the hour-glass of his life the borough that had meant so much to him was still very much in the forefront of his thoughts. Before he gave directions for the disposal of his earthly goods there was one last thing he had to do for his fellow burgesses — one last promise had to be kept.

Ever since the burgesses had abandoned their town near the river nearly 170 years earlier (around 1439), the little settlement strung along Heol Las near the church of St Mary Magdalene had been at the centre of their borough. This was what passed for the 'new' town of Kenfig, though as Evan would have been the first to admit, it was but a pale shadow of their former home. The weekly markets and the annual fairs were now but a distant memory handed down (and no doubt greatly embellished!) by word of mouth from their fathers and forefathers before them. Evan's Kenfig was no more than a straggling village of tired looking cottages and farms adjoining a tiny church that itself was no more than a chapel-of-ease to the monstrosity at neighbouring Pyle which the ecclesiastical authorities insisted was now their parish church.

Yet the borough was still in being, and this little village was its heart. Here from time to time, the burgesses from Higher Kenfig across the river, regularly met with their brethren from the Lower Borough to discuss the business of the day. Probably their meeting place was in the

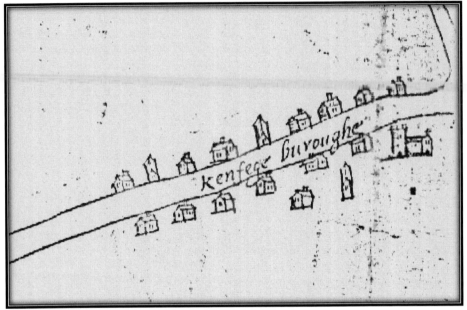

THE VILLAGE OF MAWDLAM (THEN KNOWN AS KENFIG)

FROM THE WYSEMAN MAP OF 1592. LATER MAPS SHOW FAR FEWER HOUSES WHICH MAY INDICATE A REDUCTION IN SIZE FOLLOWING THE CREATION OF THE PRESENT VILLAGE OF KENFIG. HOWEVER THIS MAP DOES CONTAIN SEVERAL INACCURACIES AS WITH THE DEPICTION OF THE CHURCH WITH THE TOWER AT THE WRONG END OF THE BUILDING!

church itself or perhaps (if it existed then as licensed premises) the bar of the local alehouse that was to become known as The Angel Inn.

Of recent years their deliberations had taken on a more urgent tone. The advancing sands had now all but obliterated the remains of the castle. Their former town had not been the last part of this conquest by nature, but steadily and remorselessly the sands continued to advance further and further inland. Every year it seemed another field, another portion of the common, vanished without trace. Up on the hill the people living along Heol Las had thought themselves beyond its reach, yet relentlessly and remorselessly the dunes crept up the slope, engulfing everything in their path. Even the windmill adjoining the road to Pyle that Evan remembered from his youth had gone, and how long now could the cottagers of the hamlet of Millhill continue to hang on before their homes also shared its fate? The people in the village near the church stared at the waves of sand advancing towards them from the plain below and shook their heads. How long indeed before their own homes would have to be abandoned, and what then would happen to their borough? The name Ty'n y Towyn (House in the Sand) applied to the farmhouse east of the church, and a huge dune that adjoined it until removed in the 1990s, indicates the realities of this threat.

Such depressing thoughts and forebodings must have figured hugely at meetings of Evan and his fellow burgesses. They were the guardians of the borough, people looked to them for leadership and for answers, yet increasingly they were having to face the fact that their re-constituted 'town' appeared as doomed as its predecessor. Gloomily they concluded that there was only one viable alternative. The town of Kenfig must be moved yet again; but where? Nobody was keen to sur-render valuable farmland for the purpose, yet where else was there that would be safe for all time from the menace of the remorseless shifting sands?

Time has forever obliterated the name of the genius that eventu-ally came up with an answer, but the legacy of his simple yet clever so-lution remains with us today. Of him we can say with some certainty that he was no scientist or engineer, indeed, it is quite probable that he was totally illiterate. What he did have was a pair of eyes in his head, and intelligence between his ears. Our anonymous hero could not have told you, for example, that winds of sufficient speed to 'roll' dry sand along the ground occur at Kenfig for roughly two thirds of the year. What he had observed was that when winds blew, they were normally from the west which was why the dunes continued their remorseless advance inland from the coast. Nor would he have known that only when wind reaches a speed of 19.3 knots, which happens for roughly 80 days a year at Kenfig, are they of sufficient strength to lift and carry sand through the air. What he did realise was that very, very rarely did they ever blow strongly enough to carry sand clear across the waters of Kenfig Pool!

So a decision was taken. A new town of Kenfig was to be built on waste land on the eastern side of the pool. Here, not only would it be free once and for all from the ravages of the sand, but would still be

THE FORMER TOWN HALL OF KENFIG BOROUGH
NOW THE PRINCE OF WALES PUBLIC HOUSE VIEWED FROM THE NORTH.
ALTHOUGH MUCH ALTERED, THE ORIGINAL PLAN OF TWO WINGS PROJECTING
FROM THE MAIN BUILDING SO AS TO ENCLOSE A SMALL COURTYARD ON THREE
SIDES IS STILL DISCERNABLE.

close to both the church and existing houses on Heol Las. They would, the burgesses decided, create a new town of Kenfig, complete with a proper town hall such as their ancestors had possessed in days of yore. Who knew, but maybe in this new environment the old glories might return, and the town of Kenfig might once again become a place of importance in South Wales?

Of course all this cost money, and on a wave of enthusiasm the burgesses hastened to pledge sums towards the building of a new town hall where they would meet to transact business, and where the manorial Courts Leet and Courts Baron would be held. Evan may well have smiled wryly at some of the enthusiastic optimism of his fellow burgesses, but at the very least the move would mean his beloved borough was safe, and would continue on into the future. Clearing his throat, and summoning his failing senses, he began to dictate his last Will and Testament.

> I give twelve pence towards Kenffig church, together with six shillings more I promised towards building a Court House at Kenfigg. (Llandaff Wills)

The New Town: The location chosen for the new town of Kenfig lay along a highway running from Nottage to Margam. Most of it still remains in use today, but the portion that continued on through the sandhills to New Mill Bridge has long been abandoned. In early documents the portion of this road along which the new town of Kenfig was built is sometimes called Heol Fawr (the 'big' or 'main' road), but once the new settlement was established it became simply Heol Kenfig. A second road or street was also constructed. This diverged eastwards from the main highway and then headed south through the fields at the foot of Paschal Hill to emerge on Kenfig Down. The burgesses christened it 'Heol y Lane' (The Lane Road) and it is still there today. This name is in itself perhaps an interesting indication of the change from English to Welsh as the language of the population. From being known simply as 'the lane' that gave access to adjoining fields it became 'Y Lane' or 'Y Lane Vach' during the period when the transition was being made. By the time it had developed into a road few, if any, probably knew what the word 'Lane' meant.

Whilst not shown on Wyseman's map, Heol y Lane certainly existed in some form in 1602 (PM 827) when it was known as Y Lane Vach. Originally it may have been just a track giving access to fields through which it passed and was consequently very narrow as the owners of the land had no wish to surrender more of their property for this purpose than was absolutely necessary.

Something of the unrealistic high hopes entertained by some burgesses for their new town comes through in a document (PM 929) by which a Kenfig yeoman named John Morgan and his wife Barbara mortgaged four acres of land adjoining Heol y Lane in 1646. This does not refer to it by name, but confers upon it the grand title "the high way leading from Newton to Margam". Newton at this time was a small 'creek' or port trading with Bristol and the West Country, and was used by the Margam estate to import goods unobtainable locally. If that traffic could be persuaded to pass through their 'new town', who knew what benefits might derive from it!

Alas for Kenfig, the goods and merchandise bound from Newton for the Mansel mansion at Margam still continued to roll along the
winding, dusty roads through North and South Cornelly, and we hear
no more of such grand titles for this narrow little lane that was Kenfig's
second street.

In the angle formed by the junction between Heol y Lane and
Heol Kenfig the Corporation built their new Town Hall. (The present
arrangement whereby Heol y Lane passes along the front of The Prince
of Wales seems to date from the early 19th century) They were attempting to recreate as far as possible the one that had existed in their old
town. Descriptions in contemporary documents show that, after the
usual fashion of such buildings, the old hall had been raised upon pillars and accessed via a stone staircase at one end. Beneath this stairway
there was a small room which served as the town's lock-up, whilst the
area in the arcade beneath the hall was where the town's weekly markets were held.

The burgesses' new Hall reproduced this layout almost exactly,
even down to the cell beneath the stairs which is mentioned in borough
minutes of the 18th century. Of course as the weekly markets had long
since ceased, the decision was taken to utilise the ground floor for some
other purpose, and it would seem that from the first it was an alehouse.
Today we know it as *The Prince of Wales*, but the earliest records call it
simply *Ty Newydd* (The New House), or The Corporation House.

From the town hall to the common on Kenfig Down, on both
sides of Heol Kenfig it was fringed by waste land separating the road
from adjoining fields. On the western side of the highway these enclosures ran down the slope to Kenfig Pool; these were mainly owned by
the lord of the manor as part of his demesne land. On Thomas Wyseman's map of 1592 the northern boundary of these fields is indicated by
a dotted line showing that here they continued (as indeed they do today) northwards to a point just beyond *The Prince of Wales*. Wyseman
did not bother to show these, as they were freehold properties and not
relevant to the purpose of his map. He only wished to show Kenfig
Down and its relationship to other main features, such as the demesne
land in the locality.

On the opposite side of Heol Kenfig, fields extended up and
over the slope of the low ridge that the burgesses called Paschal Hill.
This land had been enclosed back in the medieval period, and probably

originated as individual strips in common fields, each owned by different people. This is indicated by old maps which show many long narrow fields formed when the strips were subsequently being amalga-
mated and enclosed. If more proof were needed then there are also
many references in 17th and 18th century documents to plots of land at
Kenfig and Heol Las that were contained within larger enclosures such
as Winters Hill or Brombil.

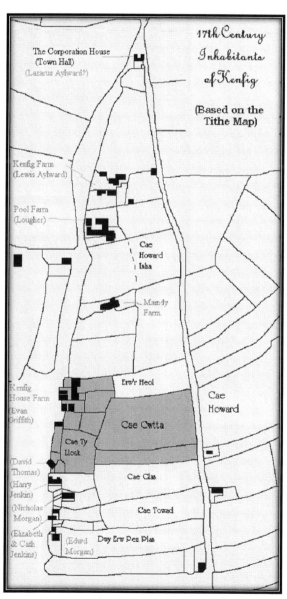

17th Century
Inhabitants
of Kenfig

(Based on the
Tithe Map)

The Corporation House
(Town Hall)
(Lazarus Aylward?)

Kenfig Farm
(Lewis Aylward)

Pool Farm
(Lougher)

Cae
Howard
Isha

Mandy
Farm

Kenfig
House Farm
(Evan
Griffith)

Erw'r Heol

Cae
Howard

Cae Cwtta

Cae Ty
Llosk

(David
Thomas)

(Harry
Jenkin)

Cae Clas

(Nicholas
Morgan)

Cae Towad

(Elizabeth
& Cath
Jenkins)

(Edwd
Morgan)

Dwy Erw Pea Plas

The earliest names
by which some of these
fields were known in the
17th century are them-
selves indicative of their
age. By 1605 Welsh was
probably the everyday
language of the commu-
nity, replacing the Eng-
lish of the earliest bur-
gesses that had persisted
for a time even after the
town's destruction. The
name Paschal Hill had
evolved from 'Pishill'.
Literally translated this
means 'the hill where
peas grow' though this
does not necessarily refer
to the common or garden
variety, but to all forms
of plants producing seeds
in a pod. In fact the 'peas'
that grew on Paschal Hill
were produced by broom
that formerly covered
most of this ridge as indicated by the name of the
lane — Heol Broom, and
the number of field
names here that also in-

corporate references to the plant. Broom Hir; Broom Mawr; and Brombil (Broom Hill) are just a few examples that illustrate the point, as well as indicating the alterations taking place as the Welsh language gained in currency. Before the century was out there would even be a Cae Banadle (Broom Field). Others bore even more archaic names that betray their English origin. Six Sax (the Field of Dry Stones); Bloody Hurst (Bloody Slope); Whitters Mead (The Community's Meadow) and Whitters Hill (The Community's Hill) are all mentioned in the 17th century and the last named would eventually evolve into Winters Mead and Winters Hill respectively.

Perhaps the most unusual field name in this area was that bestowed upon one of the freehold enclosures lying between Heol Kenfig and the pool — Cae Rha. At first glance this appears to be an amalgamation of the Welsh word for field (cae) with a possible English word 'Rha'. In fact it is most likely an English rendering of the Welsh word 'Caerau' (Fortresses), and an "encampment" was indeed noted in this vicinity by a visitor to Kenfig in 1809 but all trace has now vanished.

The first houses that were to form this new town were probably built, on their own property, by those who owned the enclosed land, and this would certainly have been true of those on Heol y Lane. It is quite clear however that many dwellings which later sprang up on Heol Kenfig were built upon the waste that fringed the road. A lease issued upon one cottage by the Margam estate in 1690 from an undated rent book of circa 1710 (PM 2192) actually states that it had been originally been built on land "dressed and inclosed upon the waste ground". Technically (and the use of the words 'waste ground' as opposed to 'common land' tends to confirm this), the land adjoining the road belonged to the lord of the manor, though the burgesses chose to regard it as part of their common. This touches upon a dispute between Margam with the Corporation and afterwards the Trustees who were their successors that rumbled on for centuries and was only finally resolved in 1971.

The Question of Ownership of Common Land: Although there was evidently a planned re-siting of the 'town' of Kenfig, the development of the settlement itself seems to have been rather haphazard and piecemeal. The town hall was probably in place by 1650, but the earliest houses were actually farmhouses like Kenfig Farm, Pool Farm, and

Maindy, standing in their own land. Landowners would have been understandably reluctant just to surrender parts of their fields for other burgesses to build on, and few of the latter could afford to purchase such plots anyway. At this point I suspect that the brave idea of a new town of Kenfig started to falter.

It then seems that some burgesses, either on their own initiative or with the tacit support of the corporation, took matters into their own hands, by building homes for themselves on the waste land bordering Heol Kenfig. In Wales there was a custom called 'Ty ai Un Nos' (a house in one night), which, whilst it had no force under English Law was apparently quite widely observed and respected, unless the interests of the great estates were involved. By this custom if a man could build a house on waste land within a single night and have a fire burning in the hearth by the time the sun rose the following day, then he could claim the ground upon which it stood. I've also heard it said that he could further enclose sufficient land for a garden, within an area determined by the distance he could throw an axe from his front door.

The Earls of Pembroke, as we have seen, took little interest in Kenfig affairs and the anarchy caused by the Civil War between King and Parliament in the 1640s would not have helped matters, so some of these earliest houses on Heol Kenfig may have come about in this manner. Be this as it may, there still remained the question of who actually **owned** this land and indeed the common lands of Kenfig as a whole.

When this came to a dramatic climax at the High Court in 1971, both parties entered the fray in the belief that they had a justifiable claim to **all** the common land at Kenfig. It was on that basis that this action was fought and a final judgement given. However, having sifted through the evidence for a number of years I am now convinced that in fact, neither party ever actually owned the common **in its entirety**.

Ownership of common land and possessing commoner's rights upon it are two entirely different things. Historically ownership of common land was normally vested in the Lord of the Manor who conceded various rights and privileges upon it to certain individuals. These rights varied from common to common, but usually they included such things as grazing livestock, taking wind-fallen timber, cutting gorse for animal feed, etc. Often commons were 'stinted', which meant that a limit was placed on the number of animals a commoner could graze there, and any 'right of common' only actually applied to certain sections of the population. At Stormy Manor, for example, it was restricted to those whose land bordered the common itself, whilst at Kenfig it was vested solely in the burgesses. Certain rights were rarely conceded to the commoners. Anyone wishing to open a limestone quarry on Stormy Common, for example, whether a commoner or not, had to pay the lord of the manor for the privilege. Nevertheless the bottom line was that whatever rights the commoners might enjoy on the surface of a common, the land itself belonged to the lord.

It was on this basis that the Margam Estate contested for Kenfig Common in 1971, claiming that they were the owners and that The Kenfig Borough Trustees were mere commoners. The latter, however, also claimed to be the true owners and thanks largely to extensive research carried out by the late Mr Ted Plumley, CBE, won the case. As I said earlier however, my own research shows that in point of fact neither side actually enjoyed complete ownership of the whole.

The burgesses for their part certainly had a good claim to the North Common (also known as Windmill Hill Common), because it had previously surrounded the medieval town at Kenfig, and was contained within the boundaries of their medieval borough. By virtue of their charter of 1397 they were also the *de facto* owners of the common at Kenfig Down further south. So far as I can discover however, they had no claim whatsoever on either the common which lay between these two elements, nor to the strip of dunes immediately inland from the foreshore.

Thomas Wyseman, the surveyor employed by the Earls of Pembroke in 1582 (Bute MSS M 15/1) and 1592 (PM 9616) to report on certain aspects of the waste and common land in the Borough of Kenfig had initially been uncertain of the ownership of the common in the dunes. In the first report he noted that the burgesses claimed "a free comon called The Sandes wch lieth between the said Borrough and the sea". His second visit however, was directly concerned with this land, and having studied the documentary evidence he was quite certain that whilst they may have enjoyed right of common there, they did not own this land in its entirety. The coastal strip was the lord's rabbit warren, and subsequently estate records show that this continued to be rented by the estate to various individuals, right into the 19th century. Wyseman also (albeit on a mistaken premise) claimed that neither did the burgesses enjoy any rights at Kenfig Pool even though apparently they had been treating it as part and parcel of their common.

The basis on which the burgesses claimed ownership of the portion of common adjoining and to the north of the Pool was their mis-identification of the 'lord's demesne land' that formed the northern boundary of Kenfig Down as granted them by their charter of 1397. This, they claimed was a field called The Earls Meadow situated near the castle ruins. On his first visit Wyseman seems to have accepted their word regarding ownership of the coastal common land, but in 1592 he examined the area more closely and read the charter that allocated part of the common to the Abbot of Neath. He would then have realised that if the burgesses' claim was right then the size of the Abbot's portion of the common should have been greater than the Grange of Sker itself! Now that he could actually see the area for himself he could also see that another block of demesne land lay between the meadow near the castle and the boundary with Sker. This was composed of fields lying between the pool and the road to Nottage. Wyseman concluded that, logically, this would have been the land that the charter referred to, since it lay immediately north of Sker.

The conclusion is indeed inescapable. All the dune land to the north of the pool and the adjoining demesne as far as the river belonged to the Earl, though he was apparently happy to concede that the burgesses enjoyed common rights upon it. To clarify the point Wyseman indicated the locations of both the castle and the Kenfig Pool demesne on his map. He went further and produced evidence to show that the lord's warren had been in existence in 1431 when a John Stradling was employed as the warrener. In fact, because of better access to even earlier documents, we can now trace such usage back as far as the early 1300s.

So did the burgesses obtain permission from the Earl of Pembroke to enclose areas of waste land adjoining Heol Kenfig? It would seem not! In 1639 they had actually sought his permission to extend their enclosure at Waun Cimla (PM 9623) though they never apparently took up the option. The jury for the manorial survey of the manor of Kenfig Borough in 1661 recorded that the Corporation had however enclosed 18 (customary) acres out of Kenfig Down some seven years earlier (circa 1653). An item in a survey of 1661 (Gray, 1909: 250) records this enclosure which the jury stated had taken place about seven years earlier. A comparison of the present boundaries of this common south of the pool, with those on Thomas Wyseman's map of 1592 do not seem to show that any such large-scale enclosure has been made from it, so this presumably relates to the enclosure of the waste adjoining Heol Kenfig. This would have legitimised the cottagers who had already built homes there and opened the way for new settlement. It is indeed quite clear from the 1661 survey that the burgesses were persisting in the claim (previously rejected by Wyseman) that the piece of demesne land adjoining the castle defined the northern boundary of 'Kenfig Down'. They also boldly stated that the common's western boundary extended to the sea and claimed the fishing rights of Kenfig Pool for good measure! The way they saw it, the land that had been enclosed was their own – part and parcel of Kenfig Down which had been granted them by charter back in 1397.

     None of these claims appears to have been contested by the Earl at this time, and indeed the burgesses' claim to *right of common* on the waste adjoining the sea and surrounding Kenfig Pool as far north as the river Kenfig never seems to have been questioned. Nevertheless, as we will see in a future chapter, later lords certainly never relinquished their right of warren in the dunes and also successfully challenged the burgesses' claim to fishing rights in the pool. This argues that in spite of the claims by the jurors of 1661, ownership of the common between the river and the southern shore of the pool had never actually been conceded to them then, previously, or afterwards.

     Whether by fair means or foul, the fact is that (in modern measure) about 22 acres were enclosed from the waste to help create the new 'town' of Kenfig. This is considerably more than was subsequently utilised for cottages, gardens and crofts, so my guess is that the Aylwards and the other farmers with land bordering the highway here took advantage of this arrangement to extend their own field boundaries closer to the road. Most of the houses on Heol Kenfig seem to have been in place by the end of 1655.

The Town Hall -- Corporation House: As one approached the settlement along Heol Kenfig from the north the first building to greet the visitor was The Corporation House set in the angle between the main road and Heol y Lane. It was whilst writing these few words that something about this building that has been staring me in the face for years suddenly became glaringly apparent! As originally built what we now think of as 'the back' of the property (facing to the north) was actually the front! The present 'front' only came into being when Heol Lane was diverted across the 'back' of the building in the early years of the 19th century to allow the premises to be extended eastwards across the original road. Previously what is now the main entrance was simply the back door giving access to a walled kitchen garden.

The 17th century frontage would have been a small courtyard open to the north enclosed on three sides by the main building and two projecting wings. It is still there now, but sealed off and roofed over in recent times — the latest of many alterations and extensions on this side of the building. A plan of the ground floor (B/K 12) of the premises dating from 1810 drawn to illustrate alterations made to the property shows that (as viewed from the north) the wing on the right formerly housed a brew-house whilst that on the left contained 'the old parlour' or 'bar'. Both were entered via doors opening onto the courtyard. On the ground floor beneath the actual town hall lay a kitchen, bedroom and another room that in 1810 was being converted into a 'new parlour'. These rooms were connected by a passage along the north side from which there was apparently then no direct access into the yard. It would not surprise me to discover, however, that originally such an entrance had existed but been blocked up prior to the 1810 alterations.

Even lacking such a central entrance, the old frontage of The Corporation House had rather a more imposing façade than the rather bland one which greets patrons today. Its appearance would also have been further enhanced by the fact that the external walls would almost certainly have been lime-washed. Later visitors to this area noted that because lime was plentiful in the locality even the humblest cottager regularly lime-washed the exterior of their home. It is also known that the walls of Mawdlam church were formerly painted a dazzling white which made it useful as a navigation point for vessels negotiating the treacherous shoals of Swansea Bay. White, the natural colour of lime, would have been the predominant colour used, but often a pigment was mixed into it to offer enterprising cottagers a palette of different shades to choose from.

Unfortunately I have yet to discover the identity of the first licensees who kept the premises now known as the _Prince of Wales_. Edmund Harry, who was the tenant in the middle of the 18th century, stated in evidence to the Corporation (B/K 11) that he had succeeded his father, William Harry (d.1741) in this role, and the latter is therefore the earliest I have identified with certainty so far. The first mention of him comes in 1695 with an entry in the Parish Registers recording his marriage to Gwenllian, a member of the Lyddon family. In 1699 he is listed as a burgess, and the same year paid just two shillings Window Tax (PM 4992). This means that he was living in a house with less than ten windows — almost certainly not The Corporation House. The earliest sure evidence I have for his connection with the premises dates from 1731 (B/K 11) when he was twice prosecuted for selling his ale at "less than measure"!

Chapter 12

Two Mills Lost

Kenfig Mill: Built not far from Kenfig Mill the first thing that occurred to me about New Mill is why the Mansels ever bothered to build it! It can scarcely have been simply for the convenience of the tenants on Water Street whose suit of mill was transferred from the one at Llanmihangel to this new establishment. People from as far away as Nottage were at one time required to grind at Kenfig Mill, whilst Margam tenants from Stormy continued to perform this duty at Llanmihangel. So just why did the Mansels suddenly decide to save their Higher Kenfig tenants the comparatively short trip to Llanmihangel?

The significance of New Mill's construction is I believe that it was erected only a hundred yards or so upstream from Kenfig Mill which, once the windmill fell victim to the sands, had been the only local alternative to the Margam mill at Llanmihangel. As such, it offered an alternative place to grind corn, right on its rival's doorstep, to those burgesses who were not bound to Margam by tenancy agreements, and also to the inhabitants of North and South Cornelly.

It is not known at exactly what point Kenfig Mill originally drew water from the river, but it was certainly above New Mill Bridge; it may be that originally it was further upstream than the weir adjoining the bridge that was used in its latter days. The Kenfig is not a large river, so if New Mill was drawing water from above the sluice gate controlling its rival's supply, and then returning it at a point further below, Kenfig Mill would have been hard pressed to operate during dry periods. The weir attached to the bridge may have been a response to this problem.

If one looks at the final years of Kenfig Mill's existence, then these initial suspicions regarding New Mill tend to harden into probabilities. There is, it has to be admitted, a possibility that it became derelict and went out of business through sand encroachment. The mill was under threat from the sand as early as 1526, as implied in a lease (PM 2815) of that year. At this time the lordship of Glamorgan (and therefore the manor of Kenfig Borough) was in the hands of the Crown (in the person of King Henry VIII) as it had been ever since the death of Earl

Jasper Tudor. The King (and the Earl before him) were also lords of what subsequently became known as 'The Pembroke manor' in Newton Nottage. Based upon Nottage House, this manor extended northwards to the boundaries of South Cornelly and Sker, but contained no mill of any kind. As well as acquiring the mill itself, the Crown's new tenants — Watkin Lougher of Tythegston and John Thomas of Llanmihangel Grange — were granted "the suit for the grindings of Newton Nottage". This meant also that those tenants on the Pembroke manor who owed suit of mill, had to lug their corn all the way to Kenfig for it to be ground into flour.

Also part of the grant were two (customary) acres of land on Grammeshill, the right to appoint the miller and "a site on the mill stream for the mill if required". It is this phrase that seems to indicate that the buildings that housed the mill may have been coming under threat from the dunes.

Whether this option was subsequently taken up is not known, but it seems that following the death of John Thomas, the Loughers continued to lease the mill and another, later, Watkin Lougher is mentioned as tenant in the Grove Survey of 1570. It is interesting to note that whereas Lougher and Thomas were paying an annual rent of twenty shillings for Kenfig Mill, another consortium, of which John Thomas of Llanmihangel was again a member, secured a lease (PM 284) on the one at Llanmihangel in 1527 at double this amount. Despite Kenfig's boost from the trade of the reluctant tenants of Nottage, it was the Margam mill that was clearly the more profitable of the two.

Somewhere along the line, this suit of the Nottage tenants was subsequently lost, putting Kenfig Mill at a further disadvantage. Nevertheless, despite this and the loss of the two acres of land formerly attached, its rent was still twenty shillings when in 1602 it was leased (PM 2944) to Richard Powell of Margam, gent. Who exactly he was I do not know, but it is at this point that Richard Powell again appears in several other documents as a close associate of the Mansels of Margam.

He may have been their steward or agent, but certainly there is evidence that he had some close connection with them. Powell's lease was for 21 years, and when it expired a fresh one (PM 9817) was taken out upon it for a like period by Sir Thomas Mansel of Margam himself. The rent was also increased to twenty-two shillings indicating that the mill was still a viable proposition.

From this point onwards however Kenfig Mill began to go downhill very quickly indeed! Following the death of Thomas Mansel a fresh lease (PM 620) was taken out by his successor Lewis in 1631, for the period of thirteen years still outstanding on the original. Notwithstanding that, it was claimed Thomas had forked out nearly £7 on repairs to the mill, and the rent now dropped back to twenty shillings.

By the time of the 1650 manorial survey nineteen years later, Kenfig Mill is described as a ruin. Yet Sir Edward Seabright (who had custody of the Margam estate was apparently still happily stumping up the twenty shillings per annum rent due upon it! The jurors requested to see his lease (presumably issued on expiry of the old one in 1644) probably hoping to discover, as was normally the case, that it required him to keep it in good repair. He ignored them and, true to form, the Earls of Pembroke did nothing either.

No mention of the mill is made in the 1661 survey, but in one carried out six years later (PM 9620) the jury reported that it had indeed ceased to exist.

> Wee know not of any water grist mill or mills now within the lordshipp, towne and burrough, but there appeareth some part of wall or walls where the Lord's mill or mills hath been.

So Kenfig Mill passed into history. We have seen how, as far back as 1526 it had probably been under threat from the sand, and its competitive edge would have been lost once the Mansels secured control, for they would have brought its charges into line with those of their own establishments at New Mill and Llanmihangel. A case therefore of 'accidental death' or was it 'murder'? To me it appears that when the rival New Mill which was built virtually on the doorstep of the Kenfig mill failed to kill it off, the Mansels acquired the tenancy, and simply ran it down. But before you make your own final verdict let me lay one further scrap of evidence before you. Once Kenfig Mill had gone, there is clear evidence that the Mansels planned to shut down either Llanmihangel or New Mill. Perhaps running two mills for existing customers, free or otherwise, was considered no longer necessary. As we will see in due course, the axe fell on the latter, and would undoubtedly have done so sooner had it not been that David Gronow, who was the remaining life of Gronow William's lease, had lived for so long!

Millhill, Hamlet and Mill, swallowed by sand: As the 17th century progressed, so it became increasingly obvious that the days of the little settlement on Millhill were numbered; the dunes had already claimed the
windmill on the crest of the ridge, and they crept steadily ever closer to
the houses. I have identified four of properties, and they all seem to
have been of the same basic pattern — cottage; outhouse or barn together with an acre of enclosed land. They all lay on the south side of
the road from Mawdlam to Marlas (sometimes referred to as Heol Millhill), though where exactly this was in relation to the landscape today is
debatable.

My own gut feeling is that originally this road ran further north
than it does now. Stand at the site of the former junction between the
long-vanished road from Kenfig to New Mill Bridge and the present
highway to Pyle. It is clear that the latter veers towards Mawdlam
church before swerving northwards again *en route* to Croes y Ddadl.
When created, the crossroads adjoining the latter would have been
closer to the base of this medieval cross than it is today, and the highway would have followed a direct route between these two junctions.
Had the road originally followed its present course then one would expect the front door of The Angel Inn to have been moved to this side of
the building long before this was done in the 1950s. Previously it had
been on the other side of the building facing the village and church, its
back turned towards the road from which it now derives its passing
trade. If this road took a more northerly and direct route in the past,
then the Millhill cottages of which I have discovered a record may now
lie beneath the present highway or even on the north side of it.

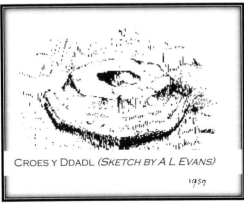

CROES Y DDADL *(SKETCH BY A L EVANS)*

1959

This hamlet had a his-
tory stretching back to the 14th
century when it was called
Millhamme, but the houses I
have noted stood outside the
borough. Taddlecross (Croes y
Ddadl) was one of the boundary
marks of the original borough,
and the road itself formed its
southern boundary as far as the
junction with Heol Kenfig. If
there were, or had been, other cottages on the north side they would

have been within the Borough, but I have discovered no references to any.

The End of the Hamlet: What I have been recounting in this chapter is in fact the final years of the hamlet at Millhill. In the second half of the century there is ample evidence that the sands were once again on the move and the burgesses in the Lower Borough had continued to lose ground to the slow but remorseless advance of the dunes. The 1666 survey of the manor of Kenfig Borough specifically mentions that freehold property had been lost to sand encroachment in recent years. The jurors also noted that boundary marks on Kenfig Down had become obscured "by reason of the driving uppe, overflowing, and covering of sand time out of mind" (PM 9620). A survey of the Herbert manor at Newton, Porthcawl in 1673 also speaks of cottages there "lying void and over-flown with sands"(D/DW 206 (iv))

Here and there in the dry records of the estate's administration it is possible to see something of what this meant on the ground. After the death of Leyson Morgan in 1679 rent ceased to be paid in respect of his cottage (The Longhouse) adjoining Kenfig castle and we hear no further mention of it. All the four cottages I identified in the hamlet of Millhill vanished at about the same time. Three were bought up by Margam in 1669, but by 1674 the one that had formerly belonged to the Jenkin Thomas, who was a merchant at Tangier, is described as "decayed". Gwenllian Thomas's former house was attached to the tenancy of Marlas Farm, but I can find no record of it after 1684, whilst the records for rent paid on the one sold by Joseph Lewis to Margam cease after 1678.

The evidence points to all four houses and Castle Cottage having succumbed to the remorseless advance of the dunes that still crept tirelessly onwards, with the village of Mawdlam the next potential victim lying in their path.

Chapter 13

Farms and Farming; Exports

One other aspect of the documents generated by Sir Edward Mansel, in his attempt to sort out the affairs of the Cradock family of Llanmihangel, is the detail they contain regarding their farming equipment. We have noted that Richard Cradock was possibly instrumental in persuading Sir Edward to add the farm buildings to the existing house, but so far as he was concerned farming the adjoining land was probably something of a hobby. Certainly none of his children, except the ill-fated Christopher, seem to have continued this interest, and consequently were not the least concerned about the fate of the "instruments of husbandry" stored on the premises. As a result these were sold off by Sir Edward with the value of the iron implements being assessed simply by weight. Fortunately his agents made a detailed written record of these which is the most complete list of farming equipment I have ever come across. Normally such mundane items are lumped together on probate inventories under the all-embracing heading 'Implements of Husbandry'.

Because Richard Cradock was a wealthy man, Llanmihangel was far better equipped than most local farms, but many of the items listed would have been used on farms. There were bill-hooks, hatchets and a saw for hedging; scythes, reap-hooks and pitchforks for harvesting; and dung-forks for 'mucking out' the stables and cattle stalls. These were all essential tools on any farm. At Llanmihangel however there were also two "wains" or wagons to do the bulk of the haulage work, and 'spare parts' in case they broke down. Two "sulls" or ploughs are listed together with their ploughshares and coulters. Mentions of yokes and "ox chains" indicate that, as on virtually all local farms oxen were used for the bulk of the haulage work, but there were also no less than six horse-drawn "carrs" which I understand were a type of sled.

Horse power also seems to have been the preferred method of transport when goods needed to be moved beyond the land of the farm. Even the major roads of this period were so rutted and potholed that transport of goods by wagon was difficult. The Llanmihangel inventories lists no less than five pack saddles, each of which enabled a horse to carry two panniers slung one on each side.

So how was all the equipment used? Unlike most of our ancestors of even a century ago, we urban and city dwellers now have very little knowledge of country life, so perhaps a picture of the rural economy of Kenfig in the late 17th century would be justified at this stage of my narrative. At the same time readers involved in agriculture will perhaps forgive me any 'howlers' I may commit for, in truth, I am myself a 'townie' whose only knowledge of farming life has come from books and information gleaned from conversations with farming folk.

Kenfig Farms

When English gentry began visiting Wales, about a century or so after Richard Cradock's day, they tended to be scathing about the standards maintained on Welsh farms. As however, the historian Joanna Martin points out in an interesting article published in the twelfth and final volume of 'Glamorgan Historian', the picture they paint is somewhat biased. In the main these visitors came from parts of England where the land was principally used for growing crops, but here in Wales it was pastoral (livestock) rather than arable farming that was important. Any cereals, beans and peas grown were mainly just to provide for the needs of the household.

This is reflected in contemporary inventories relating to local farms. Thomas Hopkin (1673) had planted just 1½ acres of wheat and a like amount of barley. Evan John Evan (1663) had two acres of wheat and 1¾ of peas whilst Rees Leyson (1664) was growing 1¼ acres each of wheat and barley with two acres of oats. Theirs were small farms, but even so these crops occupied just a small fraction of the total area. Only on farms with little or no access to surface water (such as those on Stormy Down), making them unsuitable for livestock rearing, did the arable occupy a significant proportion of the available land.

Another indication of the importance of livestock farming is that locally, it is the meadow land that, acre for acre, was considered the most valuable. Meadow was grassland carefully nurtured to provide the maximum crop of hay that could be mown and stored for use as winter fodder for the livestock. Since it was the amount of hay produced that determined how many head would avoid the annual au-

tumn cull, it tended to be the most important land on the farm. To supplement this, winter fodder farmers resorted to utilising straw, gorse,
fern and ivy which, when chopped up finely, made an acceptable sub-
stitute for hay, or could be mixed with it to make the winter supply last
longer. By such means they eked out their supply of stored fodder to
help get animals through the "hungry gap" in early spring when the
grass had not yet started to grow and hay stocks were running low.

At Kenfig unfortunately, because of the nature of the land tenure, it is not possible to make the sort of detailed analysis of local farms
that I did for the manor of Stormy. This was possible there because
every square yard of land within the manor was owned by Margam and
its dimensions usually recorded somewhere within its massive manuscript collection. Whilst this was also true of Higher Kenfig, the fields in
the lower borough, as we have seen, were parcelled out amongst many
different owners of whom the Margam estate was merely the largest.
From the information I have acquired about Kenfig farms it would seem
nevertheless, that they generally followed a similar pattern to those I
studied at Stormy and Horgrove.

It was noticeable there that farmers great and small — even

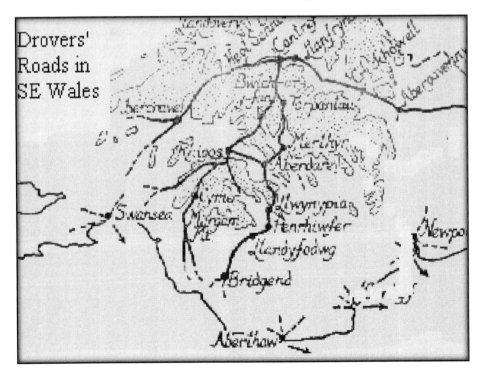

some of those who appear to have been no more than crofters — kept a few store cattle, a flock of sheep, and some dairy cattle. The only variation was one of emphasis. On Stormy Down, with its lack of standing water, it is crops and sheep that figure largely whilst the farms in the boggy valley bottom between the down and Cefn Cribwr tended to have more dairy cattle. On the south side of Cefn Cribwr ridge rearing beef cattle was more important than elsewhere in the manor.

Crofters with just an acre or so of land who had access to Stormy Common invariably kept the odd cow or a few sheep which they pastured upon it, and this practice is even more noticeable in Kenfig Borough.

Taken together, the amount of livestock at Kenfig, Stormy and Horgrove was quite large which in turn begs the question — what were they doing with the produce? This was a time when there were no large centres of population in the vicinity to provide a convenient market either for such livestock, or their products.

Some of the cattle were evidently sold to drovers, who probably visited the district annually, buying up cattle to be taken 'on the hoof' to England. There they would be fattened up before re-sale to butchers in major cities of which London was by far the most important.

One can see this process at work in the probate inventories of Kenfig burgesses who died throughout this period. On larger farms, calves were probably bred out of the dairy herd in order to improve and maintain the milk yield. Some were retained and others sold off at market or to smaller farmers and crofters, who were all eager to have a stake in the lucrative beef trade. The drove was an annual event, so the inventories show a progression of 'young cattle' from calves and yearlings through to two, three, and occasionally four year olds. Most were steers and bullocks, but there were also usually a few heifers that could be taken into the dairy herd to replace cows whose milk yield was falling. These older animals would then in turn be sold off to the drove.

Whilst the existence of the drove explains the presence of the large number of beef cattle, it does not account for the popularity of dairy herds and sheep flocks. In the second half of the 17th century the requirements of the population in towns such as Cardiff and Swansea could be more than adequately met by farms in the eastern Vale and the Gower respectively. So why did even simple crofters at Kenfig keep two or three dairy cattle when just one would have been sufficient to meet their own needs?

For the answer we need go no further than the village of Newton which has now been all but swallowed up by the modern town of Porthcawl. There are several references to a "creek" or port here in the early 16th century, and it is a pet theory of mine that it was through here that passed the goods bound to and from the medieval town of Kenfig.

Be that as it may, it was certainly a small but active port in the 17th century, and we are fortunate that some of the customs records for this period still survive. These show that in the main its trade was with Minehead on the opposite side of the channel, and Bristol, which was (after London) the second largest city in the kingdom. From ports along the South Wales seaboard, agricultural produce flowed across the channel to meet the requirements of the city throughout most of the 17th century. Unfortunately the books showing imports to Newton have not survived, so we have no corresponding record of the sort of items that they brought back on their return journey.

The Port of Newton

Perhaps the best way of illustrating the trade of this port is for me to take the entries relating to a single year when this trade in agricultural produce was at its height — 1672. In all there were 46 sailings made by eight vessels. None of these was very large, the biggest being *The Five Brothers* of Newton at 30 ton which made a total of 18 voyages.

Name of Vessel	Ton nag	Home Port	Destination	
			Bristol	Minehead
Five Brothers	30	Newton	3	15
Anne	24	Newton	1	15
Phoenix	12	Watchet	1	2
Deliverance	12	Lynmouth		2
Speedwell	16	Newton		3
Lyon	20	Watchet		2
Speedwell	16	Aberthawe	1	
Swift	26	Watchet		1

Some of these vessels left 'empty' having made a delivery but apparently failing to find a return cargo. Except for the three local vessels, Newton was probably just another port of call for several of the others. By using other port books, it is possible to occasionally trace vessels visiting three or four harbours in the Bristol Channel before returning home.

It is often said that the Newton boats of the time carried coal from the port, but this is not indicated in these records until much later. The statement is based by a comparison with the Minehead books which often show vessels from Newton arriving with coal as part of their cargo. Where, however, a direct comparison is possible between a vessel leaving the port without coal and arriving at Minehead with it, the straightforward cross-channel trip had taken three days or more! Evidently what was happening was that the vessel sailed from Newton with a part-cargo to another harbour such as Briton Ferry or Neath and loaded the coal there.

Coal may not have been an export from Newton in 1672, but a lot of other items were!

Item	Quantity	Voyages		Item	Quantity	Voyages
Wheat	1880 bushels	6		Coney skins	2 fardles	2
Barley	20 bushels	1		Hides	4	2
Beans	120 bushels	2		Cheese	3 cwt	1
Oats	1100 bushels	4		Groceries	6 cwt	1
Wool	584 stone & 2 bags			Household stuff, etc.	3 ton	1
Stockings	58 fardles & 7 packs	14		Ringo Roots	8 cwt & 5 fardles	3
Deer Skins	Not stated	1		Sheep	80	3
Mats	70 packs	1		Butter	144 firkins &	16

Oatmeal	30 bushels	4			kilder-kins; 58 pots	
Pigs	100	2				
Calf Skins	12 packs	1		Haberdashery	2 hampers & 2 boxes	1
Pewter & brass	4 ton 1 cwt	2				
Cutlery	1 trunk	1		Misc.	1 hamper & 4 boxes	1

Now if you don't know what to make of some of those quantities included in my table of exports, then rest assured, nor do I, and in truth, neither do the experts! A *bushel* was a measure of dry volume, though the size of the cauldron-like measures used tended to vary from place to place. The same can be said of other units such as the *stone, hundredweight* (cwt) and the *ton* that appear above. In old Imperial measure a *stone* was 14 pounds; there were eight *stones* to the *hundredweight* and 20 *hundredweight* made a *ton*, but in 17th century Britain every town had its own standard which often varied quite widely from those of its neighbours. As for the rest it would seem that a *fardle* was a bale of a particular size, whilst *firkins* and *kilderkins* were barrels or casks of some description. Beyond that I'm afraid I cannot go!

Of the commodities themselves, the grain and live animal exports tended to fall away to nothing after 1672, though wool, butter and stockings continued strongly. These stockings were made of wool and knitted at homesteads throughout the area. I have read somewhere that Queen Elizabeth even wore a pair to help encourage the trade in her day! Mats and bonnets ('haberdashery') were other items produced by similar cottage industries though these also tend not to occur in subsequent years.

Although three-hundredweight of cheese was shipped to Bristol in 1672, there seems to have been no great demand for this product across the channel, and it is a commodity that is rarely mentioned in other returns. At the same time large quantities of cheese are mentioned in the documents relating to the division of property at Llanmihangel, so it would seem that production was for local use only. The brass and pewter listed were probably scrap items bought up locally and shipped out for 're-cycling'. As to what "ringo roots" were, your guess is as good as mine!

Despite its imperfections the list above gives an indication of the importance of the little creek at Newton to the farms of the hinterland. Anyone who could produce a small surplus of wool or butter could get their produce to market by selling to the agents of merchants from across the channel. One final thought also occurs to me. The despatch to Bristol of the "household stuff and bedding and wearing apparel" together possibly with the cutlery, may represent the emigration of a local family to that city. Given the date however they are more likely to be Richard Cradock's long-overdue share of his inheritance en route from the house at Llanmihangel to his home in Bristol!

Although coal was not being exported at this time, the coal measures of our district were nevertheless being exploited, and if I may be excused deviating from my main theme for a few paragraphs, this is actually as good a point at which to introduce the subject. A survey of the Manor of Kenfig Borough made in 1630 (PM 9617) has a section for "mines of Coal and Iron" but the document is unfortunately badly damaged at this point. All I could make out is that a Jenkin Cradock had made a payment under this heading. Twenty years later the next survey (PM 1321) mentions a stone quarry and a coal mine on The Rugge, but gives no details. We are on firmer ground with a survey of the demesne land made in 1666 (PM 9623) which gives full details of a lease issued in 1654 to a John Leyson. It entitled him and his employees to "search, digg and mine" for coal on The Rugge and to sell or dispose of the produce as he wished. This Leyson hailed from Newton Nottage, and was probably related (father?) to the William Leyson who owned the vessel known as *The Five Brothers.* Other documents indicate that David Bowen, the owner of *Anne* was also associated with John in this venture.

This lease was due to terminate in 1675, and the mine was still operating in 1669 when it was specifically included in the deed of sale when the Earl of Pembroke disposed of the Manor of Kenfig Borough to the Mansels. After this, however, there is no mention of any mining on the common for over a century. These early mines were probably located on land there known as Tir Garw between the Waun Cimla enclosure and the river. In 1805 the Borough Council decided to "fill up the dangerous coal pits on Tir Garw under Gwain y Cimla which is of great injury and hazardous" (BK ALE).

The supply of cattle for the drove, and the steady demand for butter, wool and stockings in Bristol and The West helped bring a measure of prosperity to farmers great and small in Kenfig and the surrounding district. The fact that there was an outlet for their surplus produce enabled them to make a living and shaped the manner in which they utilised their land.

Chapter 14

Catholic Kenfig: Recusants and a local Saint

If there is one period of Kenfig's history where the lack of a diary or personal letter by one of its inhabitants is most keenly felt it is at this point during the 17ᵗʰ century. By the time of the Restoration of the monarchy in 1660, the community was a heady mixture of Nonconformists ('dissenters'), Roman Catholics ('recusants'), as well as supporters of the official Anglican church. Ideology aside, I would dearly love to know

MAWDLAM CHURCH (PHOTO BY CYRIL JAMES)

how this affected the people of the community as a whole. Were they racked by discord with members of the three factions constantly at each other's throats? Or did they take a rather more sanguine view, getting on with their own lives and allowing the others to get on with theirs? All we can say for certain is that the cold official records tell us that a 'situation' existed in the Borough of Kenfig in the second half of the century that was a microcosm of Britain in general. Nationally it led to considerable violence and even death.

It was the Turbervilles of Sker and Cornelly who still clung dog-gedly to the 'old religion', though we hear very little of their activities during the period covered by these notes. Leslie Evans devoted consid-erable time to researching the history of Sker House, but was neverthe-less unable to determine the exact relationship of the members of the family who lived there after the Elizabethan period. The best guess seems to be that the first, Matthew, was a younger son of Jenkin Turberville who originally built the house. He was therefore a brother of Christopher who held the manor of South Cornelly in 1630, and is mentioned living at Penllyn (the principal family seat) the following year.

Matthew in turn was succeeded at Sker between 1631 and 1650 by Thomas Turberville, and the latter by another Christopher between 1673 and 1675. It is assumed that the three were father, son, and grand-son, though this is no more than an educated guess. What is apparent is that the family's loyalty to Roman Catholicism remained undiminished. Matthew and his wife Alice were prosecuted for recusancy in 1622 and Leslie Evans adds that a further wave of prosecutions in 1629 netted sixteen members of the Began and Turberville families in the Pyle area, and a another six Turbervilles at Sker.

Ironically the Catholics were probably less persecuted under the Puritans than had been the case when the Anglicans occupied the seat of government. This is because under the Commonwealth many of the former restrictions upon non-Anglican forms of worship were relaxed or removed. Although intended to benefit the dissenting congregations, this also effectively removed the restraints upon the Roman Catholics, though they too were to suffer renewed persecution following the Res-toration. Like the dissenters therefore, the interlude provided by the Commonwealth proved to be no more than a temporary respite, and sterner trials lay ahead for both communities as the 17th century steadily drew to a close.

Meanwhile at Sker the Turberville's long association with the house was drawing to a close. Christopher, the last member of the fam-ily to reside there was undoubtedly a descendant of the Jenkin who had converted it out of the former monastic Grange a century earlier, though his exact relationship is a matter for conjecture. He was the owner of the property, and like his forbears clung resolutely to the Ro-man Catholic faith.

After a lull during the Commonwealth, anti-Catholic persecution had once again become a popular pastime, and the reputation of Christopher's family ensured that his name was well to the fore of local suspects. Nor did the authorities have long to wait before securing proof of his involvement. In 1678 a fugitive priest, Father Phillip Evans, was arrested at Sker though, as outlined by Leslie Evans in his book *Sker House* the circumstances of the capture had a rather bizarre aspect. Despite being forewarned of the forthcoming raid upon the house Father Evans apparently chose to remain there, and having then successfully evaded discovery by the searchers, coolly surrendered himself to them as they were about to depart.

It almost seems as though the priest was seeking martyrdom, and if so was not disappointed for, after a sham of a trial, he was publicly hung, drawn and quartered at Cardiff after the grisly fashion of the time. By his actions he had also of course ensured the prosecution of Christopher and his family who had given him shelter, and the following year we hear that Christopher was in prison for refusing to take the oath acknowledging the supremacy of the Anglican church. What seems to have crippled him however were the fines imposed upon him as a consequence. By 1684 he had let Sker out to a tenant named Thomas William and moved to London, having mortgaged the property to the Earl of Powis who was himself probably the most prominent overt Roman Catholic in Britain at this time.

In the year following, this debt was transferred to Charles Price of Badminton in Gloucester, though this too brought its own problems, in that Turberville's deeds relating to Sker had been lost when the Earl's London house was gutted by fire. Sker house and its manor was mortgaged for £1,000, though Christopher himself saw nothing of the money as it was paid directly by Price's agents to the Earl of Powis to settle the loan he already had.

In 1696 Christopher was again imprisoned, this time in the custody of G. Wyndham of Dunraven to whom he had earlier tried to sell Sker, and at this point he seems to have decided that enough was enough. There was no way he could redeem the mortgage on his property, and he had no intention of relinquishing his religious beliefs. In 1697 he, his wife Sarah, and two of their grandchildren were given permission to leave Britain for Holland, and he apparently chose to live his remaining years in exile. An entry in the court book of the Manor of

Pyle where he still retained some property indicates that he died in 1702.

The departure of Christopher and the transfer of Sker to other owners was not however the end of the Turberville connection with the district, for another branch still retained ownership of the manor of North Cornelly. Like their forebears they remained obstinately true to their religion and suffered accordingly, their house at Hall presumably replacing Sker as the focus of local recusant activity.

[Barrie omits to mention that in 1970, Pope Paul II canonised a group of 'The Six Welsh Martyrs'. Henceforth it is *Saint* Phillip Evans; the feast day is the 25th of October. *ed.*]

Chapter 15

Non-Conformists: Dissenters in Kenfig

The dissenting community which developed at Kenfig in the mid 17th century seems to have arrived in the Borough by a rather roundabout route. According to Thomas Rees in his 1861 *History of Protestant Non conformity in Wales*, the first regularly organised nonconformist church in the principality was formed at Llanvaches (in Newport, Mon.) in November 1639. Obviously there were already many nonconformists in Wales, but hitherto none had formed themselves into regular churches. The so called 'Long Parliament' with its avowed purpose of curbing both the spread of Roman Catholicism and the excesses of King Charles I, began its marathon term in November 1640, and immediately began introducing legislation easing the lot of the nation's Puritans. Shortly afterward the Civil War between Charles I and his Parliament erupted.

Initially Glamorgan and most of Wales supported the King, with many leading Welsh Nonconformists fleeing the country, taking refuge in England. By July 1645 however, the excesses of the Royal administrators had caused such ill feeling towards the Crown in Glamorgan, that King Charles himself met a delegation of the local gentry at St Fagan's on 29th of that month. The delegates did not come alone. With them was an army of yeomen of the county numbering between four and five thousand men, who drew up in battle formation to express solidarity with their leaders' grievances.

Charles left on the 5th August after apparently acceding to their demands, but his word evidently carried no weight with the general population. In September, Cardiff castle was seized from its Royalist garrison and the County declared for Parliament. Although there followed a couple of abortive uprisings, and of course the short-lived Second Civil War that ended at the battle of St Fagan's in 1649, Parliament thereafter retained control of the County, and the various Protestant Nonconformist congregations were able to worship openly.

At Kenfig the principal Nonconformist seems to have been Lewis Aylward of Kenfig Farm. He is first mentioned locally as a juror for the manorial survey held in 1650 at which time he owned a total of

56 freehold acres in the manor — over 67 acres in modern terms. Lewis in turn was closely associated with a man named Jacob Christopher about whom I would dearly love to know more.

The Restoration of the monarchy in 1660 saw the convening of a royalist parliament thirsting for revenge upon the Puritans. In 1662 the Act of Uniformity was introduced requiring the clergy of the Anglican Church (most of whom had been introduced under the Commonwealth) to either conform to its liturgy, or get out. Jacob Christopher was one of those who took the latter option and was therefore 'silenced' by this legislation. He died in 1676 and lies buried at Mawdlam church, but was evidently well known and respected beyond the bounds of the Borough.

Such information that I have been able to gather about Jacob is quite sparse and rather confusing. There are indications that he may have originated from Margam, but the first definite record of him that I have discovered places him in Newton Nottage at the time of the Commonwealth. According to Professor Leonard Higgins, the Puritans took control of this parish as early as 1644; ejected the incumbent (William Basset), and replaced him with a Presbyterian minister named Arnold Butler. He in turn was deprived of the living in 1650 and it then apparently lay vacant until January 1655 when Thomas Hilliard, an Essex man, was appointed.

It seems that during the interim, the parishioners took it upon themselves to appoint their own minister in the person of Jacob Christopher, and were therefore none too pleased at having an 'outsider' and a 'foreigner' foisted upon them by the authorities. Initially many of them continued to pay tithes to Christopher as "the lawful Rector of the Parish", which forced Hilliard to take action against them through the ecclesiastical courts.

Ultimately Jacob's former parishioners reluctantly accepted that they would never secure his re-instatement, and it was probably at this time that he joined a dissenting congregation at Cadoxton, Neath. This subsequently moved to Baglan near Port Talbot and met at the home of Robert Thomas who was also their pastor. From this congregation it seems, offshoots were subsequently established at both Kenfig and Newton Nottage.

Under the provisions of the Act of Uniformity of 1662 Lewis Aylward duly registered his house at Kenfig Farm as a meeting place for dissenters, and it seems that Christopher (described as a teaching elder with the Baglan congregation) moved to the village as their minister.

Aylward's openness about his religious activities brought problems in 1664 with the passing of the Conventicle Act. This decreed that "only five persons above sixteen years of age, besides the family" were to meet together for the purpose of worship other than at regular (Anglican) church services. It is not surprising to learn therefore, that Kenfig Farm was duly raided by the authorities whilst a service was in progress, and the preacher, Jacob Christopher, arrested and imprisoned.

If he had not lived at Kenfig previously, it is certain that Jacob and his wife Mary resided here following his release. His name appears as a witness to many local documents including several Wills which is perhaps a measure of the respect in which he was held.

I suspect that in order to circumvent the law both Christopher and his patron Lewis Aylward became 'partial conformists', attending sufficient services at Mawdlam church to satisfy legal requirements, but otherwise continuing to hold services at the farm and worship in their own way. Jacob was able to secure a preaching licence under the Declaration of Indulgence passed by Parliament in 1672, and three years later the following extract appears in a report upon the state of Nonconformity in Wales compiled by Henry Maurice the pastor of the church in Breconshire.

> There is another church, commonly called the church of Cadogstone, who meet now commonly at Baglan; Mr Robert Thomas being their pastor, Mr Jacob Christopher and Richard Cradock their teaching elders. What other officers they have I know not. Their judgement is Independent; some of them are Baptists, as hath been affirmed. Part of them also lie about Llangyfelach, as also Cynffyg in the said county.

According to Thomas Rees, Bussy Mansel of Briton Ferry was a prominent member of the Baglan Congregation. A report of 1662 states that they numbered about twenty. So who made up the Kenfig congregation? One certain candidate would be Thomas Lougher of Ty Maen, for both he and Lewis Aylward were later to be imprisoned for their religious views. Lewis was married to Jennet Lougher who from her surname would appear to be one of Thomas's family, so the two had connections beyond their church.

I also believe that Richard Cradock of Llanmihangel may have been a member, for Jacob Christopher witnessed both his will and that of his son Christopher. (He is not, however, the Richard Cradock who was a teaching elder with the Baglan congregation. The latter hailed from Newton Nottage where he held services in his own home.) Furthermore Richard christened two of his children with relatively obscure biblical names — Shadrack and Hannah — that were uncommon in the district. This seems to have been a quite usual practice amongst early Nonconformists, and Lewis Aylward himself had sons named Benjamin and Lazarus. The use of such names locally is so unusual as to make them stand out from the normal run of Richard, David, Evan, Mary, Margaret, etcetera, even though some of these are also Biblical in origin. The people who had given these more unusual names to their children knew their bible well, and bible reading played a central role in the Nonconformist religion.

With this in mind we may therefore tentatively include in their number Evan Lyddon and his wife Alice Gronow who had three children named Joshua, Noah and Hannah. There is a further connection of this family with Jacob Christopher through Alice's step-brother David Gronow. The latter was (the original inscription on the gravestone has now been almost entirely obliterated) buried with Jacob and his wife at Mawdlam[5], though their exact relationship is unknown.

Evan Lyddon was probably nothing more than a smallholder and a carpenter (several of his sons subsequently following that trade) whilst David was a local miller, so we can see that the dissenting congregation at Kenfig Farm in the 1660s probably contained a good cross section of the local community. The one thing they all had in common (besides their religion) was the fact that almost all the men-folk were apparently literate. Of the eight fathers and sons I mentioned above, for example, seven witnessed local documents with a signature. This, however, was not the case with their women who all signed similar records with their marks. This ardent desire amongst Nonconformists to learn to read the bible is perhaps illustrated by the case of Gronow William of New Mill who witnessed a document of 1650 with his mark. He was then aged 49 but eleven years later he witnessed another transaction by signing his name (albeit with some difficulty!). The chances are that he

---

[5] The inscription was noted by David Jones of Wallingford in 1889. Notebook 2.1149 23/24.

had learnt to read, but not to write — a not uncommon combination in those days.

Martyrs for the Faith: Given that the Kenfig Corporation evidently backed the formation of this short-lived school, then it is highly likely that the initiative stemmed from Lewis Aylward of Kenfig Farm. Not only was he a staunch Nonconformist but was probably the Portreeve at the time it was founded. The record of the Portreeves for this period is very fragmentary, but he certainly served in this capacity in 1668 and 1675, whilst there is persuasive evidence that he also held the post in 1666 and 1672. At this period of the Borough's history it was not unusual for the same person to be re-elected year after year, but it is significant that there is no mention of him in this capacity after 1675.

His home at Kenfig Farm continued to be a meeting place for dissenters even after the raid upon it in 1664, and under the Declaration of Indulgences in 1672, Jacob Christopher applied for and obtained a permit allowing him to hold services there. The Indulgence (which also allowed Catholics freedom of worship in their own homes) had been issued solely upon the initiative of King Charles II and was of short duration. When he recalled Parliament in January 1673 to vote funds for the war with Holland, the Members did so subject to certain conditions. One was the ending of the Indulgence; another was to give the royal assent to The Test Act. This came into force in March, and imposed severe restrictions upon all holders of public office. It was now made a condition of their holding such posts that they were to regularly take communion at an Anglican Church, and swear an oath recognising its supremacy. Naturally many Nonconformists and Roman Catholics could not find it within their consciences to do either.

Clearly Lewis Aylward was much respected both by his fellow burgesses and at Margam House for him to have been regularly re-elected as the Portreeve. Possibly therefore it was their representations that persuaded him to continue in the office for a time, but it seems that in 1675 he decided that he could not do so any longer. His position cannot have been made any easier with the death of his mentor Jacob Christopher on 1st June 1676. Such was the reputation of the latter that it was noted in the Mynydd Bach / Tirdonkin register at Llangyfelach:

> Mr Jacob Christopher of Margam, that useful and painful ser-
> vant of Christ, preacher of the Gospel for many years, departed
> this life on the last day of May 1676.

Jacob was buried at Mawdlam church, and his memorial can be seen as
a re-used flagstone in the porch. Unfortunately, because of this, part of
the inscription relating to the internment of David Gronow (possibly a
relative of his wife) has all but worn away which is sad. I know that
such re-use was in no way directed against Jacob personally – his just
happens to be the stone chosen for the purpose – but unfortunately it
does give an unfortunate impression of petty spite on the part of the
church authorities when the building was refurbished in Victorian
times.

The chapel meetings at Kenfig Farm continued, perhaps with
Lewis now as their head. Far from removing him from the notice of the
secular authorities however, his withdrawal from public service seems
to have made him a marked man. In May 1685 James, Duke of Monmouth, an illegitimate son of King Charles II landed at Lyme Regis,
with the stated objective of challenging the accession of his father's
brother, James I, to the throne of England. Probably because the new
King had already taken steps aimed at loosening the restrictions upon
Roman Catholics, the government was concerned that Monmouth
would find support amongst the country's leading Nonconformists.
Orders went out therefore

> for apprehending and securing all disaffected and suspicious
> persons, nonconformist Ministers and persons that have served
> against his Majesties Royall father or late royal brother.

Amongst those arrested were Lewis Aylward and Thomas Lougher
who were both incarcerated at Chepstow Castle.

As is well known, the attempted rebellion was easily crushed at
the battle of Sedgemoor in Somerset, and once Monmouth himself was
captured and executed the two were released, "being not accused to our
knowledge of having in any way corresponded with or otherwise abet-
ted the rebells".

Other documents relating to the area make it clear however that
the imprisonment of Aylward and Lougher was only one aspect of a
concerted drive by the authorities against dissenters here and in the
surrounding district. David Richard and Edward Frowde belonged to
the same class of petty gentry, as did most of those who formed the

congregation at Kenfig Farm. Indeed, although they were not residents of the borough themselves, it is difficult not to believe that they too were amongst its members.

Both David and Edward were staunch Nonconformists, so much so, that despite the threat of prosecution, neither would attend services at the local parish church in Tythegston. On 4th August 1684 the authorities took action against them, as described in a warrant issued to the constables of Neath Borough some time later. This ordered the arrest of dissenters who lived in that town, but included six people from outside the area, David and Edward amongst them. When the original warrants had been issued against these in their home parishes they

> had silently removed themselves for some time into such countys where the process would not run, or else so secured themselves in their houses as they could by noe means be taken.

The Nonconformist church at Kenfig Farm was itself an off-shoot of one at Baglan, Port Talbot which, in turn, had originated at Cadoxton, Neath, so this could explain why the two had fled there. Since the original warrant would have been addressed to the constables of the parish of Tythegston, it would have been meaningless outside its borders.

What the outcome was I'm not certain, but I find it very sinister that both men died shortly afterwards. Edward Frowde made his will on 24th April 1685 when he was living at home, but in poor health. He apparently lingered until the November of the following year, thereby surviving David Richard who, according to his gravestone at Tythegston, died on 22nd December 1685. In the jails of the time the unsanitary and cramped conditions meant that diseases such as gaol fever were endemic, and it seems likely that the two may have contracted some such illness whilst in custody resulting in their subsequent deaths.

Two other members of the congregation who probably fled Kenfig as a result of this wave of persecution were Lewis Aylward's sons Benjamin and Charles. The registers for the parish of Llangynwyd show that both were baptised at this church in 1683, Charles on 6th of June and his brother on 10th November. Although Benjamin's age is unknown he was almost certainly an adult whilst Charles was then 24 years of age.

It may be that the two had, like Richard and Frowde "silently removed themselves" from Kenfig when faced with the first round of warrants issued for the arrest of persistent dissenters. Alternatively, they may have been sent there by their father when he saw the way things were panning out. In either case their destination would probably have been Brynllewarch Farm which was the home of Samuel Jones, one of the leading Nonconformists of his day.

Clearly they still believed themselves to be a members of the Anglican community but free to hold their own religious views within it. This is what seems to have impressed Benjamin and Charles and led to their accepting baptism. In the case of Charles it certainly did not change his adherence to the Nonconformist cause, for he continued with the church established by his father when he in turn became owner of Kenfig Farm. Historians often refer to such people as 'partial-conformists' implying that they only went to church in order to enable them to still play an active role in public life. The case of the Aylwards, however, shows that it was not necessarily so simple

Chapter 16

Schooling comes to Kenfig

Whilst the ability to write one's name is in no way an accurate test of literacy, it does suggest that some form of education became available at Kenfig sometime after 1660. This can be seen in the table below which shows a huge increase in the proportion of men signing their names to documents (as opposed to making their mark) between 1660 and 1720. The most likely reason for such a rise which (as in this sample) tends to become more pronounced as the children who had enjoyed schooling progressed into adulthood. Furthermore, the dismal figures for women able to sign their names suggest that such a school was exclusively for boys. In several instances those few women who could write their names can be shown to have lived their early lives outside the Borough, and had presumably been educated there. In this respect therefore, the school at Kenfig seems to have differed from the one at Haregrove and also possibly from another sponsored by the Mansel family for their tenants at Margam.

Could they write their names? Everyone thinks that our ancestors were largely illiterate — that they couldn't even write their own names — or could they? When I first got interested in local history, I cheerfully accepted this widely held view, and continued to do so for a very long time, until I began digging a little deeper into the fabric of local communities in the 17th century.

Whilst carrying out my research project at Stormy in the 1980s, I became aware that far more of its inhabitants actually signed their name to legal documents than I would have expected. Even more surprising was the fact that these were not people exclusively from the upper levels of local society, but often small farmers and their families. Eventually I traced the reason to a small private school that existed at Haregrove Farm throughout the second half of the 17th century and the early decades of the 18th.

My project was by then too far advanced for me to do more than carry out some cursory research into the effect of this school upon the community, but when I started work on the Borough of Kenfig, I was forewarned and forearmed. Consequently I kept a specific record of those inhabitants who witnessed or signed a document, and whether they used a signature or made their mark.

The accompanying table shows the result of this research. It is **not** a table showing the extent of adult literacy in the Borough. If such a thing were possible, then the percentage figures for males capable of signing their names would undoubtedly be smaller. It is not even a reliable indication of the proportion of people signing documents compared to those so illiterate they could only make their mark. Because the documents were legal papers, they were generally drawn up on behalf of, and witnessed by, people from the upper levels of local society. To put it crudely, one did not invite the village idiot to be a witness to one's last Will and Testament or the lease upon one's home! Again, I cannot be sure that all those in my sample were actually raised in Kenfig, only that they were closely associated with the borough in later life. Nevertheless despite these reservations the table did serve its purpose.

People using signatures at Kenfig 1650-1720

YEAR	TOTAL SAMPLE	MALES	who signed	% signed	FEMALES signed	mark
1650	37	16	13	55.2	1	7
1660	63	29	22	56.9	2	10
1670	68	32	21	60.4	2	13
1680	62	32	18	64.0	2	10
1690	66	38	18	67.8	1	9
1700	66	41	17	70.7	1	7
1710	56	35	15	70.0	1	5
1720	62	42	15	73.7	0	5

What the figures for each year indicate is that in 1670, for example, there were 68 people in the Borough who had either in the past, or would in the future, witness a document. Of this total, 53 were adult males of whom 21 (39.6%) made their mark and 32 (60.4%) signed. Not normally included in these totals, incidentally, are those people whose only opportunity to sign was when they made their last Will and Testament. Generally this was done at the last moment when the testators were so feeble they even had difficulty making their marks!

For a time my theory regarding the existence of a school remained just that. Then I happened across two references in the Glamorgan County History proving that one had indeed existed at "Cunffig" in 1675 and 1678. It was run by The Welsh Trust, and there were 20 pupils. As to when it had started, or how it came to be there, no information is apparently available. Initially, however, the story starts in London with a remarkable man named Thomas Gouge.

Born in 1605 at Bow, London, Thomas Gouge was educated first at Eton and then King's College, Cambridge. After obtaining his degree, he went to serve the parish of Colsden near Croydon, but a few years later in 1638 took up the living of St Sepulchre's in London. This was neither a rich nor a fashionable parish, and Gouge was long remembered for his work amongst the poor and destitute families that lived there. A great believer in self-help, besides distributing alms he also provided flax for some of the unemployed to spin into linen at their homes. He then purchased the finished product and sold it where he could through friends and contacts. Retaining his living during the Commonwealth, he subsequently left it as a consequence of the Act of Uniformity of 1662.

How and why Thomas Gouge became interested in the state of education in Wales is not known, but the fact is that he did, and his work here commenced in 1670, becoming formalised as The Welsh Trust four years later. It was an undertaking financed almost entirely by himself with the aid of friends and others in the capital, together with support from the nobility and gentry in Wales. It had, as Dr Tillotson (later Archbishop of Canterbury) reminded mourners at Gouge's funeral, two main objectives.

> One, to have poor children brought up to read and write; the other, to furnish persons of grown age, the poor especially, with the necessary helps and means of knowledge, as the Bible, and other books of piety and devotion, in their own language.

It was a massive and quite extra-ordinary undertaking for one man, but he devoted the remainder of his life to its cause. Although Gouge was a

Nonconformist, and was principally concerned in enabling the Welsh nation to read their Bible and other religious publications, he was quite liberal in the manner he operated the Trust. Amongst the items it published, for example, was the Anglican Catechism and Liturgy which appeared in 1677.

> In its first year of operation (1674-5) the Trust reported that In fifty-one of the chief towns of Wales 812 poor children have been and are put to school to learn English, over and above the 500 put to school the last year, by the charity of others, before this trust began.

It is likely that the school at Kenfig was one of those 51, though it is also possible that there may have been one already in existence. Its local sponsor was almost certainly the Kenfig Corporation, and the town hall would be its schoolroom, for the Trust found little favour with the Anglican clergy and so would almost certainly not have been allowed use of the church at Mawdlam.

The decision to teach the children in English, whilst distributing Welsh publications to the adult population, earned the Welsh Trust some condemnation at the time, and subsequently. Herein, however, lay a constant problem for educationalists in Wales. The blunt truth was that no matter how well educated a child might be in his native tongue, it would not enable him to better himself in a world of commerce and administration where English was the medium. Gouge tried to bridge this with his English schools and Welsh publications but sadly his initiative proved to be of short duration. Following his death in 1681 the Trust folded and its work came to an end.

The school at Kenfig was closed, and when the Anglican SPCK established the next school in the district, it was based upon the parish church at Pyle. Given the antipathy between the two communities, the location was itself sufficient to condemn it in the eyes of many Kenfig inhabitants! Consequently after 1720 the percentages of people able to sign their name in the Borough tumbled. A striking footnote to the work of the school at Kenfig is nevertheless provided by the Suit Roll for the Manor of Kenfig Borough in 1699 (PM 5787). This lists 34 burgesses of whom 22 had or were required to sign documents at some stage in their life. Of these only four had to make their mark, and as the brother of one of the latter could certainly write his name, it seems that in his case he was simply a poor scholar!

SKER HOUSE TODAY (FOLLOWING A MAJOR RE-FURBISHMENT)
PORT TALBOT STEELWORKS AND MYNYDD MARGAM IN THE
BACKGROUND.
(PHOTO BY CYRIL JAMES)

Chapter 17

New Owners: New Survey 1660

It is my view that when a Lord of the Manor decided to hold a survey of his property, then prior notice was given to the tenants about the nature of the questions to be asked. In this way interminable debates at the actual hearing of the evidence were avoided, and the business in hand could be disposed of without unnecessary delay. That being the case therefore, towards the end of 1660[6], with the monarchy newly restored in the person of Charles II, the burgesses of Kenfig must have received a nasty shock. It was not that the Earl of Pembroke had ordered a new survey of their manor (they were quite used to those), but the nature of the questions that his steward would be requiring them to answer certainly was.

In the past such surveys had been confined to questions about the routine feudal rents, dues and duties owed by the tenants. This questionnaire however contained very pertinent questions regarding their Borough and organisation which, in truth, was none of their lord's business. It may be that the Mansels of Margam had already made tentative approaches to the Earl regarding the possibility of purchasing this manor, and the latter wanted to be sure that there was nothing due to him from the burgesses that had not been declared in earlier surveys.

Memories of the debâcle of Wyseman's visit ninety years before may still have survived in the corporate memory, and hot-heads amongst the burgesses may well have argued that they ought to refuse to answer questions regarding their organisation. In this they would have been quite justified, but the year was 1661, and it would have been a very brave (or foolhardy) tenant who risked the wrath of his lord on a point of principle in those days! Fortunately the burgesses had time,

---

[6] The Survey is actually dated January 1660, and is usually referred to as having been made at that time. However, the reference in the title to King Charles as the ruling monarch shows that the date is an ecclesiastical one – the church year starting and ending at Easter. Consequently the true date would have been January 1661 and if the burgesses were indeed notified of the survey questions beforehand, this would have been done in the closing months of 1660

and they used it to prepare a set of answers that would satisfy the Earl without revealing to him anything that he did not already know. Whilst, therefore, the details contained in this survey have always been regarded as an accurate portrayal of the Borough organisation at this time it is in fact a mixture of truths, half-truths, evasions, and down-right lies!

Those who sat on the survey jury were tenants of the manor as opposed to burgesses, but I have little doubt that most if not all were qualified under both titles — except one. So far as I can discover Jenkin William had no connection whatsoever with the Lower Borough. He was probably an educated man (certainly capable of signing his name) who operated the fulling mill in Higher Kenfig, and in 1668 is mentioned in connection with property at Pyle. Other than the mill, I have never come across any mention of him in connection with land in either portion of the borough. The most likely explanation for his inclusion within the fourteen-man jury therefore, is that he lived at the mill in Higher Kenfig, and it was probably because he was the Portreeve that he would act as their spokesman.

It was not a particularly high-powered body of jurors that he had with him. The most important was probably Thomas Hopkin Pritchard who was tenant of Marlas farm. Of the others Thomas Morgan styled himself 'gent' when conferring land upon one of his sons as part of a marriage settlement in 1665, but nobody else seems to have addressed him by this title in other documents. So far as I can discover he only owned 11 acres of freehold land in the Lower Borough though of course he may have been renting other plots as well.

Although Henry Lyddon, another juror, was very active in the district, frequently signing documents as a witness, I cannot connect him with any local property. Many other members of his family were carpenters, and it is possible that this was also his occupation. The clerk, Thomas Richard, aged 81, was included, as was a David Thomas Howell aged 72 who was tenant of land in both Higher and Lower Kenfig. They were probably there because their age gave them considerable knowledge of past events and customs in the borough. Three of the jurors were so poor that in a 1673 collection of Hearth Tax in the parish they were excused payment. Nine of the 14 appear in other documents where they had been required to sign their name, and of these nearly half could only make their mark.

The survey: On the question of the boundaries of their Borough, the jury decided to describe them as they indeed were, an account that we followed when making a comparison with those described to Thomas Wyseman in 1592. Then came the usual detailed lists of tenants, on completion of which the jurors steeled themselves to negotiate the minefield laid amidst the questions that followed. It was a quite dazzling performance — certainly good enough to pull the wool over the eyes of Robert Williams the steward!

With regard to question 4. relating to the organisation of their Borough, they could afford to be fairly open. The nature of the courts they held and the procedure for appointing the Portreeve and other officers, would have been well known to Williams anyway for (though not stated in the document), he probably held the honorary title of Constable of the Castle. In this capacity he would therefore have been involved in the Portreeve's appointment and presided over the two Courts Leet held during the year.

Rather surprisingly however the jury claimed that their courts were empowered to "determine all manner of suits, actions, and plaints between party and party to any value whatsoever". In later documents, actions brought at these 'Courts of Pleas' (held alongside the normal manorial courts) were limited to those involving sums of less than two pounds. They also rather neatly dodged the question of the Portreeve's remuneration, with an all-embracing answer regarding payments to their Borough Officers in general. Such payments, they declared, "are both uncertain and inconsiderable". This was basically true of the Sergeant, Constable, Aletasters, and Hayward, though later records show that a small annual salary was paid to the last named. Sixty years later, records show that the Portreeve was making quite a handsome profit (in the context of the times) from his year in office. Having collected the Borough rate from the burgesses, he then paid a fixed amount of £2.10s. 0d. into the Corporation's coffers and kept the rest for himself! When, early in the 19th century a decision was made to pay Portreeves a fixed annual sum, this was set at £3 — more than they had been paying in as the rate collection!

With the fifth question, the jury's answers start to become more evasive. They were not certain, they said, how many of the burgesses ought to perform suit at every court, nor were they aware of any payments due from them to the lord, except the rent for Kenfig Down and a fixed sum of ten shillings. This last, incidentally, seems to be a fixed rate to cover the burgage rent. In the medieval period this had been paid at the rate of a shilling per burgage, but following the abandonment of old Kenfig, the Corporation and their landlord seem to have settled upon this sum. These were probably honest enough answers, but on the sixth question Portreeve and Steward locked horns.

It seems that the questionnaire required to know the nature of the oath taken from a burgess on admission, and how it compared with that administered in the past. With the restoration of the monarchy so recent, this was a loaded question! It is probably no accident that the borough's two leading burgesses and prominent dissenters, Richard Cradock and Lewis Aylward were not included amongst the jurors. It is likely that both had supported the Commonwealth, during which time the oath of admission (of which to date I have found no record) was amended to remove all references to the Crown. This question was probably designed therefore to discover if this had been so, and whether it had now been changed back.

The response, presumably delivered by the Portreeve on behalf of the jury, gave nothing away — certainly not the wording of the oath!

> They say that for ought they know the oath of late years administered unto the said burgesses is agreeable in substance and effect with the oath of the burgesses time out of mind, but to declare the particulars thereof they know not.

Having delivered this statement we can almost imagine him meeting the steward's eyes with a look that declared "and short of the thumbscrew or the rack that's all you're getting from us mate"! What he was saying in effect was that so far as the jury knew, the oath was substantially the same as it had always been, though what that oath was they hadn't a clue! Put another way they were implying that the burgesses had always sworn loyalty to the country's rulers, whoever they might be, but in the changed political climate they were not going to admit that this had included Oliver Cromwell's Commonwealth!

This response was duly noted by Williams, and the enquiry continued smoothly to question 11. which again related to the admission of new burgesses. The jury could declare in all honesty that no payment was due to the Lord of the Manor at such admissions, but they were guilty of being rather economical with the truth when stating what number that might be admitted. Their reply was that this could be as many as the Portreeve and Aldermen decided upon, with the agreement and consent of the burgesses as a whole. In one sense this was perfectly correct in respect of 'out-burgesses', but as we have noted the number of in-dwelling burgesses was in practice limited to 57 or possibly 58. That, however, was their business, and they saw no good reason why the lord of the manor needed to know about such things.

The very last survey 1668: This was carried out six years later and was supplemented by a detailed survey of the Lord's demesne lands. The reason for this became evident in 1668 when Philip Herbert, Earl Pembroke, sold the manor *en bloc* to Sir Edward Mansel of Margam on 11th May. The purchase price was £525, and for the first time since its creation, both the manors within the Second Borough belonged to the same landlord.

Consolidation of the two manors that contained the elements of Kenfig Borough under one landlord was to prove something of a mixed blessing for the burgesses of the lower borough. Unlike their brethren in Higher Kenfig, many of them were freeholders who could maintain a certain independence from the whims and wishes of their lord. The Mansels however lived right on their doorstep, so their activities were under far closer scrutiny than it had been by the Earls of Pembroke who (so far as is known) never even visited the place.

This indifference had sometimes worked against the burgesses' own interests, leading in one instance to the loss of the corn mill. There had also been the inordinate delay before the Earl had taken any action over Jenkin Turberville's encroachment on the common, and this same lack of interest apparently allowed Turberville to subsequently retain the spoils of his illegal actions. At the same time the Corporation had also used this inertia on the part of the lord to their advantage. Wyseman's report written at that time makes it perfectly clear that the burgesses and other inhabitants of Kenfig enjoyed no rights whatsoever in respect of Kenfig Pool, but 70 years later they actually seem to have acquired some!

For the 1661 survey of the manor, the jurors were required to state what fish were taken there, and what profit accrued to the lord from this. The steward noted their reply that there were only eels and roach in its waters, but added:

They alsoe say that the fishing of the said pool doth belong to
the burgesses of the said town and burrough, and they know not
of any certain or considerable benefitt or profitt received by any.

Probably because of the indifferent fish stock this astonishing claim to
the fishing rights apparently went unchallenged. Later, under the eagle
eye of the Mansels and their steward at nearby Margam, such mis-
appropriations of the lord's rights would never be so simple, and a tangible example of this new and enhanced proprietary interest is apparent
in the rentals shortly after the year 1692.

Under the Earls of Pembroke, the Kenfig Portreeve had apparently acted as the bailiff for the manor, collecting the rents annually and
accounting for them to the lord's steward at Cardiff Castle. Although
not apparent in the few Pembroke rentals that survive, we may fairly
deduce that this was indeed the case, since this was the practice followed by the Mansels after they purchased the manor in 1668.

Most of the Margam rentals survive somewhere in the two major document collections at Aberystwyth and Swansea, and are invaluable to the local historian in helping to build up a picture of the estate.
With regard to the manor of Kenfig Borough, the Portreeve accounted
for two sets of rents — those due upon land and property owned and
sub-let by the lord, and then a second roll showing the fixed rents due
from the freeholders. This continued to be the case up until 1692, but
thereafter the Mansels transferred responsibility for collection of the
first group of rents to their steward or a bailiff, who was almost invariably not the Borough's Portreeve. The latter still retained responsibility for collection of the manor's freehold rents the real value of which
were diminishing with passage of time. Sadly none of his accounts for
these collections have survived, and all we have is the total amount he
paid to the steward and included on his annual rental. For the historian
this means that after 1692 it becomes almost impossible to keep track of
the changes in ownership of the various freehold lands and cottages.

One legacy of this role of the Portreeve still survived into the 19th
century in the Borough 'minute books', where sittings of the manorial
courts at the town hall were recorded. These were the monthly Courts
Baron, dealing purely with matters affecting the lord's property in the
manor, and the twice-yearly Courts Leet. The latter are sometimes described as 'criminal courts' a phrase which, whilst technically correct,
does tend to give the wrong impression. They dealt with matters relat-

ing solely to the estate's property and rights, and the most serious (and common!) 'crime' was usually the failure of tenants to trim their hedges adjoining the manor's roads and trackways.

Courts Leet were presided over by the Margam steward and the Courts Baron by the Portreeve. Since the latter was only responsible for the freehold property it is doubtful that many were actually held in any given year. Although an entry for every such monthly court is duly entered in the minute book, usually there is no mention of any business being transacted, nor of any jury being empanelled. Often when business is recorded it relates to matters of interest only to the burgesses. They seem, in fact to have utilised the Courts Baron simply as "Hall Days" — meetings of the burgesses called by the Portreeve to consider Borough matters. Generally speaking, so far as manorial business is concerned, the entries are few and far between and confined to the freehold properties.

One side effect of the use of the minute book for manorial purposes is that only occasionally are any Borough 'minutes' actually recorded in it! It was those suspicious burgesses again! Because it was a record of the manor courts, the book would have been open to inspection by the steward and his clerk. They didn't mind them seeing the record of transfers of parcels of hay and fern between burgesses, but details of their own private deliberations were another matter! So as a record of the burgesses' private business and administration the minute books are actually of very limited value until the close of the 18th century!

People and their Houses

The Kenfig Folk

Introducing the 'Folk' of Kenfig, and their homes:

It is an old truism about history that it is made by people, but it is one that past historians have often honoured in the breach rather than in the observance. Many local histories tend to focus upon buildings, places and events, ignoring the lives of the ordinary men and women to whom these are linked. This is not a criticism, merely a statement of fact. Lives of the leaders of local society both locally and nationally can often be followed from the documents they left behind and references to them in records generated by their contemporaries. Ordinary people such as those who made up the population of the Borough of Kenfig kept no diaries and wrote few letters or, if by some chance they ever did, then none have survived. Since it is also highly unlikely that any of them could ever have afforded to have their portraits painted, we will likewise never even know what they looked like.

When I first planned this second book I determined that, despite these obvious difficulties, I was going to attempt to relate the story of the second Borough of Kenfig as the story of its people. Of these earliest inhabitants, however, I can say virtually nothing, not even how many there were. The earliest reliable figures are given in the census returns commencing in 1801. That for 1831, for example, shows that the borough was then home to some 485 inhabitants of whom 276 lived in 58 houses in Kenfig Lower and the rest in Higher Kenfig. Prior to this no proper figures are available and no truly reliable method of estimating population figures from other sources has yet been developed.

In an effort to rectify this, and to identify the people of Kenfig down the ages, I created a computer record of all inhabitants listed in the borough between 1500 and 1850. Utilising this I drew up a list of those living here on 1st January 1668 on a 'heads of household' basis. When completed it identified 51 individuals dwelling in the lower borough with another 35 in Higher Kenfig – 86 households in all.

The 1831 census suggests that the average number of persons per house then was 4.75, and on that basis the population of the two halves of the borough in 1668 would have been about 408, but my gut feeling is that this is on the low side. The nature of the documents from which I drew my information is such that I would not normally expect to obtain much information about sub-tenants or labourers living in cottages attached to the farms where they worked. My figure of 408 is therefore best viewed as a minimum, and it is probable that there were as many people living within the borough boundaries then as there were in 1831. Earlier than 1668 the documentary evidence is too sparse to allow any similar calculations to be attempted.

John Thomas ap Howell of Llanmihangel Grange It may seem a little ironic that the first local character we meet in this history of the 'Second Borough' of Kenfig was at that point in life where he was preparing to depart it. This is because one of the richest sources of material concerning our ancestors is usually their Last Will and Testament and the probate inventories of their belongings drawn up immediately following their death. In the case of John Thomas ap Howell of Llanmihangel Grange it is his will provides almost my entire stock of information that I have been able to glean about him.

The date then is 9th September 1528, and the location is the former monastic Grange of St. Michael, better known to us today as Llanmihangel. This was not the lovely old rambling farmhouse that graces the spot today, but a group of buildings standing a little higher up the slope to the east. No trace of

them remain above ground today save for a fragment of the adjoining great barn hidden amongst the jumble of farm buildings on the opposite side of the lane.

John Thomas Howell whose life was slowly ebbing away on that September day in 1528 is the earliest of these tenants of whom I have discovered any record. Much of the Grange land actually lay outside the Borough boundary but, since the Grange buildings themselves did not, it was one of those Higher Kenfig residences that entitled its tenant to admission into the ranks of the burgesses and undoubtedly John was one of their number.

As he lay on his death bed, a clerk sat alongside with pen poised ready to record his decisions regarding the disposal of his earthly goods (Ridden, 1985). As a good son of the Roman Catholic Church, John's first thoughts were for his immortal soul. This he dedicated "to God and to the Blessed Lady, and to all the saints in heaven" whilst his body was "to be buried in the monastery of Our Blessed Lady of Morgan [Margam]". Then, in the spirit of the times, he made generous gifts to the church in an attempt to ensure that his soul would prove acceptable to The Almighty. A bullock apiece went to the Cathedral at Llandaff, and the houses of both the Grey and the Black Friars in Cardiff. To Margam Abbey he gave two candlesticks, and the sum of three shillings and four pence was donated to "the rood of Llangonoed". The rood was the carved and decorated screen that separated the sanctuary of a church from the congregation in the nave, and the one at Llangynwyd was probably either being replaced or renovated at this time.

His only heirs were his wife Denise and daughter Jennet. He therefore declared that his goods and chattels be divided into three parts, one portion each for them, and the third to be sold off so as to pay his debts and meet the expense of his funeral. Finally he bequeathed his lands and the remaining years on the lease at Llanmihangel to his wife and after her death, to Jennet.

Lawrence William, Llanmihangel: Our story moves on twelve years to 9th July 1540 and the will of the next tenant at the Grange — a man named Lawrence William (Ridden, 1985). I strongly suspect he had married John's daughter Jennet, but by this time he was a widower with no less than eleven children all under the age of 21. There were two sons and nine daughters, and part of the reason I suspect that Jennet may have been Lawrence's wife is that their boys were named John and Thomas (after their maternal grandfather and his father?), and two of the girls were called Jennet. Unusual as this may appear (and these are certainly the only examples of two living daughters being christened with the same name that I've ever encountered) they also had another two girls named Margaret! This may imply a

certain lack of imagination on the part of the parents, but there is actually another possible explanation.

The families that inhabited Kenfig did indeed generally show a lack of imagination when naming their children. When a baby was born they seem to have looked no further than a small pool of 'cherished names' that had been used by their ancestors. Often the eldest son was given the name of his father or grandfather, and the eldest daughter the name of her mother. Just how important this was to them is demonstrated by the fact that parents frequently christened a new baby with a family name that had originally been bestowed upon an earlier child that had died. In some instances — where the family was cursed by an unusually high child mortality rate — the same name was used time and again in the hope that the latest baby would survive and carry it on into adulthood. What perhaps happened with Lawrence's family is that the first Jennet and Margaret may have been sickly children who were thought unlikely to survive, so the name was given to the next born even though the older sister was still tenaciously clinging to life. This battle with death they obviously won and the two youngest girls were thereafter known as 'Little Jennet' and 'Little Margaret' respectively.

'Little Margaret' in fact left a legacy of her own that was to endure in the area long after she too was dead and gone. That part of the miniature gorge (which can be seen below Brynteg Road) through which the Kenfig river flows above Llanmihangel Mill is today universally known as "The Collwyn" and the wood on the Margam side of the stream was known as Coed y Gollen in the late 18th century. Documents of that period nevertheless show that it had previously been a field belonging to Llanmihangel called "Waun Maggy Fach" ("Little Margaret's Field"), though just why she should be commemorated in this way remains a mystery.

Whether or not Lawrence was John Thomas's son-in-law or merely his successor at Llanmihangel, in the short space of time that had elapsed since the latter's death developments beyond the boundaries of Glamorgan had turned the district upside down. For Lawrence, the development of most immediate concern would have been the dissolution of the monasteries by the Tudor King, Henry VIII.

Diplomatically therefore Lawrence dedicated his soul "to God and all the holy company of heaven" which would, of course, have included the Virgin even if he had not mentioned her by name. Like John Thomas before him he also made gifts to the church for the good of his soul — six shillings and eight pence to Margam, and two shillings each to the churches at Llangynwyd and Kenfig (Mawdlam). What is most interesting is that the largest amount — ten shillings — he gave "to the

maintenance of the work of the church of Llanveangell".

Lawrence's will again reflects his uncertainty regarding this new order. He was a wealthy landowner with a farm at Cardiff and land at Cilybebyll in the Swansea valley. Being of Welsh extraction he was clearly uneasy about leaving all his worldly goods to his eldest son according to the new order of things. Although he assigned varying quantities of cattle to each of his daughters, the remainder of his property was divided equally between his sons John and Thomas. The farm at Cardiff was allocated to the latter and Llanmihangel to John. As all the children were young, he appointed John Turberville to be their guardian. This was presumably the man of that name who was lord of Tythegston and a staunch Roman Catholic, so the new church order found little in his favour. Lawrence would have selected him only after a good deal of thought, and his choice together with the retention of Llanmihangel Chapel and the carefully worded dedication of his soul in his will, perhaps indicates where his true religious sympathies lay.

The will empowered Turberville to take control of Lawrence's estates until the children became of age. The dying man instructed that he should use the income from this source to "put my sons to school and to marry [off] my daughters according to his discretion" with the advice of others who had been appointed to be overseers of the will.

Administration of the estate was granted to Turberville on February 23rd in the following year, and the will was proved on August 30th, 1541. By this later date, however, young Thomas Lawrence was also dead, leaving his brother John as the sole heir to all their father's former land. In 1557 (by which time he had presumably become of age) John Lawrence surrendered his father's lease by which he held Llanmihangel to Edward Mansel of Margam. This may have been because he wished to take out a fresh lease upon the property but, as we hear nothing further of him in local records thereafter, it rather looks as though he then quit the area for good.

Evan Griffith, Portreeve

Evan was the Portreeve who presided over the enclosure at the Rugge (see Chapter 8) and was undoubtedly the inspiration behind it. He was not a rich man. The 1570 survey shows that he owned just seven acres of freehold land within the borough — a mere smallholding. At the time he made his will (Llandaff Wills) in 1605 this had been reduced to three and three quarter acres which he probably kept for growing corn to feed his household. The same document nevertheless indicates that he owned a herd of cattle and a flock of sheep which, as a burgess, he would have been able to graze on its commons, but this was not simply a case of subsistence farming

for his own needs. Mention in the will of a "yearling bullock" indicates that like other farmers of the district he was rearing young stock to sell off to the drovers once they reached the age of three years. His flock produced wool that he could sell to the agents of West-Country weavers for export via the neighbouring port of Newton. Alternatively, he and his wife Joan could spin the raw material into yarn and knit this into stockings which likewise found a ready market across the channel. Such small-scale cattle rearing and wool production was very common amongst local smallholders at this time, providing a welcome supplement to any income earned as labourers or craftsmen.

What initially may seem unusual about Evan's livestock is that his will indicates that he owned at least three 'kine' or dairy cows. Usually smallholders like him only owned just one, possibly two — sufficient to provide butter and cheese for their own needs. On larger farms the numbers were greater, for at this time butter was the chief export of Newton and indeed, of all the other Glamorgan ports. Again this seems to indicate that Evan was utilising his grazing rights on the common to maintain a slightly larger herd than required for his own needs, and was also selling off any excess butter he produced.

Two other items mentioned in his will perhaps put these other enterprises into context. One is a load of furniture that he tells us he and Watkin Thomas Griffith (perhaps a nephew), had purchased jointly. The other is a 'wain' or wagon. This last would have allowed him to take on odd haulage jobs as a carter, whilst the furniture was obviously a job-lot bought for resale. He was a man who did a bit of everything — cattle and sheep rearing; cheese and butter producing; haulage work; second-hand furniture sales; and who knows what else!

From his varied enterprises Evan may have secured enough of an income to be regarded by his neighbours as a person of some standing within the community, sufficiently so to be their Portreeve. To achieve this, the time-honoured fashion was that his name would have been submitted along with two others to the Constable of the Castle at the Autumn Leet Court. He would then have been chosen to hold office for the ensuing year. His success in achieving both the nomination and selection suggests something else about him too. Material success might have given him some status, but it was his character that won him respect; that was what secured his nomination for this office. We know that he held the post on at least two occasions and probably more.

In the class-conscious 16th century Evan, for all his enterprise, was at best a yeoman. Whilst holding the office of Portreeve however he was rated a 'gentleman' and was accorded the honorific title 'Mr' that went with this elevated status. Not just any gentleman ei-

ther! Richard Thomas of Marlas was a 'gentleman' and as Leslie Evans (1964) reminds us, he was the son of Richard ap Thomas of Ynysarwed in the Neath Valley, a very ancient Welsh family. His wife Margaret was the daughter of Hopkin Thomas Philip the soldier bard of Llandyfodwg. Richard (who had settled at Marlas in 1543) was no mere farmer. He rented out the bulk of his land to tenants and lived off the income. Tangible evidence of this family's status is that he (or his son Thomas) built the present mansion house as a fitting home for people of their quality. Yet whilst Evan held the office of Portreeve he was Thomas's superior. When admitted as a burgess, Richard Thomas would have sworn an oath to be ruled by the Portreeve of the town, and so long as Evan held office, that continued to be the case.

John Thomas, Marlas and Lewis Aylward, Kenfig Farm In the 1699 Window Tax return, only three people in Kenfig Lower are shown for payments at the higher rate. John Thomas and Lewis Aylward lived at Marlas and Kenfig Farms respectively, but the place of residence of the third so listed — **Lazarus Aylward** — is unknown and it is therefore more than likely that it was The Corporation House, as the only other building of any size in the lower Borough at the time.

There is an implication in various Margam estate documents relating to the Aylwards that Lazarus was Lewis's eldest son, but

Kenfig Farm and much of the land went to his brother Charles who is specifically stated to be his father's third son. This may hint at a family rift, but Lewis did actually settle some of his property upon Lazarus — probably at the time of the latter's marriage. Be that as it may the Poll Tax return of 1689 (PM 5139) indicates that Lazarus was then living with his wife and family in a home of his own and Window Tax returns of 1699 and 1700 (PM 4974) show that his house was sufficiently large to have more than ten windows.

Listed on the Poll Tax return with him and his (unnamed) wife are Mary and Catherine Aylward who were probably their daughters, whilst Lewis, (who from subsequent references seems to have been their son) is shown as living with his grandfather of the same name at Kenfig Farm. All these people would have to have been aged fourteen or above to be included on the return, so Lazarus's wife Ann who gave birth in 1700 to another son (christened Lazarus after his father) was probably his second wife.

Lazarus senior died in 1704 (This is the year of his will and the probate inventory drawn up following his death (Llandaff Wills)) and was clearly in some financial difficulty at the time. The reasons for this are dealt with more fully in a later chapter, but it does serve to illustrate the point that being the proprietor of licensed premises was not in itself considered to be a good living. This was true for sub-sequent tenants at The Corporation House. Even those who were proprietors of Pyle Inn, which in addition to normal licensed trade, provided refreshment and accommodation for travellers on the main road through South Wales struggled. It was therefore normal practice for the main burden of running such premises to fall upon the wives of the licensees whilst their men-folk sought other means of supplementing the family income. Lazarus had a smallholding and William Harry who succeeded him many years later took casual work in the area.

Lazarus would have been the Corporation's tenant for the premises, paying them an annual rent. As well as his garden (on the site now occupied by the car park of the present premises) his tenancy would also have included The Prince Field on the opposite side of Heol Kenfig. The name of this enclosure on the 1847 Tithe Map is 'Willona' which seems to indicate that there was a well or spring here that supplied fresh water for the household. Another name – 'Cae Ffald' – applied to the field immediately adjoining his kitchen garden indicates that part of it was taken up by the common pound in which the Hayward placed any stray livestock found wandering in the lower borough. The Borough Minute Books also mention a stable attached to the property which initially occupied the end of the eastern wing of the building, but may subsequently have been rebuilt here. Together, the fold and the stable probably account for the architectural features apparent in the boundary wall of the car park today.

The Aylwards of Kenfig Farm: South of The Corporation House the land between Heol Kenfig and Heol Lane was owned by the Aylward family, their home at Kenfig Farmhouse being set back slightly from the main road. By repute it is the oldest house in the village, and was perhaps erected by Henry Aylward who was prosecuted for his adherence to the Roman Catholic faith in 1605. On architectural grounds the earliest features of this building are dated by RCAHMW (1998) to the early 17th century, and since it stood amidst their own fields, the Aylwards would not have had to await the enclosure of common land in order to build.

The recusancy rolls refer to Henry Aylward as a "gent", indicating that he was a person of some standing, and the family are believed to be one of the oldest in the district at that time. They seem to be descendants of Aelward de Cornelly, one of a family who are the earliest known lords of the manor of South Cornelly. He is mentioned in the late 12th century and the Margam charters also mention an Adam, son of Aylward in 1213, who was probably his son. Between 1258 and 1307 the same source contains references to a William Aelward in a context that suggests he was very likely a burgess at Kenfig with business interests in Cardiff. In 1400 a Henry

Aylward is mentioned as Kenfig's 'Provost' or Portreeve — the earliest known holder of this office.

The Henry who lived at Kenfig in 1605 is first mentioned in a deed recording a land transaction (PM 5989) he concluded with Richard Thomas in 1592/3 where he is referred to as "Henry William Thomas Aylward". His father, William, was one of those who had apparently flirted with the idea of adopting the Welsh custom of using patronyms, and in his day had insisted upon being known as William ap Thomas Aylward. Although Henry too seems to have considered continuing this practice he eventually rejected the idea and reverted to being known simply as 'Henry Aylward'.

Henry's religious beliefs were undoubtedly influenced by the fact that his mother, Margaret, was a member of the Turbervilles of Penllyn, and a sister to Jenkin Turberville who built Sker House. No doubt it was this family connection that secured for her husband William the stewardship of the Turberville's manor at North Cornelly, a post he is mentioned as holding in 1560 (Evans, 1964: 60-1). Further bolstering Henry's religious convictions was the fact that his own wife, Catherine Thomas, was a daughter of Thomas Began of Pyle who is listed for recusancy in 1590 and 1591. Ominously, perhaps, Henry's prosecution is the last record I can find of him. The conditions in which such people were held at the gaol awaiting trial were often horrendous, and in these overcrowded, unsanitary conditions, gaol fever was rife.

On the 1570 Grove Survey one or two of the jurors named in this survey are worth a brief mention. **Rees Thomas Melyn**, as his name implies was a local miller. He also farmed some land in the district, since the survey shows he was renting nine acres of the demesne from William Jenkin. His occupation was added to his name in order to distinguish him from two other residents of the borough who were also called Rees Thomas. One other was *Rees Thomas Evan*; his grandfather's name had been added to his own in order to distinguish him from the other two.

Of the other jurors **John Nicholas** had probably moved here from Newton Nottage. A man of this name and parish is mentioned as owning land in the Borough in 1557. Robert John and Thomas Began both held to the 'old religion' and rejected the new form of Christianity that had now been introduced at their little church in Mawdlam. As religious persecution increased later in the century their names appear amongst those from the parish arrested and prosecuted for their beliefs.

The 1570 survey of the manor of Kenfig Borough also records that **William Aylward**, Henry's father, owned 33 acres of land in the manor. He was also one of the Eight Elected Burgesses who, two years later, approved Portreeve Evan Griffith's scheme to enclose part of the borough common at Cefn Cribwr. Henry's widow, Catherine, held these thirty-three acres at the time of another survey carried out in 1630 (PM 9617) and died on 23rd October, 1635. Her will (Llandaff Wills) and the probate inventory accompanying it are so faded that they were difficult to decipher, but it would seem that the value of her worldly goods amounted to just £4. 3s. 3d. Even by the standards of her day this was quite a small sum, but probably it was because the farm itself was actually in the hands of one of her sons. Most likely she lived with him in her own portion of the house or an adjoining cottage, retaining just sufficient land to grow an acre of corn and keep a few head of cattle and a pig so as to be self-sufficient in the matter of food.

As to which of her children actually succeeded her is a moot point. She and Henry are known to have had at least three sons — Francis, Charles, and William — though only the last of these appears to be mentioned in her will. Strangely too, it is her daughter Anne whom she appointed to be her executor, and this may point to a rift within the family that could well have been because of differences over religion.

As we have noted both Catherine and her husband were Roman Catholics who had been prepared to suffer for their faith. Fifteen years after her death, the farm was in the hands of a Lewis Aylward who was presumably her grandchild by one of the sons. We will get to know Lewis better in due course, but he too was to suffer for his faith — but as a 'dissenter' —one whose religious persuasion tended towards the Puritan beliefs, diametrically opposed to those of the Roman Catholics. The Aylwards had gone from one religious extreme to the other in just three generations!

Pool Farm and The Loughers: The next homestead in our perambulation along Heol Kenfig is the one we know as Pool Farm. This name is first used in the 18th century, and if it had an earlier one I have yet to discover it. For the purpose of this account I shall, however, continue to refer to it as Pool Farm. It is now the last remaining thatched house in the village. Again the RCAHMW report dates the building to "circa 1600" but unlike Kenfig Farm we are able to narrow down the time of construction of this property a little more closely. The earliest occupants were a junior branch of the Lougher family who were lords of the manor of Tythegston. Consequently they were near the very top of the social tree within the Borough, though they probably never actually owned Pool Farmhouse. The subsequent history of this building is tied to that of the Demesne Lands in the lower borough — property that was actually owned by the lord of the manor from whom the Loughers rented it. Some of the demesne, as I have mentioned, adjoined Kenfig Pool, but the whole consisted of fields scattered throughout the manor

and in total amounted to some 120 acres (modern measure).

Historically there was a close connection between the Loughers and the Turbervilles. Richard Lougher, who was living at Sker in 1467 as a tenant of the Abbot of Neath, claimed descent from the Welsh Lords of Aberavon, and acquired his surname from an earlier tenancy of another Abbey Grange on the Lougher river. His son Watkin married Gwenllian, a daughter of the John Turberville of Tythegston whom we met briefly in an earlier chapter, when he was chosen by Lawrence William of Llanmihangel to act as guardian for his children.

When John died an almighty legal wrangle broke out between the now widowed Gwenllian and her cousin Christopher Turberville as a result of which he got the bulk of the family estate including Penllyn and Sker. She, on the other hand, had to settle for Tythegston and Newton Nottage, and through her, these passed into the hands of her Lougher descendants.

The bad blood between the two families continued into the period covered by this chapter. In 1631 the Council of the Marches of Wales heard a complaint from Matthew Turberville and the widowed Cecile Turberville of Sker, backed by Christopher Turberville of Penllyn. This alleged that Watkin Lougher of Tythegston and John Lougher of Cornelly had destroyed a ditch at Sker that separated a field known as Cae Barbour from the highway leading to Nottage. To add insult to injury they then, so it was alleged, turned cattle into the enclosure thereby ruining the wheat crop planted therein (D/D Ty 100).

Watkin and John claimed that the land upon which they had entered was part of the highway from Cowbridge to Neath and was "common waste", presumably alleging that it had been illegally enclosed by the Turbervilles. Matthew however was stunned! As he pointed out, that particular road then ran across Ewenny Bridge to Pyle via Newton Down passing nowhere near this property! Unfortunately the end result of this action is not recorded.

In 1602 Robert Lougher of Tythegston obtained a lease from the Earl of Pembroke to the demesne lands within the manor of Kenfig Borough (PM 826). It seems likely that he was one of the younger sons of Watkin Lougher of Tythegston, (a son or nephew of the Watkin mentioned above). To secure this lease he was probably given financial backing by his father and in this manner was provided with a small estate from which to earn a living, for generally speaking this branch of the Lougher family preferred to rent out their property rather than farm it themselves.

In 1628 a fresh lease (PM 888) was taken out upon the demesne by Robert's son Richard who is stated to be "of Kenfig" indicating that he actually lived within the manor. He subsequently took out an amended lease (PM 903) in 1632, but neither of these documents nor his father's mentions that a house was included in the demesne lands. This is only referred to for the first time in a manorial survey of 1650 when the property was in the hands of Thomas, Richard's son.

Pool Farmhouse we can therefore say was built sometime between 1632 and 1650 prior to the enclosure of common land in 1653. We may also surmise that the house was built by the Pembroke estate for either Richard or Thomas and that the latter probably lived there. It is also clear however, that before this, the family had been living in a home of their own within the lower borough, but where this was I have been unable to determine with any certainty but, as outlined in a later chapter, it may actually have adjoined Pool Farmhouse. There is mention of "Richard Lougher's House" in an undated document created about the year 1600 (D/D Ty 56), though this had actually been let to tenants at that time. By virtue of their residence in Kenfig, these early Loughers would of course have been burgesses, but unfortunately we know very little else about them.

By 1661 Thomas had left Kenfig to live at Ty Maen in South Cornelly which thereafter became the family's principal home, but his connection with the manor continued when he was appointed by the Earl of Pembroke to be its steward and Constable of the Castle for the forthcoming year. After his departure, the Loughers utilised Pool Farm like the Turbervilles of Penllyn used Sker — as a convenient small estate to support junior members of the family or, if there were none, subletting it to other tenants.

Kenfig Land: One cottage about which I have so far failed to discover anything prior to the middle of the 18th century is the one that formerly stood on the west side of Heol Kenfig near Pool Farm. It was the only dwelling on this side of the road and is now in ruins. Evidently it was built on a strip of waste land that separated the fields of the demesne from the highway which was enclosed to create a garden and a long narrow croft known as 'Kenfig Land'. Neither cottage nor croft were new creations when they eventually appear in the records, but how far back their history extends is at the moment impossible to say.

Maindy Farmhouse, set in its fields, well back from the road, has a rather obscure past but also a strong claim to be the oldest in the village — I can actually take its documented history further back than any other dwelling. Its first owner was a Thomas Griffiths of Bettws, who in 1628 sold (PM 889) the house, a barn, yard and eight acres of land (approx 9.5 modern measure) to a Griffith Howard for £40. Griffith was acting as the agent for a William Howard of Llysworney, but the identity of

their tenant at the farm is not mentioned. This indeed is the problem with this little property. It is a fairly simple matter to determine who owned it in the middle of the 17th century, but the records I have seen are silent as to who actually lived there. The only tenant that I have so far actually identified is a Jenkin Savours listed in the manorial survey of 1650. The Savours were a Margam family, members of whom are frequently met with in records appertaining to the Kenfig area, but of Jenkin I have so far discovered nothing other than this one stray reference.

Of the eight customary acres mentioned in the sale, three surrounded the house and extended between Heol Kenfig and Heol y Lane. Another four lay on the opposite side of the latter in a field that later became known as 'Howards Land' but at this time was known as Brombil, to which the eighth and last acre adjoined. In 1650 an Alice Howell, 'alias Howard' of Llysworney (who was presumably William's widow) and her son Jenkin placed this property in trust with Morgan Gibbon of St George's-super-Ely as part of a marriage settlement made when he married Morgan's sister Barbara. This secured her right to the property in the future and Morgan in return gave the groom the sum of £100 (PM 942).

Whether either of them ever actually laid eyes on their Kenfig property has to be doubted, for Jenkin Howard is described as living at Bedwas in Monmouthshire. In 1665 the land on the east side of Heol y Lane was in the occupation of Lewis Aylward of Kenfig Farm, presumably as the couple's tenant.

By 1672 Jenkin , now described as a cleric, was living at Llanishen north of Cardiff, and with his son William sold most of their land (but not, apparently, the house) to Sir Edward Mansel of Margam for £70. As the sitting tenant, Lewis Aylward continued in occupation of 'Howards Lands' for which he was paying £4. 10s. 0d. rent in 1675.

Kenfig Farm circa 1900
Gad

Kenfig House Farm. All of the first three houses of the new Kenfig we have looked at so far were farmhouses, all set back from the roadside. This, I believe is because when originally built, they stood at the edge of the owner's land fronting onto a strip of waste that separated them from the road. When the enclosure programme of 1653 went through, the occupants then merely appropriated this strip and incorporated most of it into their own fields. Certainly at the south-

ern end of the village (as indicated on the Tithe map of 1846 the cottages and gardens that sprang up here were erected in quite a wide strip of waste between the road and the enclosed fields.

Kenfig House Farm is the first of these properties and actually borders the road, but its origins and early history are obscure. From what I can make of the documentary material, my bet is that it actually originated with the family of Griffith Evan, eldest son of the Elizabethan Portreeve Evan Griffith. He seems to have lived in a house on the north side of Heol Las, and on his death in 1605 it was Griffith who succeeded him. When Rees Leyson married Griffith's sister Catherine, he helped establish his new brother-in-law in the district by selling him some of this property, but apparently continued to reside on Heol Las until the last mention I have of him in 1630.

Griffith had two sons, Evan and Jenkin, and two daughters named Catherine and Margaret — the latter married to a John William of Margam. Evan Griffith died in 1645, and in his will mentions that he owned a cottage (probably the family home on Heol Las) that he had let out to a Rees ab Owen, and another house where he lived, to which there were attached three acres of land. The house and two of the acres were to pass to his wife, but the third acre was to go to his brother Jenkin provided that he paid thirty shillings to each of their sisters (Llandaff Wills).

This acre I have identified as a strip field bordering the south side of one called Cae Cwtta that lies on the west side (i.e. Heol Kenfig side) of Heol y Lane. The only way, however, that I can make sense of the data in these documents relating to this and the adjoining fields is if Kenfig House Farm (now confusingly known as Kenfig Farm House!) and an adjoining enclosure, actually started life as Evan's house and his two acres of land.

Although Evan's will mentions a son named Yorwerth Evan, he was evidently no more than a baby and died without reaching adulthood. His land is mentioned as a boundary in a document created the following year, but he does not seem to have survived for long afterwards. Under the terms of the will, Evan's house and land therefore descended to his (unnamed) widow.

In 1652 Evan's brother Jenkin Griffith, married Margaret, the daughter of Evan John Evan of South Cornelly, and a marriage settlement (PM 949) was drawn up to protect her rights to a certain portion of his property. This was in fact the house and land that had belonged to his brother Evan, so either the latter's widow had also passed away by then, or she and Jenkin had arrived at some sort of accommodation. In 1663 he augmented this property with the purchase of a field called Cae Cwtta that lay between his house and Heol y Lane (PM 4081). Then five years later he added another property, one lying on the south side of his home, consisting of a house, barn and three acres of land (PM 1012). Also included in this last deal was a small field on Heol Cornelly.

We cannot say whether Jenkin's marriage to Margaret was a happy one or not, but like his brother's it produced no children that survived into adulthood. When he came to make his own will on 15th October, 1673, she was, therefore his sole beneficiary (Llandaff Wills). The settlement he had made on their marriage already guaranteed her the house and land he had inherited from his brother, so the property he bequeathed her amounted to the cottage on the south of their home with its three acres of land. He tells us that this land had been divided up into several closes, and this indeed is the way it appears on the Tithe Map. There is no mention of Cae Cwtta in the will, but an acre field called Erw Heol Lane was included. This appears to be a field that Margaret in her own will calls "Yr Erw Uchaf yn y Cae Cwtta", undoubtedly the one marked on the Tithe Map as "Erw'r Heol". The Cae Cwtta field on this map is an acre smaller than the field of that name purchased by Jenkin, so he had evidently sold these two acres on and kept the third one for himself. Other documents indicate that he also occupied other land on the opposite side of Heol y Lane, presumably as a tenant.

If I am correct, what is now Kenfig Farmhouse was indeed the home of Jenkin and Margaret, and so her will(Llandaff Wills; PM 1040) made in 1697 indicates it was quite different to the building that stands there today. By then the original house had been divided up into three cottages sharing a common "court and garden before ye doores". Margaret and a woman named Joan Hooks lived in the two end houses, but the tenant of the middle house is not named.

This conversion had probably been made by Margaret during her widowhood. When her husband had been alive the house and the barn that adjoined it had been the centre of a small farm, conveniently situated to take advantage of his right as a burgess to pasture livestock on the common. Consequently the probate inventory made on his death lists a cow, two heifers, a calf, mare, twenty-six sheep and some poultry. With corn from the fields and the produce of the garden, it had been enough to provide them with the wherewithal to survive with a little extra from the sale of wool and cattle. They were, nevertheless, far from being amongst the better-off in Kenfig circles. The entire contents of his home were worth just ten shillings which shows that this was a very humble dwelling. At neighbouring Llanmihangel farm, Richard Cradock's 'great kettle' alone was worth more than this, as was Jenkin's own cow, valued at 13s. 4d!

The life of an elderly person in 17th century Kenfig was not easy. Assuming that Margaret was aged twenty when she married in 1652 (and most brides seem to have been older) then by 1689 she would have at least been in her late fifties, but was working as a labourer for her living. In 1691 she found it necessary to sell three-quarters of an acre of her land to the Margam estate for £9 (PM 742-4). Clearly she was struggling to make ends meet, so converting her home into three cottages would have made sense. Not being a farmer herself her income would have been supplemented by the rent from two cottages and also from letting the fields she had inherited from her husband.

As Margaret entered her sixties the eventual disposal of this property seems to have become a matter of concern to. A period of illness during the winter of 1697/8 had rendered her "indisposed in my bodily health". She decided then, to order her affairs, even though she was not to die for another four years. Accordingly she made out her will on 17th February 1698.

Margaret's only personal possessions were her clothing (2s 6d.) and the contents of her home (£1), but there were, of course, the cottages and land that she was renting to tenants. There lay the rub! She had no children of her own, and several of those who paid her rent were more than mere tenants; they were also her neighbours and more than that, her friends. Joan Hooks (d. 1723) for example was evidently a family friend of long standing to whom Margaret's father had bequeathed a sheep in

1663. Whilst bequeathing the cottage in which Joan lived to her niece Martha Cradock for 10 years, Margaret nevertheless stipulated that Joan was to have the barn attached to the cottages for her lifetime. The cottage that was her own home she gave to Margaret, the wife of Morgan John of Kenfig, and the middle one of the three to Jane, wife of a labourer named Richard Thomas. Margaret is quite specific that these cottages would be theirs for life, only if and when they became widows. She knew only too well from her own experience the hardships of this condition, and how much such 'rent free' accommodation would mean to them! After the lives of the people named (or in Martha's case the ten years tenure of Joan Hooks' cottage) then ownership of all three would pass to others. Joan's cottage was to go to Catherine, the daughter of David Richard, and the barn together with the other two would become the property of Evan Richard.

Evan Richard, who seems to have been only a labourer, was also inherited her orchard, garden and two crofts adjoining the barn, and she appointed him her executor. The interesting thing for me is that with the exception of Martha Cradock all those I have mentioned were not (so far as I can discover) close relatives of Margaret, nor is any such connection expressed or implied in her will. Several family members, including her brother Robert, were indeed the recipients of various bequests, but the remainder went to people Margaret

cared about and who had, presumably, cared about her. Continuing this theme Jenkin Yorwerth was given the sum of ten shillings and to his wife "a wastcoate & pettycoat of the best I have". Her oatmeal chest went to Morgan John; and Rees Thomas was to have the acre called Erw Heol Lane after her niece Martha Cradock had enjoyed it for ten years. From her slender resources she also bequeathed twenty shilling (equal to the value of the entire contents of her house!) to the poor of the parish.

That's why I rather like old Margaret. Similar wills I've read from the period invariably leave almost everything to relatives. Having no children of her own, one would normally expect her property to have been dispersed amongst nephews and nieces who may, or may not have bothered much with her in life. For her, those who had been her friends were equally, if not more important, and she was clearly aware that even in her straightened circumstances she was still a lot better off than many others living in the community.

Thomas John's House: The next house on Heol Kenfig was the one Jenkin Griffith had purchased in 1668, together with three acres of land. The vendor was a Thomas John of Pyle, who may be the son of the man of the same name who had been the previous owner. Jenkin is shown for the holding with this earlier Thomas John on the Manor survey of 1661, which probably indicates he was renting it from him at that time. The two were in fact related, Thomas being the son of Jenkin's sister Catherine to whom he had paid thirty shillings under the will of their brother Evan. She was married to John William who was a Margam man and apparently never had any connection with the borough. The deed of sale for the property mentions that by 1668 this first Thomas John was already dead, which leads me to assume that the person of the same name who sealed the deed was his son. Unfortunately none of this enables us to identify the people who actually lived there for the Johns were clearly absentee landlords.

Margaret's will makes no mention of this cottage but it adjoins the three-quarters of an acre she sold to Margam — a field called Cae Ty Llosk on the Tithe Map. Although the deed of sale also makes no mention of the house it would seem that it was part and parcel of this transaction. Both properties were subsequently leased to a David Thomas in 1690, and the description of the cottage tells us that originally it and the garden had been "dressed & inclosed upon the waste ground of the said Burrough on the east side of a lane or highway there called Heol Kenfigg". A clause was also added protecting David's right of access to his field at the rear by a lane nine feet wide along the northern boundary of this property.

The name David Thomas was a very common one in the Borough at this time, and this one is normally distinguished by being referred to as David Thomas ab Owen. He seems to have been on good terms with old Margaret Evan for he witnessed her will and helped make the subsequent probate inventory of her meagre belongings. Referred to as a labourer tho last trace I have of him in the records is in 1713 and 1714, when he paid tithes on crops of barley that had presumably been raised on this land.

Harry Jenkin. South of David Thomas's cottage there lay three houses the early history of which is provided by documents relating to the two fields that bordered them on the east known as Cae Glas and Cae Towad. In 1646 the owner of these, John Morgan, used them as security for a loan of £30 raised from an Edward John of Newton Nottage (PM 929). At that time the western end nearest Heol Kenfig bordered "the Common called Mynnith Kenfigg", so clearly it had not then been built upon. John Morgan evidently failed to redeem this loan and nine years later, in 1655, John Edward seized the property and sold it to Hopkin Thomas of Pyle for £45. He in turn sold it on the following year to Thomas Morgan of Kenfig. In these documents the description of the western boundary shows that it bordered several properties variously held by Harry Jenkin, Nicholas Morgan, Elizabeth Jenkin and Catherine Jenkin.

These are evidently the cottages and gardens belonging to the individuals named, of which Harry (Henry) Jenkin's seems to have been the northernmost. In his will (Llandaff Wills) Harry styles himself as a "yeoman", thereby putting himself a step above the common herd of labourers and craftsmen. In this he may have been aspiring to a status that was not rightfully his, but in truth he does rather seem to have been more than a simple settler of the 1650s. Indeed, his father Jenkin Howell had been one of the churchwardens at St Mary Magdalene's; this is recorded in an inscription on the church bell dated 1664.

His will indicates that Harry held a lease upon other land somewhere in the area, though where and from whom I have not identified. He owned two old horses (the 17th century equivalent of two motor cars) upon which he and his wife Ann Gwillym would have ridden through the village. They slept upon a feather bed or mattress raised up from the floor upon a bedstead, and whilst they only ate their food from a set of "longe wooden dishes", they nevertheless did so with pewter spoons!

On his smallholding Harry had a small herd of cattle which included two oxen for haulage work, and these he possibly hired out for work on farms at harvest and other such times. Three cows provided his household with butter and cheese, with perhaps a small surplus for resale. It was probably from them that he had bred the two calves listed. Like the "three yearlings" mentioned, these would be reared to the age of three years before being sold off to the drovers. Completing his smallholding was a flock of twenty sheep which, together with the horses and cattle were probably turned out to graze upon the common, for although the acreage of his farm is not stated, the amount of freehold rent he paid indicates that it cannot have been great.

Like Evan Griffith before him therefore Harry Jenkin seems to have been one of those 'Del Boy' type characters one frequently comes across at Kenfig during this period — making a living as and where they could, often with no little success. He also seems to have lived to a ripe old age[7]. When David Jones of Wallington visited Mawdlam church in 1889 (Jones, 1994) he saw his gravestone set into the floor of the nave which showed that Harry died in 1721. Jones noted his age as 78, but for him to be a property owner back in the 1650s he would have had to be even older. Probably therefore the passage of feet across his tombstone had somewhat obliterated the original inscription, and what was read as a '7' may have been either an '8' or even a '9'.

---

[7] Contrary to popular belief, many inhabitants of the period lived well beyond their fiftieth birthday – see "A Question of Age" later in this Chapter

Nicholas Morgan is first mentioned as a witness to a document of 1654, significantly the year following the supposed date of the permit to enclose common land. He served as a juror for the 1661 manorial survey: on this he is listed as owning 1½ acres of freehold land on Paschal Hill. The final mention of him comes in another deed relating to Cae Glas and Cae Towad in 1676. To date these sparse facts are all I have been able to gather about him, but he was very likely a brother of Edward Morgan, Pen Plas (see below).

Elizabeth & Catherine Jenkin. It is not entirely clear whether these two ladies, who were both widows and sisters to Harry Jenkin, shared a single cottage or lived in two separate ones. The records relating to the adjoining fields tend to indicate the latter, but other sources seem to show that they combined with a man named George Thomas to create a single house — he taking one part, and they the other. It seems, in fact, that the trio may have pre-empted the burgesses' enclosure plans and done this between 1646 and 1650, for in a survey drawn up in the latter year (PM 1321) they are already shown as paying a freehold rent of a penny in respect of a cottage in Paschal Hill hold. Bubbling up irresistibly in my mind at this point comes a fantasy image of a formidable lady in 17th century costume determinedly casting about her with an axe in order to establish the boundaries of her Ty ar Un

Nos! The local womenfolk were indeed formidable folk in their day, but here I think my sense of humour is getting the better of me, so I had best return to more sober reflections!

In pre-empting the 'official' enclosure the trio may have been assisted by the fact that George is later mentioned as a servant to Lewis Aylward of Kenfig Farm. At the time this cottage was built, the Aylwards' change of religion to Nonconformity had brought its own reward when, following the execution of King Charles I (January, 1649), the Puritans and their allies took control of the land. As a leading Nonconformist and one of the largest private landowners in the Borough, Lewis's prestige was consequently enhanced and his support for the trio's enclosure plans may have been crucial.

The sisters continued to live together at the house until 1665 when Catherine remarried a local man named Morgan Thomas and went to live with him. The last mention of both comes in the year 1676, and Elizabeth was certainly dead by 1692 when their former half of the cottage was in the hands of Margaret Evan's neighbour, David Thomas.

Pen Plas — The Top House — was, as its name implies the last house on the main road towards Newton. Behind it, extending right the way to Heol Lane, was a two-acre field separated from the common to the south by another strip field where the bungalows of Ton Kenfig stand today. My Welsh is rather sketchy to say the least, but I have always understood that the word 'plas' indicated something more than a simple dwelling house, yet that is all that ever seems to have stood here. Perhaps it was used in a comparative sense to indicate that the original building was something rather more substantial than its neighbours'.

One curious fact is that on Wyseman's map of 1592 a house is indicated standing in the field that then formed the northern limit of the common in this direction. This would place it beneath the bungalows there today, but I suspect that

the building "John ap Morgan's House" indicating that it was the home of one of the burgesses who had authorised the enclosure of Waun Cimla and was the Portreeve in 1588 and 1599. He is also referred to at the time of the Waun Cimla enclosure as a 'gentleman', so perhaps this house was the original 'Plas' which was later abandoned. Then a new one may have been built on Heol Kenfig, when the field fronting the common was enclosed. John ap Morgan is last mentioned in 1602.

At first glance it might appear that John was of the same family as Edward Morgan who

PEN PLAS, NOW CALLED CAE RHYD

the field in which they were built only came into being as part of the 1653 enclosure. Wyseman labelled

was the owner of Pen Plas in 1646, but the latter was actually the son of a Morgan Howell who was a contemporary of John's, so there is really no obvious direct link. Is it therefore just coincidence that as well as Edward this Morgan Howell had another son named John Morgan? Could indeed Morgan Howell have been a nephew of the first John ap Morgan? Here again I am entering the realms of supposition. The fact is that Edward was the owner of Pen Plas in 1646 and, as the 1650 manorial survey tells us, it formed part of an estate of 45 (customary) acres of freehold land in the lower borough — about 54 in modern terms. Stray references to this property show that it was quite a scattered holding, with some of the land spread along Heol Las. In 1671 Edward paid tax upon two hearths (PRO. E.179 221/294) but such is the nature of these returns that there is no way of knowing if this relates to two hearths in a single large house or single hearths in two houses.

A document that mentions some of his property forming a boundary in 1656 styles him a "gentleman" though there is no other such reference to him. The 1661 manorial survey states that he was then living at Llantwit, Neath which again is not repeated elsewhere. Given the religious history of the neighbourhood and its Nonconformist connections with Neath, one is led to wonder if he was perhaps a dissenter who, at the restoration of the monarchy, deemed it prudent to quit the district for a time.

Edward is last mentioned on the 1677 rentals for the Manor of Kenfig Borough. By this time the extent of his freehold properties had reduced slightly to 43 (customary) acres. His land then passed to a Griffith Morgan who may have been his son. He in turn sold over half this land to Lewis Aylward and Thomas Edmund. From subsequent events we know that Pen Plas itself was included in the Aylward portion.

Thomas Edmund, who died in 1692, purchased the other half. He was a minor gentleman living at Old Park, Margam and also owned considerable property in and about Laleston. His brother David, was recorded as the Rector of Newton Nottage from 1678 to 1709. Of his sons, Thomas was briefly Vicar of Llangynwyd before dying at a young age in 1707; William was Rector of Coity from 1708 to 1727 (Jones, 1994).

Despite these strong religious connections the family became involved in the scandals associated with the marriage of Jocelyn Sidney (1682-1743), who was the Last Earl of Leicester. He made his home in The Great House at Laleston which the Edmunds owned.

Those who would know more must read Neville Granville's article that appeared in *Morgannwg* (1992: 39-), for although the Edmunds had a Kenfig connection, they are not a Kenfig family and fascinating though it is their story has no place here.

With Edward's death and Griffith's sale of Pen Plas their connection with Kenfig ceases, but

Edward's brother John Morgan (the same who owned Cae Glas and Cae Towad) remained, and his descendants continued in the borough. These included a son called Nicholas (Nicholas John Morgan), a perpetuation of a rather unusual name for the district which may indicate that the Nicholas Morgan mentioned earlier living in the cottage on Heol Kenfig was another brother.

Thanks to the survival of a small group of records from the middle and latter part of the 17th century it has been possible for me to attempt a house-by-house reconstruction of the residents of Heol Kenfig at that time. Sadly this is not possible at this early date for the other centres of population in the Borough such as Water Street, Heol Las, or Heol y Lane, nor indeed can it again be attempted for Heol Kenfig until the census returns of the mid 19th century. However in the case of most of the farms, and some cottages and smallholdings, it is possible to follow the succession of occupants down the centuries. Many are little more than lists of names, but here and there some individuals do stand out.

David Richard was a younger son of Richard David of Pencastell Farm near Kenfig Hill. His father having died in 1671, the tenancy passed to his mother, Margaret Thomas, and under the terms of her lease from the Margam estate was due to pass after her day to David's eldest brother James who seems to have been living elsewhere at this time. Consequently David remained at home and probably did the actual work upon the farm up until the time of his mother's death in 1682.

Pencastell at this time was an average sized holding of just 30-40 acres, but David's status rose dramatically following his marriage to the widow Thomasin Tucker of Stormy Issa Farm which lay at the foot of the ridge upon which Pencastell stands. For widows living in Stormy manor to re-marry during this period was very rare, so it was either a love-match or (more likely) a marriage of convenience on her part.

Thomasin's first husband was Edward Lewis, the eldest son of William Lewis who had turned Stormy Issa into a farm of some 120 acres by adding to it other properties in the vicinity when the tenancies fell vacant. To judge by his signature Edward had received a very good education and was being groomed to take over the farm after his father's day. In the meantime he, Thomasin and their young children lived with the rest of the family at Stormy Issa of which all trace has now been obliterated.

In the 1670s the family was struck by complete and total disaster. Christopher, Edward's brother, died in 1670 and was quickly followed by his sister Alice (1672); Edward himself (1673); his father (1674) and mother (1677). These deaths had left Thomasin as the family's sole survivor, with the second largest farm in the district to run and at least three very young children to provide for. In this respect therefore her marriage to David Richard was perhaps made less for love than to ensure the future of her children, and may have taken place whilst her mother-in-law was still alive — certainly by 1678 at the very latest.

After Catherine's death, David and Thomasin re-organised the farm, giving up one large, but not particularly fertile holding that had been held in her name. This enabled David to continue to work Pencastell on behalf of his own mother which practice he continued after her death by an arrangement with his brother James.

One assumes that at this time David was quite a young man, but Edward Frowde, his companion in the misfortune that was to follow, was probably a lot older. A member of a Cardiff family, he had arrived in the area about 1649 when he purchased twelve acres of land at Horgrove (modern Haregrove) between Stormy and Laleston. This seems to have followed his marriage to Ann, the daughter of Jenkin Griffith of Horgrove who was then an important local landowner who had established a school on his property. The couple set up home in the hamlet (which has long since been abandoned) and the ruin of their substantial house (three up; three down) is still visible. In 1685 Edward shared his home with his eldest son Stephen and family, on the rather unequal basis that they occupied two rooms whilst he retained the other four!

The Origin of the Yorwerths The Yorwerths are a family who figure prominently in the records of Kenfig in the 18th and 19th century. For practical purposes I have adopted this particular spelling of their name, which is the version used by many of them down to the present day. When contacted by possible descendants today, almost their first remark is "We don't spell our name that way!" to which the short answer is "Well your ancestors may well have!"

Jean Evans of Llandough who is a descendant of this family has made quite a collection of all the local variations of this name which include Yorath, Iorwerth, Joruard, Jorward, Jorwerth, Jorworth, Yoruard, Yorwarth, Yorwath, and Yorwed! It depended upon the preferred spelling of the person who wrote it down, and in contemporary documents several different variations are frequently applied to the same person during their own lifetime. One of the earliest family members actually signed his name with yet another variation — Yorreth! As is my normal practice in these notes I will stick to just the one variation.

It is fairly easy to trace the family back to two brothers named David and Richard Yorwerth who lived in North Cornelly about the year 1700, but beyond that, things become more difficult. In fact prior to this, the name Yorwerth (with all its variations) is quite rare in Kenfig either as a first or second name. In the entire period between 1500 and 1850 I have come across only four instances of it being used as a first name. One of these is a Yorwerth Yorwerth born in 1783, another is the son of Evan Griffith mentioned in 1645 who died in infancy. The other two also belong to the 17th century, and it is they who provided the clue that has enabled me to advance a conjectural origin for the family which takes it back as far as the reign of the first Queen Elizabeth.

A Catherine Yorwerth is listed as living on Heol Las in the survey of 1570, and was allocated a parcel of hay at Waun Cimla, following the enclosure of 1572; this would indicate that she was the widow or sole heiress of a former burgess. Her relationship to other members of this family is however uncertain, for wives did not normally take their husband's surname at this time. We start to get on slightly firmer ground in the early 1600s with the occurrence of three people with Yorwerth as their second name — Jennet (b. 1573); Evan (b. 1585) and Thomas (b. 1587). Their dates of birth indicate that they were almost certainly two brothers and a sister, and to them we can add Alice Yorwerth first mentioned in 1623 and a widow by 1630.

Who their father was I have yet to discover, but almost certainly his first name was Yorwerth (or some such variation) for the family was evidently at this time using patronyms. Evan Yorwerth's son, for example, was Morgan Evan whilst the children of Thomas were known as John and Yorwerth Thomas respectively. In actual fact the Yorwerth name does not seem to have continued through the two sons but rather via their sister Jennet.

In the early 17th century Evan Yorwerth was the leading figure in the clan. A survey of the manor of Higher Kenfig in 1633 (PM 1280) states that "Jevan Yorath" by virtue of a copyhold lease of 1602 "houldeth one tenement called Cae y Kwtyer contayning one messuage, one house, one garden, one close called Y Ka Issa contayning five acres or thereabouts & halfe one acre; & [a] close called Ka Pcell contayning seven acres & halfe or thereabouts; one close called Y Ka y Rha contayninge one acre three quarters or thereabouts". What is strange is that some of these properties do not seem to have been situated in Higher Kenfig. As mentioned earlier 'Cae y Rha' is a very unusual name, and later documents indicate that it was a field that lay between The Prince of Wales public house and Kenfig Pool. Cae Cwtta (Short Cut Field) has also been mentioned lying between Heol y Lane and Heol Kenfig (There was also another one between Heol Las and Heol Fach).

It seems therefore that all or part of this small farm was actually in Kenfig Lower — within the Pembroke manor of Kenfig Borough, rather than that of Higher Kenfig, to which the survey relates. This is actually not unusual either here or elsewhere. Later Higher Kenfig rentals include freehold rents that actually relate to property situated in the lower manor. Perhaps, therefore, these originally belonged to Margam Abbey and, for administrative purposes, were included in Higher Kenfig. What is strange is that both Cae Cwtta and Cae y Rha were subsequently freehold properties bought up by the Mansels in the 18ᵗʰ century! As the survey states they were held by lease in 1633 this clearly was not the case then. A possible explanation seems to be that the estate was itself renting these fields from the owners, and sub-let them to Evan with other land it owned in Higher Kenfig.

The Yorwerth lease upon Cae Cwtta etcetera, was originally taken out in 1602 upon three lives, although only those of Evan and his brother Thomas were current at the time of the survey. The missing third member was probably either their father or mother. After some brief mentions of Evan and Thomas's sons, all trace of this male branch of the family is then lost in the Kenfig district.

Of their sisters, Alice married a man named Morgan Llewelyn who, in 1623 took out a lease (PM 1321) upon "one cottage and a little plott of grounde there unto adjoining at and lyeing within the walls of the castle of Kynffige, contayning one quarter of one acre or there abouts at the yearly rent of six pens". The ruins of this cottage lie in a small thicket just east of the castle ruins and were excavated in the 1930s by the Port Talbot and Margam Historical Society. Unfortunately no record of this excavation exists though some of the artefacts recovered were deposited with the National Museum at Cardiff

These finds are consistent with the occupation of the house during this period, and remarkably include a shoe that has been preserved by the boggy nature of the site. Significantly there is no mention of this property in the survey of 1570, so it is likely that it was Morgan who obtained permission from the Earl of Pembroke to build this house and enclose the surrounding land. Traces of ridge and furrow ploughing south of the castle-keep probably mark the location of the land that he was farming. By 1630 Morgan was dead and the property was in the hands of his widow Alice, who in turn was replaced by their son Leyson Morgan by 1650.

From the above it is clear that the family name 'Yorwerth' was not continued by the descendants of these family members, and it would seem that in this respect it is their sister Jennet who is the key member for the origins of the Kenfig family.

Of the man she married we can say only that his first name was probably David, for the couple christened their son 'Yorwerth' and he was thereafter known as Yorwerth David. They lived on a small farm in Higher Kenfig which, at the time of the 1633 survey was held by 38 year old Yorwerth David and his widowed mother under a lease issued in 1596. It contained 10 acres of land (about 12 acres modern measure) and I previously believed it to be a tenancy that appears in estate records of the 17th century as "Yorath's Land" or "Yorath's Tenement". This turned out to be a holding called Morfa Bach, and the one held by Jennet and Yorwerth was known after their day as Tir Evan Owen from a subsequent tenant. Much later in time, the two tenancies were combined to create the farm called Morfa Bach Uchaf which was subsequently absorbed into Ty'n Cellar Farm in the latter part of the 18th century.

There is no mention of a house in the survey entry relating to Jennet's tenancy, but one is mentioned when the farm was transferred to new owners in 1663 following Yorwerth's death. Presumably therefore it was he who built one on the property during the interim, and it may in fact be the farmhouse subsequently known as Morfa Bach Uchaf.

Yorwerth's son was christened David after his grandfather, and as 'David Yorwerth' he chose residence at North Cornelly where he and his descendants kept an alehouse and ran a small farm. He was the last of the family to be named under the Welsh practice of patronyms, and thereafter Yorwerth (in its many and varied forms) became the family surname. For a time their direct connection with Kenfig Borough was broken, but in due course their descendants returned to play important roles in its later history.

Mansions The optimism of the people of Kenfig apparent in the creation of their new town was not just confined to those who now made their homes there. Elsewhere in the borough two of its largest and most impressive houses — virtually small mansions — were also erected during these early years of the 17th century.

Marlas House and Thomas Richard The house at Marlas has a long history though it was never (as is frequently claimed) one of Margam Abbey's granges. There was a house known as 'La Marle' on this spot in the 13th century (Birch, 1897: 192-3) when the occupants were the Grammas family who owned most of the land in the immediate vicinity. Their history can in turn be traced as far back as the closing decades of the 12th century, so arguably there has been a house on this spot for over eight hundred years. A memory of these early inhabitants was retained in the name of the ridge upon which it stands between the River Kenfig and the Afon Fach. Although now long forgotten, this was known as 'Grammes' or 'Grammas' Hill, a name that still held its own in the early 17th century.

When the Lovel Family quit the Hall in North Cornelly in the early decades of the 14th century it seems the Grammus family moved there, and the history of their former home becomes rather vague. In 1344 a character named William de Marle is mentioned in the Margam Abbey records (Birch, 1897: 310-11). He claimed pasturage rights on land belonging to the adjoining Abbey Grange at Llanmihangel but eventually admitted that he had only done so in a fit of "levity of mind" and, "moved by the spirit of truth", withdrew his claim.

After this the paucity of records surviving from the 15th and early 16th centuries mean that we lose track of the farm's history al-

family living at Ynysarwed, near Melincourt in the Neath Valley and, according to Leslie Evans (1964), acquired Marlas in 1543 when he purchased 25 acres of land at Kenfig from Sir George Herbert. In the year following the Grove survey however, he and his wife transferred the property to an Anne verch William of Ynysarwed who was the widow of Jenkin ap Thomas, possibly Richard's brother. Coupled with her in this

MARLAS FARMHOUSE (SKETCH BY A L EVANS)

together until the 'Grove Survey' (see Ch 7) of the Manor of Kenfig in 1570. At this time the house and its lands were the property of Richard Thomas who, for some reason which we can no longer fathom, had bought up no less than fifteen derelict burgages in the old town of Kenfig.

Richard was a member of an ancient and respected Welsh

tenancy was their own son Thomas Richard, and, from the date placed upon the house by the Royal Commission on Ancient & Historic Monuments in Wales, it is probably he who built it.

Thomas was apparently a man with grand ideas, for what he built for himself was no mere farmhouse but rather a small mansion sufficiently large to accommodate two family homes today. As originally conceived it was 'U' shaped, with two projecting wings flanking a courtyard that opened to the west. At some later date this open side was blocked off by the construction of another wing to create a square building with a central courtyard. By local standards it was a very imposing house.

Although some of the outbuildings also seem to date from his time, it is unlikely that Thomas Richard actually farmed the land attached to the house, save perhaps for a small portion to provide for his own household. Rather, he rented his property out to other local farmers and lived a gentleman's life on the income.

An undated note added to Thomas Wyseman's report on the dispute with Jenkin Turberville mentions that Thomas was renting an acre of land at Kenfig Pool, but was two years behind with his rent which was a bushel of oats "Cardiff measure". Although such 'corn rents' continued at nearby Stormy manor until the early years of the 18th century, this is the only instance I have come across at Kenfig. The document alleged that Thomas had felled two elm trees valued five shillings (25p) on this property "and caryed them to his freeholde". For this, the note continued, he owed the lord a fine of ten shillings.

One wonders, indeed, if the timber from these elms ended up as part of the fabric of Marlas House, for the building of this 'dream home' seems to have

proved an undertaking that was beyond Thomas's resources. By 1612 he was in serious financial difficulty, and that year mortgaged forty [customary] acres of his property to Thomas Mansel of Margam (PM 1243). Although it is uncertain how big the farm was at this time, later documents describe it as encompassing eighty acres (96 in modern measure).

The fields involved in the mortgage are listed by name, and with the exception of 'Yateland' (The land by the stile) and 'Yaterw' (The stile acre) all are Welsh. One named Cae'r Bont Garreg (Stone Bridge Field) indicates that a stone bridge already existed to carry the Mawdlam to Pyle road across the Afon Fach stream.

Thomas was unable to redeem the loan of £133 that he thus raised, far less the accumulated interest charges. By 1633 he was forced to surrender the property to the Mansels. In 1642 Thomas and his wife found it necessary to sell another 12 acres of their land to Margam (PM 1307) and shortly afterwards the house followed. In 1646 the estate gave power of attorney (PM 1310-11) to David Bennet to take possession of the mansion from Thomas on behalf of the Mansels. This apparently marks the departure of this colourful character from our area, for we hear no more of him in local records thereafter.

The Mansels had not, however, got the entire Marlas holding for a manorial survey of 1650 makes it clear that they then owned only a part of the property. The house certainly impressed the new owners. In 1686 it is said to have been utilised as suitable accommodation for Sir Edward Mansel's eldest son, Thomas and his new bride (PM 6662). This Thomas succeeded his father in 1706, and went on to become the First Lord Mansel in 1711, but other than this note from later estate records, I can find no other reference relating to his alleged period of residence there.

Llanmihangel and the Cradocks
Unfortunately I have been unable to discover any references to the former Abbey Grange at Llanmihangel, from the time John Lawrence surrendered his lease upon it in 1557 until a mention in the one and only surviving survey (PM 1280) of the manor of Higher Kenfig made in 1633.

This lack of information is all the more unfortunate as the RCAHMW report(RCAHMW, 1988: 418) on the farm suggests that, like Marlas, the earliest portions of the house date from "circa 1600". It seems to have been, from the first, a very impressive building — not quite a mansion, but certainly something more than a mere farmhouse. The Grange buildings that had previously been home to Lawrence William were abandoned and eventually demolished so that no traces of them now remain above ground.

Of William Meyrick who is listed as the tenant in 1633 I know virtually nothing. What I can say is that he was probably a person of some importance in his day, if only from the fact that he could afford to rent the property and live in a house of this size. The survey is also rather uninformative about the extent of the land attached to it.

LLANMIHANGEL FARMHOUSE TODAY *(PICTURE BY CYRIL JAMES)*

The jurors say only that the portion which lay within the boundary of their manor amounted to some 110 acres of which ten were woodland, thereby implying (as we know to have been the case before and after) that the farm included other land beyond the borders of their manor.

Shortly after this, in 1638, the picture begins to clear somewhat with a brief mention in a Margam MSS (PM 2191) recording receipt of the sum of £37.11s.4d. from Richard Cradock "in full rent for Lanmihangell". Four years later Cradock secured a lease to 17 [customary] acres of rough ground called Gorse Fawr (PM 2190, record of the Court of the manors of Pyle & (Higher) Kenfig, 23rd June, 1668.) and then in 1645 another upon "that mansion house, ffarme, or grange called & known by ye name of Llanvihangell" for the lives of himself, his wife Elizabeth and their son Richard junior (PM 2190). By 1651 he had added the tenancy of the nearby corn mill as well.

Although I have not been able to ascertain Richard's true origins, the indications are that he hailed from the Swansea area and was obviously from a family of some standing. He seems, in fact, to have been on intimate terms with his landlords, the Mansels, and the value set upon his goods and chattels at the time of his death in 1668 suggest that he then ranked amongst the top elements of the Glamorgan gentry. We will not dwell further here on Richard and his family, for they will make an appearance a little later in my narrative because of a family scandal that must have entertained the gossips of Kenfig for many years afterwards!

New Mill and Gronow William

In 1628, a lease (PM 1280) was issued by the Margam estate to a Gronow William which reveals for the first time that the Mansels had gone to the expense of erecting a new corn mill near the bridge carrying Water Street across the River Kenfig. Known simply as New Mill it had a very short history but afterwards the bridge was (and still is) known as New Mill Bridge (Pont Felin Newydd). Gronow was not its first tenant for he had taken the property over from a Rees ap John, but it is doubtful that the latter had been there very long.

William Gronow of New Mill was the son of a man named William Watkin who was tenant of a property on the Ffrwdwyllt stream somewhere in the vicinity of modern Taibach. A précis of a lease issued in 1673 (PM 6349/586) shows David Gronow held this property consisting of a house and unspecified amount of land. At the same time the name 'Gronow' is rather unusual in this area and they may have originated in the Neath district. A family surnamed Gronow were later people of some importance there in the 18th century, and when in 1650 Gronow William purchased some land in the lower borough, three of the witnesses to the transaction (PM

943 & 946) were from Cadoxton, Neath.

Born about 1601 William wasted little time in establishing himself as a person of stature in the district. Attached to the mill was a house and a small farm of very modest proportions.

> 2 acres ar[able] & pasture, ... one other close called Ynys y Pandy contayning 5 acr or thereabout, ar[able] & past[ure]; one other close called The Hamme contayning 1 acre or thereabout in pasture; one other parcell of medow called The Moores contaying one acre or thereabout (PM 1280).

In modern terms this amounted to only 8.4 acres, but William was a man who apparently had come here with money in his pocket, and soon set about expanding his holding north and south of the river. By the time of the 1630 survey of the Manor of Kenfig Borough (PM 1321) he had acquired a further 4.8 acres freehold land on Paschal Hill, and the following year added another 9.6 acres he bought from a John Rosser (PM 899-901). The Higher Kenfig Survey of 1633 also lists him as tenant of Watkin Lougher for 7.2 acres of freehold south of the river, but held under that manor. Within five years of acquiring New Mill therefore he was the tenant or owner of an averaged-sized (if somewhat scattered) farm of about thirty acres.

Of Gronow's first wife I know only that her name was Margaret; that she was born about 1602; and that by her he had at least six children of whom Alice Gronow (1625-1698) was included as a life on her husband's lease to the mill. Of their other children Evan was living at Kenfig in 1663 where he owned 11.2 acres of freehold presumably inherited from his father. He left the borough shortly afterwards, selling his holding to the Margam estate in 1671 (PM 698), and I have noted stray subsequent references to him at both Pyle and South Cornelly. Another daughter, Mary (d. 1694) married Morgan Evan the son of Evan Yorwerth of Kenfig, who had left to take over the tenancy of land in the manor of Horgrove, where the couple are mentioned in 1666 (PM 6349/179). William Gronow, whom we will meet again, inherited 8.4 acres of his father's freehold in Kenfig Lower. Both of the boys (but none of their four sisters) could sign their name which seems to indicate that they had received some education. Gronow himself, incidentally, was only able to make his mark to a document in 1650, but eleven years later signed his name when he took out a fresh lease on New Mill (PM 4082).

The reason for this new lease was that his wife Margaret had died sometime after 1633, and Gronow subsequently remarried a woman called Catherine Gamage (d.1694). She was related to an Alice Gamage of South Cornelly who mentions both Gronow and Catherine in her will of 1645 (Llandaff Wills). To Catherine she bequeathed a cow, four ewes, a feather bed and a cauldron, but she was not apparently very impressed with her husband.

> Gronow Wm of Newmyle is indepted unto mee ... of eighteen pounds unless hee doth assure eight acres of free lands wich was bought by John ? ... unto John Gronow his sonne.

There then follows arrangements for recovering the debt if Gronow failed to perform his part of this bargain.

John was the son of Gronow and Catherine, and evidently something of a favourite with Alice. As well as taking steps to secure him an inheritance from his father she bequeathed him a cow, a mare, six ewes, a feather bed and a "crock". She also made a bequest of six sheep and a yearling calf to the couple's daughter Elsie, but completely ignored Catherine's step-children. As we hear nothing further of Catherine's two children, both presumably died in childhood. There was, however, a third child (presumably born after 1645) that she and Gronow christened David. He grew to manhood and in due course played his own part in the saga of New Mill.

By 1650 Gronow owned 18 acres of freehold land in the lower borough and further increased this with the purchase of a holding on Heol Las from a Richard Lewis (PM 943 & 946). The property consisted of a house, barn, bakehouse, orchard and garden together with 3.6 acres of land, and was sold subject to the continuation of the tenancy of Jane John, the widow of William Began. The first surviving rental for Higher Kenfig dates from the following year, and this shows that in addition to New Mill, Gronow had, since 1633, acquired the tenancy of the holding called Yorath's land. So thirteen years on from his arrival at New Mill Gronow had expanded his original smallholding to roughly 57 acres (modern measure).

By 1661 Gronow seems to have realised that the sands of his life were running out, and he set about making provisions for his family. What particularly concerned him was the future of David, his sole surviving child by Catherine. As things stood, the tenancy of New Mill would pass, under the terms of his original lease, to his daughter Alice and her husband Evan Lyddon. With their consent, and that of Sir Edward Mansel his landlord, he therefore made a new agreement concerning the property. The land known as Ynys y Pandy (7.2 acres) was detached from the original farm and let separately on a new lease to Evan and Alice with their son Joshua (PM 8057). Other land amounting to roughly 10 acres (modern measure) was then added to the mill, and this was re-let to Gronow on the lives of himself, Catherine and David (PM 4082).

Amongst this new land was a property called 'Hamma' and in other documents as 'Hamme' — a name that indicates it was a water meadow periodically flooded by the river. This was valuable land, in that the flooding by the river during the winter, which was often deliberately caused by building dams and weirs, meant the field would produce two, and possibly three crops of hay per year, whereas an ordinary meadow normally produced only one, or two at best.

Having thus provided for both Catherine and her son, Gronow died the following year. His will (PM 1362) appointed her as his executrix, and made bequests to his seven surviving children and his grandchildren. It also includes gifts of a peck of barley or oatmeal to seven named individuals, and a peck of wheat to his aunt Alsod Jenkin. Whether the other seven were his servants, or just some of the 'deserving poor' I'm not sure.

Thomas Thomas. A Proper Gentleman?

Most of what I have been able to learn about Thomas stems from his will drawn up shortly before his death in 1640 (Llandaff Wills). Taken at face value this, together with the accompanying probate inventory, suggest at first sight that he was nothing more than a prosperous cottager. On the acre of land attached to his home he was growing 'neckale' (Winter Wheat?). He owned three dairy cattle and a horse that he probably grazed on the adjoining common. His poultry likewise presumably scratched their living there. He was also the tenant of some four [customary] acres of land on the road to Cornelly.

On that basis there is nothing to indicate why he should have any claim to the title of 'gentleman'. Yet a closer perusal of the contents of his home hints that here was no mere peasant with delusions of grandeur. In the kitchen of his humble cottage the pans were made of brass, and there are pewter items listed amongst the tableware. His bed was equipped with sheets, bolsters and pillows, and why would he require four coffers or chests to hold just the few clothes and valuables (if any) of a simple labourer? Furthermore, he was apparently sufficiently wealthy to have loaned out several small sums totalling £4. 14s. 0d.

Thomas acquired one of his cottages as early as 1612 when a woman named Alice Glas surrendered the property to him (PM 841). The strange thing about this transaction is that it took place at the Court of the manor of North Cornelly, but such curiosities are actually quite common in the feudal system. We have already seen how some freehold property in Kenfig Lower was inherited from Margam Abbey by the Mansels, and are accounted for under their manor of Higher Kenfig. Here we are looking at a similar instance involving a freehold property that had somehow or other passed into the possession of the Turbervilles of North Cornelly.

Piecing together his story as best I can, it would appear that Thomas ap Thomas was indeed of good stock, and had possibly been a former tenant of Llanmihangel farm. He married an Elizabeth Howard, but the couple had no children and, either the marriage went sour or, he fell in love with a woman named Mary William. Thomas already owned the two cottages on Millhill, so he abandoned Elizabeth and went to live there with Mary as his servant. In due course she bore him a son they christened Jenkin.

The survey of the manor of Higher Kenfig made in 1633 shows Elizabeth was then tenant of Llanmihangel Mill in her own right, though where she actually lived is unknown as there is no evidence that there was a house attached to it at this time. Thomas apparently left her comfortably provided for, and in his will bequeathed his "beloved wife" (his words – not mine!) two acres of wheat growing in a field called Longland and all the goods and chattels on her land in the parish of Margam. The remainder of his property all went to his 'supposed son' Jenkin who was to remain in Mary's custody for the following two years (suggesting that he was aged 19 at the time of his father's death).

Excluding the money owed to him, the total value of Thomas's property came to just under £29 but no cash is mentioned and I suspect from subsequent events that this might have been quite considerable. In 1670, for example, the executors of the will of Christopher Cradock of Llanmihangel recorded that there was an outstanding debt of nearly £75 owing to a Jenkin Thomas – Thomas's son (PM 5154).

Although he is subsequently shown as the owner of the cottage on Millhill, Jenkin Thomas left the district by 1662, and when next we hear of him six years later was a merchant at the town of Tangier in North Africa (PM 5994). This was a newly acquired British possession which, together with Bombay in India, had been part of the dowry of King Charles II's wife, the Portuguese Princess Catherine of Braganza. Portugal had only just secured its independence after a period of Spanish domination, and in return for this generous gift Britain undertook to support it against any future aggression from its larger neighbour.

Little seems to have been written about this former British colony at Tangier, but clearly Jenkin had seized the opportunity it offered to set up in business there, and to do so would have required more capital than could be raised on the property listed in his father's probate inventory. He probably retained ownership of the cottage so long as his mother lived, but by 1668 she was presumably dead so he gave directions to his agents in the district to sell it off and it was subsequently bought by the Margam estate (PM 700).

The identities of some of the occupants of the Millhill cottages in the early part of the 17th century are known. At one time, two seem to have belonged to Thomas Thomas, who lived in one and, presumably, let the other to some unidentified individuals. Thomas styled himself a 'gentleman', so what was he doing living in such a humble abode? Thereby hangs a tale!

Joseph Lewis Sometime during his life Thomas ap Thomas sold or gave his second cottage at Millhill (which was also held under the manor of North Cornelly) to his nephew Thomas Hopkin who was the tenant at Marlas Farm. In 1661 the latter, together with John Turberville as Lord of the Manor of North Cornelly, sold the property to Joseph Lewis for £21 (PM 3662). Whether Joseph ever actually lived in it is doubtful however, for his interests seem to have lain in Pyle where he served as a churchwarden and his name is cast on the church bell. A prosperous local farmer, there is a memorial to him and his wife Ann David on the chancel wall there adjoining the altar. They presumably let out the cottage on Millhill, though I cannot identify their tenants. In 1669 the couple sold the cottage and its adjoining acre to Sir Edward Mansel of Margam (PM 687) who had purchased Kenfig Borough manor the previous year. It was a transaction that represented a saving on their part for whereas they had previously been paying a freehold rent of a shilling per annum, the annual rent demanded by their new landlord was only sixpence. This no doubt indicates the increasing threat from the sand, as does the fact that they received only £15 for the property — considerably less than they had paid for it just eight years earlier.

Jennet William Other than to say that she was the widow of a man named Jenkin Evan, there is very little I can say about this lady who lived in one of the Millhill cottages in 1666. These facts survive by virtue of some information passed to the Earl of Pembroke's steward (PM 9622) by the Kenfig Portreeve, Lewis Aylward. The steward's note of their conversation is rather confusing and difficult to read, but appears to indicate that this property had been held by Jennet and her husband under the manor of South Cornelly. Because of this the only suite they owed to the Earl's manorial court was as "resiants". This meant that although they were 'resident' within the manor, the property in which they lived was not held directly from its lord. Aylward further mentioned that according to the court records in his possession, back in 1589 the occupant had been a Thomas Morgan who was then tenant of a Joseph Lewis (though not the same person as the one mentioned above!). This is the only record I can identify relating to this property.

Thomas Richard So far as I can ascertain, the parish of Pyle & Kenfig did not enjoy a vicar of its own until the late 18th century. Previous to this it was combined with the neighbouring parish of Margam. The vicar there provided for the spiritual needs of both. Nevertheless, during the early part of the 17th century the parish may have been provided with a curate of its own, though it has to be said that the value of the gentleman in question appears to have been somewhat dubious. He was Thomas Richard, the resident of the fourth cottage I have identified in the hamlet of Millhill.

When his property was granted to his daughter Catherine is was described as "one mansion house, barne, one other pound or chamber with one acre of free land" (PM 938), but the term "mansion" in no way reflects the size of his house, merely the fact that although it was a humble cottage, it was his own! Documents of the period invariably describe him as a "clerk of Kenfig" which presumably means that he was in Holy Orders, and probably therefore the curate serving perhaps both Pyle and Mawdlam churches.

It was a frequent complaint of the Puritans that the Anglican clergy of the day were often illiterate, and Thomas seems to be a case in point; when called upon to witness various documents he invariably signed with his mark. He had arrived in the area sometime prior to the year 1622 when he took out a lease with the Margam estate upon a holding called Craig y Collwyn (alias Waun Maggy Fach) in Higher Kenfig (PM 1280). Since he was aged 44 at the time it is possible that I am doing him an injustice, for his later inability to sign documents (first apparent in 1635)

may actually have been due to the fact that his eyesight had failed.

He probably acquired the cottage at Millhill about 1628, and lived there the rest of his life. In the lease of 1622 his wife is named as Elizabeth who was still living eleven years later. She was five years her husband's junior, though in the event, he not only outlived her, but remarried as well. He and Elizabeth had a son named Hopkin Thomas included with them on the Craig y Collwyn lease, but he also seems to have died sometime after 1633. By his second wife, Ann Jenkin, Thomas had four daughters and as the end of his life loomed large, appears to have been particularly concerned about one named Catherine, probably because she alone of the four remained unmarried. To protect her interests he therefore had a document drawn up in 1649 (PM 938) securing her right of succession to the cottage on Millhill "as if this [were] my last will & testament"

How Thomas fared during the Commonwealth is not recorded. One suspects that he was turned out of his living but probably managed to scrape along. He had the land adjoining the cottage upon which to grow corn, peas and beans, and since he was presumably a burgess, would also have had right of pasture on the adjoining waste. If his eyesight had indeed failed then much of the work would have been done by his wife and Catherine, perhaps another reason why he was so keen to ensure that the cottage passed to the latter after his day. In addition he may have been able to sub-let Craig y Collwyn so, even if incapacitated, he and his womenfolk would have been able to survive The Commonwealth with a little to spare.

Thomas lived to see the restoration of the monarchy in 1660, for the last mention of him is made in a document of that year. He would then have been aged 82, and did not survive for long afterwards. When his wife Ann made her will (Llandaff Wills) six years later she is described as a widow.

Under the terms of this document, Ann left sums of money to their three remaining daughters. Only £4 was bequeathed to Gwenllian, but Ann and Catherine were generously endowed with the sum of £20 apiece. Catherine was once again probably well provided for because she was single. In Ann's case however their mother seems to have been playing upon the cupidity of her son-in-law by leaving her such a large sum, for it came with strings attached! Ann's husband, Hopkin Watkin, was the owner of a farm, and in order for his wife to receive the money he was required to draw up a legally binding document ensuring that the property would descend to their children "according to his former promise". Whether the ruse succeeded, alas, we do not know.

Catherine seems to have died shortly after her mother, and in accordance with the document her father had drawn up in 1649 the property passed to her sister

Gwenllian who sold it to the Margam estate in 1668 (PM 684-5).

At a manorial Court Leet (PM 2190) for the manors of Pyle & Higher Kenfig held on 23rd June, 1668, the jurors reported to the steward that Richard Cradock, one of the lord's tenants in the latter manor, had passed away. Under the terms of his lease a heriot of "ye best beast" that he owned was therefore due to the lord, and David Bennet the steward later endorsed the record that this had subsequently been "paid in kind". Having reported the death, the jury added (as was normal practice) that Richard's widow, Elizabeth Cradock, was now "tenant in his stead according to ye same lease upon ye farme of Llanvihangel". We may note in passing that Elizabeth is referred to by her 'married name', an indication that (as related in an earlier chapter) the Cradocks were people of some station in life. At this time in Kenfig's history, English practices in this respect were still a novelty, and most married women continued to be known by their maiden names.

We would assume that Richard's passing was mourned by his family, friends and neighbours, but although we do not know how old he was at the time they would also have declared (to borrow a phrase from a later age) that he had had 'a pretty good innings'. He had lived at Llanmihangel for over 30 years, raised eight children, and enjoyed the comforts and prestige that his wealth had brought him in this quiet corner of Glamorgan.

Whilst, therefore, his death was probably noted by the jurors with sorrow tinged perhaps with respect, there was no hint of the family crisis that was to follow, which was to generate a whole file of documents in the Margam estate records.

Richard made his will (Llandaff Wills) on 19th March 1668 when he was "weake in bodie", and in it are clear indications that, however things might appear to outsiders, all was not entirely well within his family. His son Morgan was a clerk in holy orders who, for example, was bequeathed the sum of £20 but only "if he doth personally appear" to collect it. A hint therefore that he had not been visiting his parents, and that his father was somewhat piqued about it. Perhaps there was a rift between them over the question of religion, for it seems that despite the bequest of a shilling to Llandaff Cathedral and five shillings "towards the reparacon of the parish church of Margam" Richard (as suggested in a previous chapter) may have been a Nonconformist. Morgan, on the other hand, was an Anglican clergyman.

The eldest son, named Richard after his father, had probably already left home by this time to take up residence in Bristol, but he was the heir to Llanmihangel by virtue of the lease the family held upon it. Whilst therefore his father bequeathed him land at Cwrt Rhyd Hir in Port Talbot, and other property at Neath, he nevertheless willed that after his death, and that of his wife, Llanmihangel was to go to Christopher. He was another son, who apparently, was the only one that had remained at home. The fourth son, Shadrack, is later mentioned as living in London. Furthermore all bequests to his sons and their four sisters (Elizabeth, Jane, Hannah and Mary who received sums of money ranging between twenty and fifty pounds) were conditional upon their accepting this bequest of the farm and its contents to Christopher.

The dying Richard also apparently foresaw problems between Christopher and his mother. Having appointed them joint executors of his will he urged them "oute of my affectionate love, to carry on their business joyntley and not severally" – i.e. to work together in implementing the terms of the will and running the estate. He then continued, "And if any diffrence happen to be, as I hope there will not, I do require them by this my last will and testament to reffer themselves unto the overseer hereafter to be named".

There is perhaps no better indication of Richard Cradock's status, than that the persons who consented to be the overseers of his will were none other than Sir Edward Mansel of Margam and the Right Honourable Bussey Mansel of Briton Ferry. In the event, most of the work sorting out the subsequent mess seems to have fallen upon Sir Edward who, by the time everything was finally 'done and dusted' must have heartily wished that he had ever agreed to put himself in such a position!

An inventory was duly made of Richard's property on 11th June 1668, shortly after his death. It is a comparatively uninformative document, but tells us that, including over £70 owed to him as debts (but not including any cash, investments, or bonds) his worldly good totalled over £350 — a massive sum in the context of that time and place. According to his will, Richard had actually farmed at least a part of the land at Llanmihangel, for he refers to his "stocke of oxen, kine, young cattle, horses, mares, sheepe, corn and graine in the ground and in the houses and barnes". Only the "corn in the ground" finds mention in the inventory, the livestock apparently being lumped together under the heading "Movable goods".

Richard's widow Elizabeth (nominally at least) now took over the tenancy of the property, though it was probably Christopher who actually ran the farm and estate. As I related in my _Five Mills of Kenfig,_ she became embroiled in actions at the manorial court up to her death in (or shortly after) 1671, which is the last record I have found of her. In February of 1670 she and Christopher had still not settled her late husband's will, for it seems he had left them as many debts as he had assets. "A true and perfect scheduell of the debts" for which they were liable was drawn up at that time showing that these totalled £341.10s.8d, and that £200 due in

legacies had still not been paid to Richard's beneficiaries (PM 5154).

Two years later, almost to the day, Christopher himself lay seriously ill (he apparently died sometime later that year) with these matters still unresolved. He further complicated things by making a will of his own (Llandaff Wills) leaving all his possessions to his brother Shadrack, with instructions to settle the debts and bequests inherited from their father's will, appointing him and their eldest brother Richard as his executors. From documents in the Margam file relating to the subsequent disposal of Richard's property (PM 5155 & 5301-6), it is clear that (if this had not been the case at their father's death) both these brothers were now living away from the area, Shadrack in London and Richard junior in Bristol. At this juncture their sisters and brother Morgan seem to have decided enough was enough, so with Christopher ill and helpless, they apparently took matters into their own hands and helped themselves to whatever took their fancy at the family home. At this point Sir Edward Mansel decided that as the original overseer of Richard Cradock's will, the time had come for him to take a hand.

Sir Edward seems to have taken the view that Richard's original property (which had been in Christopher's custody) should be shared equally between the surviving children. To this end he despatched his servants to recover the stolen items, and the list of property recovered under this head grew quickly. On 2nd May 1672 Hannah and Elizabeth (Betty) surrendered a huge quantity of items including two sides of bacon weighing 77lb; 15 cheeses; a pewter chamber pot; a saw; curtains, linen, wheat, barley and hay! Nor was this all.

Martha Cradock (the niece of Margaret Evan of Kenfig) is described in Richard's will as his daughter-in-law though not, apparently, the wife of any son then living. She disgorged a whole host of items she had apparently taken from the farm on behalf of her sister-in-law, Elizabeth — 23 sheep, a cupboard, table, bench, three bedsteads, two pots of butter, a flitch of bacon, and two stone of cheese. She had also removed a quantity of brass, pewter and silver which she had given to another sister, Mary the wife of Humphrey Audley of Swansea. Rather than surrender any of these, Audley paid Sir Edward their value in cash.

As property was recovered, so it had to be re-distributed evenly amongst the family. On 4th November the prodigal son Morgan, together with his sisters Elizabeth and Hannah, produced for the inspection by Mansel's agents, all the property they were apparently allowed to keep. This included three chairs covered in "Rushia Leather" and various utensils of brass and pewter. Mansel also further allocated them certain other items such as a table and cupboard that still remained at the house. Other property seized from Han-

nah and Elizabeth (including the pewter chamber pot) were delivered to Richard who, being away in Bristol had of course not had an opportunity to participate in the free-for-all at Llanmihangel.

Having made this division of the late Richard's property, Sir Edward also seems to have acted as broker in a process whereby some items allocated to one sibling could be purchased by another. Thus some furniture from the "Hall Chamber" was sold to Richard for £5 which sum was then paid to Mary Audley.

Gradually Sir Edward's agents worked their way through the mass of property, itemising, evaluating, listing and allocating the various articles until eventually in 1675 and 76 the file closes, with receipts from the various parties for the cash and property they had received. There was however apparently one final complication. The Rev Morgan Cradock, apparently 'went missing' again, and in consequence had not received his full share of the property when he died in 1680. Presumably he must have made a will leaving all his worldly goods to his brother Shadrack, so not until 10th January of the following year was Mansel able to dispose of the final items and cash to him, thereby finally drawing a line under the whole sorry affair.

So much for the estate of the deceased Richard, but what of Llanmihangel Farm itself? After the death of his mother, Richard Cradock had apparently been content to allow his brother Christopher to continue at the property and even to run the holding he himself had inherited at Cwrt Rhyd Hir on his behalf. Christopher was still living in January 1672, but his health was failing when he dictated his last Will and Testament on 15th February (Llandaff Wills). He died shortly afterwards but although Richard returned briefly to Llanmihangel he had little interest in settling there. Instead he and Shadrack seem to have come to an arrangement whereby the latter would take over Richard's interest in the lease. The subject was broached with Sir Edward Mansel as the landlord, and he gave his permission in writing for the lease to be amended subject to the payment of £40. Accordingly on 6th January 1673 the farm was duly assigned to Shadrack (PM 5299), but by the August he had had enough of 'playing farmers' and surrendered it back to Sir Edward (PM 5301) before presumably heading back to the bright lights of London. In his will (PM 5305) Shadrack nevertheless directed that on his death he be buried at Margam near his parents and Christopher. With his departure I once again temporarily lose track of the tenancy of the farm and its land.

Through a Kenfig Keyhole: Llanmihangel

One benefit for the historian from the events at Llanmihangel is that despite the lack of detail in the probate inventory made at the death of Richard Cradock, the reams of paper-work associated with the subsequent division of his property does give some idea of his home and furniture.

Then as now, the house was divided between living quarters and a portion connected with the work of the farm. Basically, as illustrated in the report of the Royal Commission on Ancient & Historical Monuments in Wales (RCAHMW, 1988) the building is 'T' shaped. The 'cross-piece' is the main house facing south up the valley towards Marlas, the 'stem' extending away northwards and terminating in farm buildings. As originally conceived it seems to have consisted purely of the domestic element which appears to date from the early years of the 17th century. Prior to 1668, and possibly at the instigation of Richard Cradock, the 'stem' was extended further north to create the stable with a "corn loft" or granary above. This last is reached by an external stone stairway, and rows of pigeon holes were added beneath the eves as nesting boxes for these birds which were reared for their eggs and meat.

With the aid of the commission's plan of the house it is possible to attempt some sort of reconstruction of the interior, as described in the documents drawn up after Richard Cradock's death in 1668. The main entrance in the south front of the 'cross-piece' of the 'T' led into a small lobby from which doors led left and right into the 'hall' and the 'hall chamber' respectively. Internally separate doors then led on from these rooms into a large kitchen set in the northern extension. Here there would also have presumably been a smaller room (called "the Buttery" in the probate inventory) which was a pantry where foodstuff and other provisions were stored.

The hall was the 'living room' of the house used, not only by Richard and his family, but by their servants as well. The 'hall chamber' on the other hand would have been the 'best room' or, what we of an older generation knew as 'the parlour'. It would have held the finest furniture in the house, but it was used only when an important visitor came calling, or on special family occasions including funerals. Richard's body would have lain here in its coffin, until removed for burial, so that family and friends could pay their last respects.

Identifying the upstairs rooms in the commission's plan with those of the inventory is a little more difficult. The inventory names them as the cross-chamber; the middle cross chamber; the little chamber; and "ye speere" which is probably 'spare' as in spare room. Certainly it contained little of value, for its entire contents were costed at less than a pound, compared with £11. 14. 8d. for those in the "cross-chamber" which was the most important of these upstairs rooms.

The Commission's plan of the house indicates two large rooms, one each above the hall and

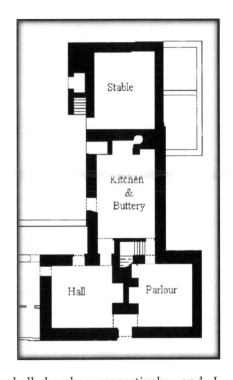

hall-chamber respectively, and I would assume that the cross-chamber was one of these, and the other was perhaps the 'speere'. The middle-cross chamber was then probably the room set immediately behind them in the kitchen extension, and the room beyond this was the 'little chamber'. I would also hazard a guess that as it was the main bedroom the cross-chamber was the one above the hall. This last being the 'living room' of the house a fire would have been kept burning during the winter, thereby heating the room above. The same applied to the two bedrooms above the kitchen. Although the parlour had a fireplace (set in the wall separating it from the one in the hall and sharing its chimney) its spasmodic use meant both it, and the room above would have been rather cold in winter. Hence, presumably, the reason why 'the spare' was not in general use.

The two other rooms mentioned in the inventory are the dairy and the bake-house. In the present building the dairy and a kitchen are in 'lean-to' type buildings on the north and west side of the hall respectively. The RCAHMW report indicates that these are more modern than the rest of the building, but when repairs were being carried out to a small section of the dairy floor in 2003 it was found that underneath lay the footings of a substantial wall about a metre wide. This was at the western end of the room, and roughly parallel with the north wall of the hall indicating that some building at one time abutted onto it. The thickness of the footings suggests that this was perhaps the dairy where substantial walls would help keep the interior cool.

Across the yard on the north side of the kitchen extension are the remains of a building containing an oven, and presumably this was the 'bakehouse' such buildings being normally detached from the main house to minimise the risk of fire.

Unfortunately the probate inventory of 1668 does not list the contents of each room, just their total value. Nevertheless, thanks to the family squabble that erupted in 1672, we are able to gain some idea of how they may have been furnished.

Although its contents are valued at only £6.17s 0d, the hall was the heart of the house. Here the family and their servants took their meals together sitting about 'the great table'. As head of the household Richard senior would probably have sat in 'the great chair' and perhaps the 'turned chair' (made of timber 'turned' on a lathe) was used by his wife Elizabeth. The four ordinary chairs were possibly those of family members still living at home, whilst the servants and farm labourers made do with the stools and the 'form' or bench that are listed.

The other hall furnishings included a cupboard, a truckle board; a bed, and a sideboard. But these are terms that are not quite what they might seem to us today. A cupboard at this period was a table with two or three shelves on which the family's sliver, pewter, and earthenware was displayed. As such it was the ancestor both of the Welsh dresser and (when doors began to be added in the 17th century), the modern cupboard. The 'sideboard' was actually a side table, perhaps the round one mentioned in another document as belonging to the hall. Food and drink brought from the buttery and kitchen would be placed on this, prior to being served at the main table.

The bed in the hall is described as a "cupboard bed", a type that will be familiar to visitors to the museum at St Fagan's. It stood within a large cabinet fitted with sliding doors, thus affording the occupant some privacy when others were using the hall. The truckle board was another type of bed fitted with wheels so that it could be pushed under other furniture (in this case perhaps the table) whilst not in use. On the walls there would have been hung some guns with their equipment. Used for shooting vermin and game in the adjoining fields, the weapons themselves are not included in the various lists, but there is mention of the hooks upon which they hung and a "gun scourer" (for cleaning out the gun barrels).

At £16.19s.0d. the value set upon the furnishings of the adjoining parlour made them the most expensive in the house, and it was undoubtedly Elizabeth Cradock's pride and joy. Here would have been the three chairs of Russian leather — a durable material made from skins impregnated with oil made from birch tree bark. Although the records tells us that there was a carpet on the floor, we do not know what other articles of furniture may have been displayed here. Significantly however one item that is specifically said to have come from this room is a bed sheet — evidence that the furniture was covered to protect it from dust and sunlight when not in use. This confirms that it was the 'best room' or 'parlour' only used on special occasions or to receive important guests. If the latter arrived unexpectedly the sheets could quickly be whisked away displaying the furnishings in pristine condition.

Second in value to the contents of the Hall chamber were those of the main bedroom. Beds in those days were simply mattresses on the floor, and only the better-off had them raised on bedsteads, of which four are listed here. The one in the main bedroom (the cross-chamber) was probably the 'French' bedstead which was a full four-poster with canopy above and curtains about the sides. These protected the occupants from the draughts that crept down chimneys and through gaps in doors and windows. They slept on a comfortable mattress stuffed with feathers, and the same filling was used for the bolster and pillows. The bed linen probably included the pair of 'Holland' sheets, a term that indicates they were of the finest quality.

Mats mentioned elsewhere in the inventory probably covered the floor, and here too were most likely a number of coffers or chests (including 'the great chest') containing clothing, spare bedding, and the family's valuables. Another item would have been the pewter chamber pot "with the name of Watkin Jenkin upon the bottome". Whether inside or outside the receptacle is unfortunately not stated. The one would mean that it was the name of the maker or former owner, but the other? Let us just say that this was a time when the chamber pots of ardent royalists often sported a depiction of Oliver Cromwell — on the inside!

Of the contents of the other occupied bedrooms, what was apparently the second-best bed is described as a "half-headed bedstead", upon which the mattress and bolster had been stuffed with "flocking" — waste wool. This bedstead had a headboard and a post at each corner to support hangings round the outside, but no canopy above like the one in the main bedroom.

Just behind the value of the contents of the master bedroom were the items in the kitchen. About the only thing that I can definitely say belonged here was a cupboard, though furnishings such as chairs and a large table would also have been essential. What is particularly fascinating is the list of utensils, crockery, and other kitchen equipment contained in the lists drawn up by Sir Edward's agents. Not all would have been kept here. We can imagine that the finest pieces of family silver and plate would be displayed in a cupboard in the parlour and used only on special occasions. The ordinary crockery for everyday use would have been stacked in the cupboard in the hall, and included both wooden trenchers and earthenware plates. In the kitchen cupboard would have been some of the utensils used in cooking, an activity that centred upon the great fireplace at the north end of the room. This "equipment of the hearth" is listed in some detail.

In front of the fire were a pair of andirons such as were to be found on every fireplace in the house. These were a pair of stands consisting of parallel iron rails with pillars (often ornamental) at the front. Placed on either side of the hearth, they supported the logs which fuelled the fire. Alongside, were two shovels and tongs to tend the fire itself, and ranged about it various different items connected with cooking. Meat could be roasted on one of the three spits in front of the fire, turned regularly by one of the lowlier members of the household staff. At Llanmihangel however they may have mechanised this operation as there is mention of "a bitt of chain that hung ye weights". With associated gears and pulleys the weights acted rather like those on a grandfather clock, turning the spits at a steady rate as they slowly descended. Beneath the spits on an iron stand was a large shallow pan — the dripping pan — to catch fat that oozed from the joints of meat above. Very valuable stuff dripping! Besides being used for cooking it went to make rush-lights and candles and to grease the axles of carts and wagons.

As an alternative to using the spits there were two "great racks" for roasting meat directly over the fire, and an "iron grate" which was probably a gridiron. This was a platform of iron bars with short feet and a long handle, again used for roasting small joints of meat over the fire. Probably suspended above the fire was a rack from which pots and cauldrons were suspended on hooks. Since there were four pairs of hooks it is therefore not surprising to discover eight iron "potts" listed elsewhere in the papers.

The best of the kitchenware had undoubtedly been spirited away in the family free-for-all, and we know of just a few of the better items of brass recovered from certain family members. A brass ladle, a posnet (a little pot for boiling with a handle and three feet); a chaffing dish (a dish with a small heater beneath) and the "great kettle". This last was not the utensil we know today but a large round pan with semi-circular handles on the sides used for heating water.

Richard Cradock's home at Llanmihangel was far better furnished than most in the district, save for the Mansel mansion at Margam. Added together, the value of the purely domestic contents of the building amounted to well over £60. By way of comparison the contents of the home of Leyson Morgan (son of Morgan Llewelyn and Alice Yorwerth) who lived in the cottage at the castle, was value at £2.1s. 0d. in 1679. This actually compares quite well with those of several small farmers who died locally at about this time. The entire contents of the house of Jenkin Griffith, grandson of former Portreeve Evan Griffith, amounted to just ten shillings (1673), and those of Thomas Rees the son of Rees Leyson to only 12 shillings (1672). His father (who died about 1664-7) had lived in what was actually one of the better furnished homes, the contents of which were

valued at £3. In 1696 even the contents of the home of a petty gentleman such as Richard Lougher at Ty Maen, South Cornelly (d. 1698) amounted to only ten guineas (£10.50p)! Where his contemporaries in Kenfig were concerned, it has to be said that Richard Cradock had been in a class of his own!

Note: At the time of writing this portion of my history I was unable to identify the origins of this family, but later (2008) I was able to ascertain that they were from Cwrt Rhydhir (Longford Court) Neath Abbey, and descended from a John Cradock who rented it from Richard Williams (alias Cromwell) in 1544. The tenancy was surrendered by Richard & Shadrack in 1672.

Hopkin Edward of Caeau Gollen
Caeau Gollen was a peculiar holding, in that part of its land lay on the north side of the river Kenfig, whilst the house and the remainder lay on the south. The house, in fact is probably what we now know as Glasfryn Boarding Kennels. Because of this split, it is a property that constantly keeps 'dodging round' in the records. The Margam estate, for example, considered it part of Higher Kenfig, but with the house standing in the lower borough its occupants were assessed for Poll Tax there. Such a division was probably confusing and inconvenient for them, but I can also assure you it is also a considerable nuisance for a local historian!

Hopkin took over this tenancy in 1682, but had been active in the area since 1661 when he was one of the jurors for the manorial survey made that year. He may have briefly spent a period of residence in North Cornelly where he is mentioned as a juror in 1673 (CL Deeds 1/1 203/240), and in that year was made the executor of the will of another Kenfig resident called Thomas Hopkin. The latter had no children of his own, and although no relationship is mentioned it is highly likely that one existed for Hopkin replaced the deceased as owner of 1½ acres of freehold land in the Paschal Hill Hold.

In 1677 Hopkin acquired the tenancy of Maes Mawr, a 3.6 acre field lying on the north side of Heol Las bordered, incidentally, by land that had also formerly belonged to Thomas Hopkin. He still retained other property in North Cornelly, and may actually still have been living there, but moved back into the borough once he acquired Caeau Gollen five years later.

The amount of land attached to this holding was not great. Estate records say it amounted to ten acres which would be about twelve in modern measure. Access to the land across the Kenfig had also been a problem in the past. The river could be forded easily enough, but beyond it on the north side lay a leat carrying water to power New Mill. In 1668 there had been a row at the Higher Kenfig manorial court when the jury reported that a bridge over the leat leading to "ye houses of 2 or 3 of ye tenants" had broken. John David Bowen of nearby Farm Fach, one of the oldest inhabitants was called forward to give evidence, and placed responsibility on the widowed Catherine Gamage the mill tenant by declaring that "they yt live in ye new mill did usually put it there" (PM 2190). Twelve months later it had still not been replaced, so Catherine was fined five shillings and this apparently spurred her to take action for we hear no more of the matter.

So far as I can discover Hopkin and his wife Jennet Deere had no children, and only they are mentioned as living in the house at the time of the 1689 Poll Tax return (PM 6189). He was a smallholder in the Evan Griffith mould, with probably less than twenty acres of land in total, but seems to have done quite well out of it. His will (Llandaff Wills) is a simple affair in which he left all his worldly possessions to his wife, but the value placed upon these was over £30 — a 'tidy sum' for the district. As was to be expected, he had two cows to supply milk from which to produce butter and cheese; four steers and three yearlings being reared for sale to the drovers; and 40 sheep that he probably pastured on the adjoining common land.

Like Evan Griffith before him Hopkin owned a wagon which, whilst it would have been useful for fetching produce harvested from Maes Mawr, also enabled him to undertake occasional haulage work. He also seems to have dabbled in horse breeding in

a small way, for the inventory includes a horse, two mares, and a
colt. With their corn in the field
and the eggs from their poultry, he
and Jennet his wife would have
been largely self-sufficient in the
matter of food. Small wonder then
that they were able to purchase
some small luxuries for their home,
the contents of which were valued
at £5.

Hopkin died in 1693, and
his widow Jennet continued at
Caeau Gollen until her own death
ten years later. One small facet of
his latter days may be of interest as
showing the inflexibility of the customs of the times. Hopkin failed to
turn up to perform his 'suit of
court' on 1st September, 1692,
probably because he was already
very ill (he made his will on 30th
November). His absence was duly
noted, and there is little doubt that
he was subsequently fined for his
omission.

Rees Leyson Rees Leyson was the
ancestor of a family that subsequently continued at Kenfig for
some two centuries. Almost
throughout this entire period they
stuck with the practice of Welsh
patronyms, the name chosen for
the eldest son alternating between
Thomas and Rees. Consequently
Thomas Rees is succeeded by Rees
Thomas whose son was Thomas
Rees, etc, etc. For convenience sake
therefore I generally refer to them
as the Rees/Thomas family.

Born in 1585, Rees may or
may not have been a local man, but
married Catherine Evan, the
daughter of former Portreeve, Evan
Griffith whom we met in an earlier
chapter. Although illiterate (he invariably signed documents with
his mark) Rees was a man of some
ambition, and utilised contacts
within his wife's family to build up
a small farm based upon a house
on the north side of Heol Las. This
last was settled upon the couple in
1618 by her brother Griffith Evan
as a gift which also included some
3½ acres of adjoining land (PM
9590).

Eight years later Rees
added some fields called Ynys y
Pandy, Longrove, and Y Wern, that
he acquired under a lease from the
Margam estate (PM 1280). At the
same time he also purchased 7¾
acres (approximately 9¼ modern
measure) of freehold land within
the manor of Kenfig Borough
which gave him a holding of over
30 acres (modern measure) in total
— about the area of a normal sized
farm of this period. It is indeed
possible that it was larger, for he
could have been leasing other land
of which I have no record.

The house in which Rees
lived on the north side of Heol Las
has long since vanished, buried
beneath modern housing. Unlike
many he made his will (Llandaff
Wills) in 1664 when he was "in
good health and perfect memory"
rather than leaving things until the
last moment. The inventory made
at the time of his death two years
later shows that only four acres of
his land had been put down to
crops — one each of wheat and
barley with oats being grown on

the other two. The reason oats predominated is because Rees seems to have been engaged in rearing horses. Whilst only a single mare and colt are mentioned he owned five fillies between two and four years old. These he could have bought as colts at a horse fair such as the one held annually at St Mary Hill and then raised on the farm for eventual re-sale.

His seven dairy cows indicate that he was producing butter and cheese, and there is the usual mix of younger cattle being reared for the drove. His 28 sheep and lambs together with an unspecified number of poultry complete the list which (except for the horses) is typical of the composition of other farms of this size in the district at this time.

The People of Heol Kenfig Together with Heol y Lane, the main highway called Heol Kenfig formed the 'New Town' that the Burgesses of Kenfig had created for themselves. But what of the people who now made their homes there? There is no roll or census recording these details, but there survives from the latter part of the 17th century a number of marriage settlements, deeds, leases and other such documents relating to property that bordered both these roads. The evidence contained in these and other contemporary records is not simple or straightforward, but piecing the fragmentary information together as best I can I believe I have identified the approximate location of the houses and their occupants in the mid and late 17th century with some degree of accuracy.

Some Kenfig Women
The consequences of a deal (PM 2929) in which Rees Leyson was involved in 1622 ultimately further added to his growing land holding. In that year he financed the purchase of a field called Cae Mawr on Heol Fach by a spinster named Cecile Thomas from his brother-in-law Griffith Evan and an Evan Richard Saunders. It is likely in fact that he was in some way related to Cecile, and paid over £120 for the property on her behalf. Cecile never married, and towards the end of her life in 1653 she returned the favour by selling this property, together with another acre of land she owned, to Rees's daughter, Catherine, for just £1 (PM 953 & 4). The two women enjoyed a close friendship, but like Cecile, Catherine also never married and then as now it seems that the local gossips had been at work. In the document Cecile therefore firmly and clearly makes the point that she made this gift purely because of "the natural love and affection that I beare to and towards Katherine Rees".

Cecile died shortly afterwards, and Catherine continued to enjoy possession of the fields until her own death in 1664. Probably she, and Cecile before her, rented them out to local farmers to provide themselves with a small income. By her will (PM 5923) Catherine bequeathed the property to her married sister Joanne for her life, and upon her death to their brother Evan. If he had no heirs, then it was to pass to their eldest brother Thomas Rees. Exactly what happened next is not recorded, but by 1666 the fields were in the hands of her father Rees Leyson, and after his death indeed passed on to Thomas Rees as the eldest son.

One point this simple story illustrates, is the degree of independence accorded to the womenfolk of Kenfig compared with their counterparts in English society of the day. There, women were regarded as the responsibility of their fathers whilst single, and of their husbands once married. Society apparently believed members of the fair sex incapable of ordering their own affairs, and as a consequence the pressure upon them to marry (or re-marry in the case of widows) was immense. Here at Kenfig we have a case involving two women, Cecile Thomas and Catherine Rees, who had chosen not to take a husband and who were quite clearly ordering their own affairs.

Although even more marked in the nearby manor of Stormy (where virtually all the inhabitants were of Welsh stock) this aspect even extended into the workings of the borough itself. It will be recalled that when setting out the provisions regarding tenancy of the plots of hay within the enclosure at Waun Cimla, the burgesses had been careful to include clauses protecting the rights of the

occupant's womenfolk. Ordinance No 53 provided that in respect of such parcels "every widow shall enjoy the priviledge of her husband during her widowhood" and added that nobody was to "interrupt the said widow of her priviledge as long as she liveth and dwelleth within the said burrough and town". Later we find widows of burgesses exercising full burgess rights (other than that they could neither hold any office nor vote at elections) and being included on the roll of burgesses. Only if they died, remarried, or left the borough was somebody appointed to take their place.

This attitude towards the women of the community seems to have been introduced into Kenfig as part of the wave of interest in things Welsh apparent during the Tudor and early Stuart period. Under Welsh law, women had been responsible for their own destiny once they achieved the age of fourteen. Thereafter they were free to make their own way in the world, marry whom they wished, and entitled to half a son's share of their parent's goods and chattels upon their decease. Even after the arrival of the Normans, native laws and customs continued to be practised in the Welsh lordships and 'Welshries' of Glamorgan. Only with the introduction of King Henry VIII's Act of Union had these been swept away and replaced by the English code but, as examples from both Kenfig and Stormy illustrate, the former laws coloured local customs and practices regarding the treatment of women for several centuries afterwards.

Two local women who certainly showed themselves capable of standing up for themselves were the widows Elizabeth Cradock of Llanmihangel and Catherine Gamage of New Mill as recorded in the surviving records of the manorial court for Higher Kenfig. These records commence in 1667, and continue into the first decade of the 18th century, and make fascinating reading. The courts were held at Pyle alongside those for that manor, and presided over by the Margam steward. They may have sat in the church as the largest building in the village, but generally one would expect them to meet in the bar of a local alehouse. Pyle boasted two at this time, one run by a man named Charles William and the other, situated somewhere near the cross, kept by Anne Nicholas. We know this from their frequent appearances at these sittings for breaches of the licensing laws! Later, about 1689, *The Tap* (then known as *The White Hart*) came into being. Purpose-built by the Margam estate as an inn designed to serve travellers, this was a roomier building, and one suspects that after its construction it became the regular venue for these hearings.

There were basically two types of court. Courts Baron dealt purely with matters relating to the property of the Lord of the Manor, and in theory were held every month. According to the 1633 survey of Higher Kenfig, however, the one for this manor only actually sat when requested by one of the Lord's tenants there. The petty constable would then notify those required to perform suit of court that their presence was required. The other courts (one in the spring; the other in the autumn) were the Courts Leet that dealt with a wider range of matters — such as the failure of licensees to adhere to the law! Alongside these might be held a Court of Pleas that dealt with debts valued less than £2.

Everyone who was a tenant of the Lord of the Manor was expected to attend such courts, and failure to do so resulted in a fine. Once assembled the first task at any court was to appoint a jury from these tenants. The number was not fixed and could be as few as eight though generally they seem to have aimed if possible to select twelve who were of course all male. This was a "jury of presentment" whose task was to 'present' or 'report' to the steward any matters relating to the lord's tenants and their holdings in the manor. If required the Steward would then make a decision and perhaps impose a sentence arrived at (in the case of Leet Courts) with the help of two 'assessors'. Normally these were two of the oldest inhabitants of the manor chosen for their knowledge of its customs and practices in the past.

The Courts Baron, supervised the property of the Lord, reporting the death of tenants and what heriot was due from the next of kin. Normally this was the 'best beast' that the deceased had owned, though usually the family had the option of paying a fixed cash sum instead. For those who owned no livestock then 'the best' of their belongings were taken. Evan William's daughter, Wenllian, handed over an iron pot when he died. In the manor of Pyle an anvil was seized on the death of a smith named Richard John, and the worldly goods of a widow named Mary Jenkin were so few that the bailiff had to be content with her petticoat! These were all tenants of property within the manor, but in Higher Kenfig a "turf heriot" was apparently applied to anyone who died there who was not the member of a tenant's family. When John Thomas, a servant employed by Elizabeth Cradock died in 1671, the bailiff seized his doublet which was then sold for ten shillings. In 1667 a pauper named David Richard was being escorted back to his own parish, being passed on from constable to constable along the way, when he died in Higher Kenfig. His most valuable possession was "an ould hatt". One can only wonder what the bailiff did with that!

Ensuring that the estate's property was kept in good repair was another important role of the manor court. The tenants accepted this responsibility as part of their tenancy agreement, but the estate undertook to provide them with the necessary materials. These included lime for painting the walls and thatch for the roof, as well as timber and stone. It was under this

head that Catherine Gamage got herself into a running battle with the manor court, and I cannot but help feel that there may have been an element of petty spite at work amongst the jurors. I have often noticed that new tenants were frequently called to account for the state of their property about which there had been no mention hitherto. It seems to me that often the jurors turned a blind eye in the case of somebody who was 'one of them', but cheerfully did their duty in the case of a newcomer! Catherine's laxity in maintaining her property to acceptable standards may just have been too blatant to ignore, but she was the proprietor of New Mill and as I have noted in an earlier chapter, millers were not particularly well liked anyway!

At a Court Baron held in October 1667 the jury reported that Catherine's dwelling house was out of repair (PM 2190), and David Bennet the steward ordered that this was to be done before the month of February, or else she would be fined the sum of 13s 4d. The next court was one in March of 1668 and the jury reported that this fine had fallen due as she had not carried out the work as ordered. "We doe allsoe present the same to be still out of repaire" they continued, and Bennet gave her until the end of May subject to another fine of £1. 8s. 8d.

Catherine seems to have complied with this order, but the jury at the Spring Leet were still not satisfied with the standard of her property, or that of four other tenants, who were all given a month to effect repairs or else pay fines of 5s. 8d. each. The entry is endorsed with the note that on this occasion, Catherine completed the work on time. At the same sitting, however, she and the widowed Jennet Morgan of Burlake Cottage clashed over responsibility for a length of ditch that adjoined their properties. Tenants were expected to 'scour' and keep these clean, but this section was probably a drainage ditch alongside the road fronting the cottage, and as such Catherine evidently felt that it should not be her responsibility.

The Court appointed a special jury to meet and look into the matter, and when they reported back to the June court, they found that this length of ditch was indeed Catherine's. Their decision indicates that the cottage had most likely originally been built in a pre-existing field belonging to Morfa Bach Isha Farm (which was part of Catherine's holding) so, as the jurors saw it, responsibility for the ditch remained with the original tenant.

At the same Leet Court, the death of Richard Cradock of Llanmihangel was noted, and his widow Elizabeth formally admitted to his tenancies. Both she and Catherine however were again embroiled with the jury at the next Leet held in September. On this occasion it was because the two of them were in dispute over responsibility for the maintenance of one of their common boundaries. Catherine was also under fire from

some of her neighbours regarding the state of a bridge "leading over ye mil pound to ye houses of 2 or 3 of ye tenants" as reported earlier in this chapter.

The steward gave her until 5th October to effect repairs or else forfeit the sum of 3s. 4d. There is no mention of this at the next court held on 26th of that month, nor of the outcome of her dispute with Elizabeth Cradock, but the beleaguered Catherine was now assailed with complaints about the state of her barn!

This Catherine seems to have reformed to the court's satisfaction, for at the first sitting held in 1669 it was Elizabeth's problems that exercised the jury's mind. Apparently in response to a query from her concerning responsibility for maintaining the river boundaries above Llanmihangel Mill, they reported that from the mill to the weir it was that of the tenant of Llanmihangel Farm. Above this as far as the Puckwall[8] was the responsibility of the occupant of Coed y Collwyn. With regard the weir itself they stated that it was "allwaies repaired by ye farmer of Llanvihangel mill".

At the autumn Leet, Catherine was back in the firing line again, fined for failing to restore the bridge over the mill leat and threatened with a ten shilling fine unless she did something about the state of the thatch on her house.

---

[8] The Puckwall was the field on the north side of Pyle church, now occupied by modern housing.

Having mulled over the jury's response to her query about the boundaries adjoining the weir for her mill, Elizabeth Cradock presented herself at the Spring Leet in 1670 demanding to know how, given their response, she was to effect repairs to the weir! To do so would require hauling timber and stones to the site which could only be conveyed by wagons. The access path along the mill leat was clearly too narrow for this and the jury had declared that adjoining land was not part of her property.

Accordingly the court appointed another jury to visit the site and make recommendations, in the meantime taking another swipe at Catherine Gamage for the state of her barn "in the moors" and letting her "little house by ye New Mill" fall into disrepair. This may relate to a cottage or outbuilding, but 'little house' (ty bach) is of course a colloquialism for an outside toilet! This she failed to do and was duly fined at the next sitting in June.

At this court the jury that had looked into the question of Elizabeth's access to the weir in the Collwyn, reported back that they had secured access for her through the land of Gwenllian Thomas (of Millhill) via "ye road or high waie by ye church yard at Pile". This, apparently, was the fore-runner of the footpath that runs down the Collwyn today, though at this time it probably only led down to the spring adjoining the river. Elizabeth, however, had now really got the bit between her teeth and was

on the offensive. Another jury had to be appointed to determine the boundary between her land and the Borough common, and she brought three charges of debt against a local tenant named Llewelyn George. Each was for the sum of 39s. 11d — just inside the £2 limit and therefore within the jurisdiction of the court.

The result of these actions is not recorded, but Elizabeth's belligerence appears to have had the desired effect, for the jury did not cite her for any alleged infringements again. Whilst Catherine had repaired her 'ty bach' however, the matter of her barn dragged on until the summer of 1671 when she at last repaired the building to everyone's satisfaction. From then on she too seems to have been largely left in peace.

They may not have been able to vote in elections, sit on juries or to have held any local office, but to judge from these examples the women of 17th century Kenfig were certainly capable of taking care of themselves where their own interests were involved!

Cordwainers, Morgan Jenkin; Richard Thomas The making and working of leather was perhaps the principal industry practiced within the old medieval town of Kenfig. Certainly the one craft guild that we know existed there was that of the Cordwainers and Glovers. A cordwainer was a shoemaker, and as several inhabitants of the borough carried on this trade in the late 18th century it is tempting to postulate that the trade had continued here after the abandonment of the old town. Unfortunately the available documentary evidence is insufficient to support such a hypothesis. A document of 1591 makes reference to a Kenfig cordwainer named Morgan Jenkin, but there is no mention of another for very nearly an entire century.

The next cordwainer I know of was a bachelor named Richard Thomas who died in 1684. He was the son of a Thomas Evan who owned two acres of land called Cae yr Mynydd, a field I have not identified but which extended from Heol y Lane to waste land alongside Heol Kenfig. The meagre contents of his home were valued together at £2.15.0d. when he died in 1665, but he does seem to have been more than just a simple crofter. The previous year, for example, he had witnessed the will of Rees Leyson and may even have written the document himself. There is also an undated survey of the parish made by a man of this name in the Margam manuscript collection.

Strangely Richard is not mentioned in his father's will, which relates solely to the disposition of the two-acre field. This went to his elder brother Evan provided that he paid the sum of £20 in two instalments to be divided equally between their three sisters. If he failed, then the land was to go to them, and for good measure the three were appointed joint executors of the will thereby ensuring

this provision would be implemented in full.

Richard never married, and one of the few references to him is an entry on the Margam rental for 1684 for the sum of six shillings and eight pence due in respect of part of a cottage on Heol Las. This entry had not appeared on the previous surviving rental (1682) and it is doubtful that he ever occupied it for he was dead before the year was out. As his next of kin, probate was granted to his brother Evan on 1st January 1685, and it seems clear that at the time he died Richard was living with him and his wife. Other than his clothes, the only items he possessed were a coverlet, two sheets, a small sum of money, and his stock in trade as a shoemaker. These included six pairs of "ready shoes" valued together at 8s. 8d. and a stock of leather worth over £5. Given the cost of the shoes, Richard seems to have been quite generous in the matter of allowing credit to his customers for when he died there was still owing to him "by his booke" the sum of £2.10.0d. A stock of pitch also mentioned by the "appraisers" would have been used by him to waterproof the finished footwear.

Appended to the inventory is a list of Richard's debts. This was not unusual as they would have to be met by Evan as his legally acknowledged heir. What I found strange however is that Evan included debts to himself of 12 shillings for "his service during his sickness" and £2 for "funerall expences". Disposing of the dead was a costly business even in those days! The inclusion of these two items by the next of kin are however so unusual (they are in fact the only instances I have come across), that I cannot help wondering if the brothers had fallen out rather badly. This would perhaps explain why Richard had apparently taken steps to find alternative accommodation shortly before his death.

So how did Evan spend £2 on burying his brother? There was no funeral director to walk in and remove the burden of making the necessary arrangements from the grieving family. They had to do everything themselves. Almost as soon as Richard had drawn his last breath, Evan would have sent out for somebody in the community (usually a woman) to 'lay the body out'. She would probably have been on 'stand-by' expecting such a message at any time of the day or night. Speed was essential here before *rigor mortis* set in, and there were probably a number of people within the community that normally undertook this gruesome but necessary task, unheralded and unmentioned in the dry and dusty records that survive today.

History is likewise silent about any local customs or rituals associated with death, but logically the body of the deceased would have remained at the house whilst the carpenter made a coffin and the sexton of the church dug the grave. Whilst there, friends, neighbours and relatives probably called to offer condolences to the bereaved and pay their last respects. This would perhaps give the family an opportunity to assess how best to convey the body to the churchyard. Until fairly recent times the coffin of a popular and respected member of the community would make the journey to its final resting place, carried on the shoulders of teams of bearers happy to perform this last service for a friend or relative. Otherwise the family would have to hire a horse and cart for the purpose.

The date of the funeral would then depend upon the availability of the local clergyman, but normally it would take place within two or three days of the death. Then, as now, refreshments would be provided for the mourners some of whom might have walked or ridden quite a considerable distance to be there. A funeral in the community was by its very nature a sad event, but it was also a social occasion that offered a break from the normal daily round and sometimes a little more. Mary Savours (alias Thomas), who originally hailed from Ballas on Stormy Down, retired to live at Kenfig following the death of her husband, and made her will in September 1704 (Llandaff Wills). She ordered that a bushel of wheat be baked into loaves to be distributed amongst the poor at her funeral in Pyle church.

Add all the little expenses together and the two pounds Evan claimed for the funeral expenses, whilst a large sum in the context of the time, does not seem too far-fetched. One thing that it would not have included would have been a memorial stone to mark the grave, as this practice only became common in the late 18th century.

Like their father, Evan was apparently somebody rather more substantial than a mere Kenfig freeholder with two acres of land. He could write his name, and may have written Richard's probate inventory himself. The 1689 Poll Tax return for the lower borough also shows that he and his (unnamed) wife were sufficiently wealthy to hire two servants. Three years later she inherited a Margam holding in Pyle manor, and at the time of the 1694 Poll Tax they were living with Thomas Rees in South Cornelly. With them was a Robert Evan who may have been their son. Evan died in 1697 and his burial is recorded in the parish register on the 9th of July.

Burials of some of those who could afford it were made inside the church itself and here a memorial was often erected over the tomb or somewhere nearby. Several such are affixed to the walls of Mawdlam church, and one of the earliest is that to Richard Lougher of Cornelly who was buried here on 28th March, 1698. It is a fine tablet on the north wall of the sanctuary displaying his coat of arms surmounted by a horse (or possibly a unicorn) which were originally painted – some traces of colour still being apparent.

The location of Richard's grave, in the holiest part of the church, is an indication of his status within the local community, yet it would probably be true to say that by rights it does not belong here in Kenfig at all.

Richard Lougher was one of the Loughers of Ty Maen, South Cornelly, who (as we have seen) had a close association with Kenfig. Normally however they, together with members of the main family from Tythegston Court, were buried at Newton, where indeed Richard's son Thomas is interred, as commemorated by a memorial inside the church. So why therefore did Richard chose to be buried at Mawdlam?

Born in 1653 Richard was the eldest son of Thomas Lougher, and was one of the 'lives' on a lease taken out by the latter upon the demesne lands of Kenfig two years later. As was the family practice, and probably following his marriage, Richard set up home in Pool Farm, perhaps as early as 1672, when he was one of the witnesses to the will of Christopher Cradock of Llanmihangel.

His father Thomas died in 1685/6, but the rental for the manor of 1686 indicates that Richard was then the borough Portreeve, which means he was still living at Kenfig and had not yet taken up residence at the family home in South Cornelly. Ty Maen was a far grander establishment than Pool Farm, but it seems as though he was very much torn between his two. In 1689, for example, he and his wife Ann are listed for Poll Tax in South Cornelly, but in that same year he was obviously very active within the borough. Not only was he the collector of the Poll Tax, but was one of the witnesses to the marriage settlement drawn up when Lewis Aylward's son Charles married Ann Evan. The following year he is mentioned as a burgess, which could not have been the case had he been permanently residing outside the borough boundary, yet the 1694 Poll Tax again shows him as living at South Cornelly. When, however, he took out a fresh lease upon the demesne land the following year he appears as Richard Lougher "of Kenfig".

The inescapable conclusion is that Richard loved Kenfig and the house at Pool Farm so much that he spent part of every year living here with his family. Part of the attraction may have been that he was running a small farm here. The probate inventory drawn up at his death lists a crop of corn, his cattle, sheep, poultry and pigs, yet he was a man who was one of the local gentry. It seems therefore that because of his affection for the area Richard chose to be buried near the altar at Mawdlam, with the fine memorial erected by his widow close by.

The Waters Family By a very short margin Richard's is not, however, the earliest memorial in the church. Opposite, on the south wall of the sanctuary, are two memorials that together commemorate several members of the Waters family. On the one are Richard Waters (1647-

1696), his daughter Mary (d.1687) and son David (d. 1689)[9]. The inscription on the other is actually rather confusing. It commemorates his niece Margery Waters who died at the age of 18 in 1694, and actually states that her parents were "Evan and Anne Morgan". Evan was in fact Evan Waters and the brother of Richard, and Morgan was actually the maiden name of his wife Ann..

Although they are known to have lived in the district since at least the 15th century, historically the Waters family seems to have had little or no connection with Kenfig. So far as I can ascertain they lived at South Cornelly, probably in a house on the site of the present Ty Draw farm. Evan and Richard were the sons of David Waters who was one who reverted to the Welsh system of patronyms and insisted on being known as "David ap Evan". It is by this name that he first appears in local records as the bailiff for the manor of Pyle in 1637, but the clerks in the office at Margam usually refer to him either as "David Waters" or "David ap Evan Waters". Although resident in South Cornelly, the 1650 survey of Kenfig Borough Manor shows that he owned 33½ acres of freehold land here, and he is mentioned for this again in the survey made ten years later, this time as "David Bevan" — yet another variation on his name!

---

[9] This was evidently a child that died in infancy as the couple baptised another son named David in 1695.

Neither of his sons seems to have continued the old man's affectation, and when he died in 1689 he was succeeded by Richard as the elder of the two. As this memorial indicates, his wife was Catherine (Kate) Lougher, who was perhaps Richard Lougher's sister, as the latter's son Thomas later refers to Richard and Catherine's son as his cousin. This son was named David after the brother listed on the memorial who died before he was born.

This marriage seems to have cemented what was already a close relationship between the two families. The two Waters men and Richard Lougher were of about the same age, and of similar social status, so the three had probably been playmates from childhood. Richard Lougher witnessed the will of Richard Waters and drew up the probate inventory of his property. Similarly Evan Waters performed the same services for Richard's family when he died.

Why Richard Waters should, like his namesake Richard Lougher, choose to be buried at Mawdlam is a puzzle because the bulk of the family land in the Borough — 31½ acres — was given to his brother Evan during their father's lifetime. Perhaps he had been living here hitherto, but returned to the family home to run the estate because their father, old David ab Evan. would have been into his 70s by this time.

Ann Morgan, the wife of Evan Waters, was the daughter of Morgan Thomas of Stormy Vawr farm whose descendants (much to the confusion of their 19th century family historian!) later adopted the surname Waters themselves. Evan subsequently inherited some free land in South Cornelly from his father, but where exactly he lived in Kenfig Borough I have been unable to ascertain. He was certainly a burgess, because he is twice mentioned as the Portreeve (1690 and 1692), but the tablet in the sanctuary records the tragedy that struck him and his wife in 1694 with the death of their daughter. Eighteen year old Margery was, in the words of the inscription "a virtuous virgin and the only child" of the couple. Through the medium of the verse they chose to have inscribed on her memorial we can still feel something of their emptiness and despair following this loss.

Gentle reader doe not weep
I am not dead but faln asleep,
Bestow thy teares upon thy sins.
Out of my grave I call to thee,
Prepare to dye and follow me".

Evan lived until 1724, and his widow Ann until 1740 whereafter their property reverted to their nephew, Richard's son David.

These three memorials in the sanctuary at Mawdlam therefore commemorate more than the deaths of the people named on them. They recall a life-long friendship of three people for whom, over 300 years ago, Kenfig was a special place.

Before moving on, there is one point that I feel I should make about what I have written so far regarding the people of Kenfig we have met and which I have categorised into social classes, which they themselves recognised. At the same time I believe that too much emphasis should not be placed upon these divisions within local society. The Begans of Cornelly, who appear at best to have been only small farmers, were closely associated with the Turbervilles of Sker through their adherence to the Roman Catholic faith. Similarly the Cradocks, Loughers and the Aylwards rubbed shoulders with dissenting worshipers from lowlier stations in life at the embattled congregation in Kenfig Farm. Greatest leveller of all, however, was the Borough organisation itself, where admittance to the ranks of the burgesses depended upon neither wealth nor social status.

Everyone knew and respected the boundaries of their status in life but there was considerable interaction between the various classes in local society. The Cradocks may have been one of the largest fish in the local pond, but Martha the grandaughter of Richard Cradock was related (probably by marriage) to a grandson of our 'Del Boy' character Evan Griffith. So the impression I have from my years of study is that whilst the people of Kenfig were very aware of their status as gentlemen, yeomen, craftsmen and labourers, these divisions were not perceived as insurmountable obstacles to love, friendship and mutual respect.

THE SUIT ROLL OF 1699 Manor of Kenfig Borough

This is actually the only Suit Roll for the Court of the Manor of Kenfig Borough that I have come across, and is of interest in that it provides us with the first (but albeit, incomplete) roll of Kenfig Burgesses. The purpose of the roll was to provide an up-to-date list of those tenants who owed suit of court, and would be checked on each occasion that it sat to ensure that all were present. Absentees were duly fined for their omission.

Those listed on the roll are divided into three groups. The first section is entitled *"Burges Kenfig"*, which is simply "Kenfig Borough".

This lists just five people. Edward Herbert, esquire appears for the Manor of South Cornelly and Christopher Turberville esquire for its neighbour on the north. Christopher Turberville, gent of Sker is included for his portion of Kenfig Down Common and perhaps some freehold property as well. The other 'gentlemen' listed were Richard and Thomas Lougher, the first being the lord of the manor at Tythegston who owned freehold land in the manor, and the other the ten-year old son of Richard Lougher of Ty Maen, South Cornelly, who was tenant of the demesne lands.

None of these lived within the Borough, and it is unlikely that any of them ever attended the manor courts but simply paid their fines for absence instead. They were all petty gentry, a cut above the others listed, and it is for this reason alone that they are shown in a group of their own at the very start.

The other two groups are the Burgesses (of which 34 are listed) and eight free tenants who owned freehold in the manor but did not enjoy this status. Five of the latter are widows and, with the exception of Mary Savours, are probably the former wives of deceased burgesses. Elsewhere I describe these as "female burgesses" though technically there was no such thing. Whilst they could not vote in general elections; sit on the borough and manor juries, or hold any office, they paid the borough rates and otherwise enjoyed the same burgess' privileges as their late husbands. Indeed, it appears from the first 'full' burgess roll drawn up in 1783 that whilst they lived they also technically occupied their husband's place within it as a burgess, and the vacancy his death had caused was only filled when they too died, remarried, or moved outside the borough.

In all therefore the Suit Roll gives us the identities of 38 burgesses or burgesses' widows most of whom lived in the Lower Borough but including several from Higher Kenfig. These last were presumably required to attend the court in respect of property they held south of the river although I have been unable to verify this in some cases. (I show which burgesses could sign their own names, and which used a mark.)

1. John Thomas, gent (1659-1723) (signed) . Born the son of William Thomas of Laleston he became an apothecary in London, and returned to this area about 1686. In 1691 he took out a lease upon Marlas Farm which became the basis for a small estate he built up consisting of freehold as well as leasehold properties that he sub-let to other tenants. Whilst at London he married Elizabeth the daughter of John and Sarah Cocks, and his mother-in-law (d. 1719) is buried in the family plot in Pyle Churchyard. JT died 11th October 1723 at the age of 64, but his son, William Thomas of the Custom House, London showed little interest in continuing the estate and after a period in the hands of John's executors the estate was broken up. His position at the head of this roll may indicate that he was the Portreeve at this time, an office he is known to have held in 1714.

2. Lewis Aylward, gent (d.1705) (signed) . The descendent of one of the oldest families in Kenfig who had been burgesses in the medieval borough, he owned several plots of freehold land centred upon Kenfig Farm. First mentioned at Kenfig in 1650 he is known to have held the

Portreeveship on two and possibly four occasions between 1666 and 1675 but not after this last date. This is probably because he was a dissenter who turned his home into a meeting house for Nonconformist services. In 1664 this was raided by the authorities and the preacher arrested, whilst in 1685 he was imprisoned in Chepstow Castle as a precautionary measure during the Duke of Monmouth's rebellion. He was married to Jennet Lougher, possibly a sister of Thomas Lougher of Ty Maen, South Cornelly. The couple had at least five children of whom Lazarus (d.1704) appears to have been the eldest, and Lewis seems to have provided him with land of his own sometime prior to 1687. Kenfig Farm he gifted to his third eldest son, Charles, on the occasion of the latter's marriage in 1689 though he himself continued to be shown as the tenant on the rentals. By 1699 Lewis's health was failing, and on the 1704 Margam rental Charles is shown for his holdings although his father did not actually die until the April of the following year. Interestingly neither Lazarus nor Charles appears on this Suit Roll.

3. Evan Waters, gent (d.1724) (signed) . The Waters were a South Cornelly family, probably living at Ty Draw. Evan may therefore have been a younger son given a farm at Kenfig where the family owned over thirty acres of freehold land. His father David ap Evan Waters of Cornelly, in addition to this freehold held more under the manor of

Higher Kenfig and was renting two acres from Richard Lougher. EW is mentioned as holding the office of Portreeve in 1690 and 1692. He was married to Ann Morgan the daughter of Morgan Thomas of Stormy Fawr farm, but the couple only had one daughter named Margery who died *"a virtuous virgin"* in 1694. At this time Evan Waers was living in South Cornelly where the family property descended to him three years later following the death of his brother Richard. Indeed, other than his inclusion as a burgess (rather than a freeholder) on this roll there is no indication that he ever returned to Kenfig prior to his death.

4. Joshua Lyddon (d. 1715) (signed) . The eldest son of Evan Lyddon and Alice Gronow (1625-1698) dau of Gronow William of New Mill and therefore a sister of **William Gronow** (No 6) and a half-sister to **David Gronow** (no 5). Joshua was also the brother of **Noah Lyddon** (No 24), and his wife Catherine was a daughter of Thomas Rees (1620-1672) of the Rees/Thomas family and therefore the sister of **Rees Thomas** (No 14). The couple married circa 1686. Joshua Lyddon is first mentioned on his parent's lease to Ynis Pandy in 1661, at which time he was apparently old enough to sign his own name to the document as one of the 'lives'. He succeeded to Ynis Pandy (held under Higher Kenfig) on his mother's death, but also owned several freehold properties in the lower borough. Mentioned as Portreeve in 1711 and 1712. He and his wife (last mentioned in 1699) apparently had no children that survived to adulthood, and on his death in 1715 his property was inherited by his brother Noah.

5. David Gronow (d. 1723) (signed) . The son of Gronow William (d. 1662) by his second wife Catherine Gamage (d. 1694), and therefore a half-brother to **William Gronow** (No 6) and Alice the mother of **Joshua Lyddon** (No 4). Prior to his death Gronow William arranged that the mill and the small farm attached would pass to David and his mother, and from 1678 until her death he also operated the other Margam Corn Mill at Llanmihangel. He therefore lived in Higher Kenfig where most of his land was, but the Land Tax return of 1695 indicates that he also occupied an unidentified property in the Lower Borough which is why he appears in this Suit Roll. When Margam closed down the New Mill circa 1702 David left the area and although he made a brief return five years later eventually went to live at Taibach. On his death he was buried at Mawdlam in the grave of the Nonconformist preacher Jacob Christopher, but what his connection with him was I have so far not been able to ascertain. I can find no evidence that he ever married.

6. William Gronow (signed) . A son of Gronow William by his first wife Margaret he was therefore a brother-in-law to Jenkin Lyddon (No 4) and a half-brother to David Gronow (No 5). From his father he inherited seven acres (approx eight ½ modern measure) in Kenfig Lower and a house that probably stood on Heol Las. From 1687 to 1688 he was the tenant of Newlands Farm in Higher Kenfig, and went to live there. From 1690 he was constantly in trouble with the manor court over the state of the property and, although he had repaired the main house the labourers' houses attached were still giving cause for complaint at the time he left. At this time he was married to a woman named Elizabeth by whom he had at least two children (Gronow and Gwenllian William), but by 1692 she was dead, and at the time of his return to Heol Las he married Barbara Morgan a sister of William Morgan of Bettws. About 1708 the couple mortgaged the property at Kenfig and then sold it two years later at which time they were living at Coity.

7. Nicholas David (d. 1727) (signed) . The son of a Margam farmer named David Nicholas Nicholas David is first mentioned on his lease to a property called Court Llygad there in 1661. His father also owned three and a half (customary) acres in Kenfig Lower which descended to Nicholas upon his death in 1669. His admission as a burgess seems to have come about when he became tenant of Llanmihangel Farm in 1687. Five years later he inherited a further three properties in Pyle and Higher

Kenfig following the death of his mother Ann Bowman. He served as the Margam bailiff for these manors 1701-4, and for Higher Kenfig alone in 1708. Nicholas David surrendered his tenancy of Llanmihangel shortly after 1706 and thereafter apparently lived at Pyle. Although he retained the freehold land at Kenfig which led to his inclusion on this Suit Roll (about eight ½ acres at the time of his death), he would of course have ceased to be a burgess. He had six daughters and one son by his wife Gwenllian (alias "Gillian") Leyson of whom Mary was the executrix and sole beneficiary at the time of his death whilst through another daughter, Jennet, he was the grandfather of a Kenfig burgess named David Rees.

8. Thomas Hopkin Thomas (d.1740). One of three persons named Thomas Hopkin in the roll who are very difficult to differentiate between. I believe that he was probably the son of **Thomas Hopkin** of Pyle (No 13), a view shared by A.Leslie Evans who thought he might be the person who sheltered two Jesuit priests in the 1730s.

9. Hugh Howell (d. 1702) (signed) . Became the tenant of Farm Fach in Higher Kenfig (and thereby a burgess) between 1678 and 1672, he appears on this roll by virtue of three (customary) acres of freehold land belonging to his wife Catherine John whom he married circa 1678. She succeeded him at Farm Fach and is last mentioned in 1706.

There are no known children of the marriage.

10. Morgan John (d.1754?) (signed) . In 1663 a person of this name was bequeathed three sheep in the will of Evan John Evan who may be a relative. The first certain mention of him comes in 1689 when he, his wife Margaret William, and a servant are listed for Poll Tax in Kenfig Lower. MJ frequently appears as a witness to local documents, and drew up several local probate inventories. In 1695 was the Land Tax collector for the Lower Borough, and himself paid the tax in respect of certain unspecified lands. Later (1704) documents relate to the sale of three (customary) acres of land he had purchased in the borough. In the will of Margaret Evan of Kenfig (1698) was bequeathed an oatmeal chest and a field called Cae'r Ty Bach (unidentified) whilst his wife was bequeathed a cottage adjoining Margaret's on Heol y Lane. After 1715 his history becomes difficult to follow because a man of the same name lived on Heol Las.

11. Jenkin Evan (d. 1724) (signed) . Is probably a Jenkin "Bevan" mentioned in a Hearth Tax return of 1673 at which time he was probably living at Pyle. In 1698 he replaced William Gronow (No 6) as tenant of Newlands farm at Kenfig, but to date I have found no mention of him connected with land in the lower borough that would explain his inclusion on this roll. He and his wife had at least two children.

12. Richard (?). Unable to decipher second name.

13. Thomas Hopkin of Pyle The second Thomas Hopkin on the list and probably the father of **Thomas Hopkin Thomas** (No 8). His wife was Nest Griffith (d.1712) whose mother, Tanglwst Mitchell, took out a lease on a house at Pyle in 1687 on the lives of herself, Nest, and Nest's son Thomas Hopkin. In 1684 Thomas Hopkin himself is shown on the Higher Kenfig rent roll as tenant of a drying kiln that actually lay in the Manor of Kenfig Borough somewhere on the north side of the road from Mawdlam to Pyle. The kiln had previously been in the hands of Nest, and Thomas is shown as holding it "in right of his wife". A document of 1711 shows that he owned a house in the Lower Borough as well as being the occupant or tenant of various other properties besides the drying kiln. His inclusion as a burgess on this roll therefore seems to suggest that he was actually living in the manor, and "of Pyle" relates to his origins and not his current abode. It was added in an attempt to differentiate him from the other two with this name. The last certain mention of Thomas Hopkin is in a tithe return of 1714.

14. Rees Thomas (d. 1721) Eldest son of Thomas Rees (1620-1672) by his wife Mary Thomas, and therefore the current head of the Rees/Thomas family and a brother of the wife of **Joshua Lyddon** (No 4). Rees also had a connection with **Thomas Davies** (No 26) as his eldest son Thomas was married to a daughter of the latter, and **David Thomas Rees** (No 30) may have been his uncle. Is first mentioned in the will of his Aunt, Catherine Rees, in which he was willed lands called Pant y Shrinkin (on Heol Fach) and Maes Mawr (on Heol Las) subject to certain conditions. There is mention of his children as early as 1667, but I have been unable to discover the identity of his wife. Initially seems to have lived at Pyle, but succeeded his father as tenant of the Higher Kenfig tenancy known as Ynys y Pandy, and then surrendered this to Jenkin Lyddon at about the time of the latter's marriage to his sister. The Poll Tax return of 1689 then shows him living with the couple in the Lower Borough where in 1692 he is shown as tenant of a house on Heol Las. His wife was still living (though not mentioned in 1689), and they are both listed for Poll Tax in 1694, at which time they were presumably living in the house on Heol Las. This had become the centre of a smallholding made up of rented and freehold property. In 1708 Rees succeeded Jenkin Lyddon as tenant of Llanmihangel Corn mill. His will mentions three daughters, (but not his son, Thomas Rees) and three grandchildren.

15. Thomas Hopkin (d. 1728) (signed) . The third person of this name on the roll, and once again very difficult to place. He seems to have been the son of Hopkin Thomas of Pyle (1633-1668) by his wife Mary Nicholl and to have inherited certain freehold land in the lower borough from them. To this was added another acre that he inherited from his (unidentified wife) by whom he had a daughter called Mary. On the death of his first wife he married Mary the daughter of William Cuffe of Margam. Of their children Thomas (b.1699) died after a few weeks and Sarah (b.1695) later married John Tanner. Confusingly this TH is also referred to on different occasions as Thomas Hopkin Thomas, Thomas Hopkin of Pyle and Thomas Hopkin of Greenstreet, which are also used to identify other individuals of this name on different occasions. It seems, however, that whilst he and his wife were living at Pyle in 1689, they moved to a house on Heol Las ("Greenstreet") about 1692 when he inherited 18 acres of freehold land on the death of his mother.

16. John Leyson (d.1715) (signed) . The son of Leyson Morgan, and in 1666 included by him as a life on his lease to "The Longhouse" adjoining the ruins of Kenfig Castle. This became operative in 1679 on his father's death, but John seems to have been content to abandon the holding to the sand for it is not listed on that year's rental nor subsequently. In 1682 he appears for the rent of Burlake Cottage adjoining Water Street in Higher Kenfig in place of a Margaret Morgan

whom he may have married. The tenant before her had been his father. He continued the tenant here for ten years, then in 1692 abandoned it for Ty Du farm in Higher Kenfig which he retained until his death. Mentioned as the Constable of Higher Kenfig in 1698, and its bailiff in 1702. Fined 2s 6d. for failing to grind his corn at New Mill in 1699. In 1703 he either surrendered or was stripped of his holdings in Higher Kenfig and the following year was also the subject of a distress warrant by the Margam estate whereby his property to the value of £6. 12s. 0d. was seized to meet his debts. Presumably owned some freehold property in Kenfig Lower to have appeared on the suit roll, but I have found no mention of any to date.

17. Evan Richard (d. 1725) (signed) . First mentioned in 1683 when he took over the tenancy of Cae Tywod in Kenfig Lower, and is described as a labourer when he and his unnamed wife appeared in the Poll Tax return of 1689. He may in some way have been a relative of Margaret Evan of Kenfig who made him the executor of her will. By it he and his wife were to have an orchard, garden and two crofts, and also some houses a barn and another garden once the current occupants had died or moved away. So far as I am aware the couple had no children.

18. Hugh Owen (d. 1726) (signed) . The son of Leyson Owen by his wife Gwenllian Thomas who was one of the daughters of Thomas Richard the clerk of Kenfig. Under provisions drawn up by Thomas in 1650 Gwenllian and Hugh were to succeed to his cottage at Millhill if both her sisters died without heirs. This seems to have indeed been the case and Hugh sold off the property to the Margam estate in 1669. In the Poll Tax Assessment of 1689 he is listed as a labourer. Hugh married a woman named Alice, and in 1693 took out a lease upon a holding called Cae'r Gollen on their lives and that of their daughter Catherine. Also known as Waun Maggy Fach this holding lay on the Margam side of the river Kenfig between Llanmihangel Mill and "The Black Path" near Pyle church. Thereafter he is frequently referred to as "Hugh of Collwn". Sometime prior to 1704 he built a house here as well, but this may have been on the building on the opposite bank of the river near Llanmihangel bridge (where the stable stands today) and therefore in the manor of Kenfig Borough. This would account for his inclusion upon the roll, and perhaps the origin of the 8d Land Tax for which he is shown in returns for the lower borough in the 1720s. His lease of 1704 also gave him rights to a 'creek', which is presumably the river Kenfig at this point. Not the least curious fact about Hugh is that the parish register records that he and his (unnamed) wife were buried together on 3rd January, 1726. I have not so far found a record of any children.

19. George William (d. circa 1724) (mark). Son of William George and Mary John he and his brother John William shared the tenancy of a Higher Kenfig holding later known as Tir David John by virtue of a lease taken out by their widowed mother in 1678. In the Poll Tax return of 1689 he, his wife, John and their sister Gwenllian, were all apparently living together at the same house. Following John's death about 1693 George continued as the sole tenant. I have not come across any mention of him holding land in the lower borough that would justify his appearance on this roll. George is several times mentioned as the petty constable for Higher Kenfig. He and his wife Abigail had a daughter, Margaret George, who paid the heriot that fell due on her father's death in 1725. Strangely, although George signed documents with his mark, his brother John signed with his name.

20. John David. This being a fairly common name in the district, there is some difficulty determining his true identity. We know he had children, so possibly he is one of two men of this name who baptised children in Margam parish during the period, but on the 1689 Poll Tax assessment he alone is listed as a labourer living in Kenfig Lower. He is also probably the JD of the Parish of Pyle & Kenfig who leased two acres of land at Kenfig from the Tythegston estate in 1691, and is again listed on his own for Poll Tax in 1694. In 1704 he is shown for 8d. Land Tax. He is described as a nephew by Margaret Evan in her will of 1698, and she bequeathed a house that she owned to his (unnamed children). A man of this name had been employed to take care of Llanmihangel Farm whilst it was vacant, but was dismissed in 1712, and is probably the same person shown for a small amount of tithes in 1713 and 1714. Less certain is that he is identical with a JD who, with his partners paid to operate a lime kiln on Newton Down in 1727 or another mentioned as a mason in 1729.

21. Evan Owen (d. 1734) (signed) . Is mentioned as a life on a lease taken out by his parents Owen ap Evan and Ann Gamage on Morfa Bach in 1663. He seems to have been a juvenile at this time, and his mother then remarried (circa 1666) a Henry Lyddon who became the next tenant. Ann Gamage died late in 1670, and presumably Evan was still a minor so the estate re-let it to an Evan Howell who held it until Evan took possession in 1684/5. This suggests that he was only a child when the original lease was taken out. He could only make his mark on the 1663 lease, but signed his name to a later document. Evan Howell was probably married to Evan's sister, Margaret who was a widow by the Poll Tax of 1689 when the two were living together. He later succeeded her as tenant of an unidentified holding in HK that had previously been her husband's. In 1700 was appointed both petty constable and bailiff for HK,

and in 1702 was the assessor and collector of the Poll Tax there. Not known to have had any land in the lower borough.

22. Henry Jenkin (d. 1721). According to the inscription on his gravestone as recorded by David Jones of Wallington, Henry was 78 at the time of his death. This is probably incorrect (the stone being in the floor of the church the inscription was probably worn) and he was most likely at least ten years older. He is mentioned as owning property on Paschal Hill in 1655, and in 1660 this is listed as a freehold cottage that probably lay on Heol Kenfig where his sisters Catherine & Elizabeth Jenkin also lived. They were the children of Jenkin Howell and Alice Jenkin. His will of 1712 mentions that his wife was named Ann Gwillim, and names their children as Edward (1697-1755) and Jonnet Jenkin.

23. Hopkin John . In 1667 he and his brother Edward were presented as tenants of a tenement near Newlands that had formerly been held by their father John Hopkin. Edward died later that year, and Hopkin who was a blacksmith, seems to have abandoned the holding and the following year rented a house and garden elsewhere in the manor which he subsequently converted into a smithy. In 1673 took out a lease on a house and garden with six (customary) acres of land attached *"over Kenfig river, infested with the sands, near Portland"*. This therefore lay within the lower borough and the Poll Tax return of 1689 confirms that it was where he actually lived. Although I have found no mention of his wife he did have a daughter named Mary Hopkin who succeeded to his holdings following his death which occurred about 1724.

24. Noah Lyddon (d. 1716) (signed) . The son of Evan Lyddon and Alice Gronow, he was a younger brother of **Joshua Lyddon** (No 4). Although listed as a labourer for Poll Tax in 1689 he was a carpenter by trade, and is first mentioned in 1685 when Evan, the first of his seven known children by his wife Mary was baptised. He acquired the tenancy of several plots of land in the borough over the years, and between 1702 and 1706 was the tenant of New Mill when David Gronow left it for the first time. In 1713 he was the collector of the Land Tax. Interestingly when he and his sons took out a lease on the tithe barn in 1715 he used an unusual seal that had also used by Charles Aylward in 1712.

25. Hopkin Thomas (1671-1743) (signed) . Son of David (d.1695) and Mary Thomas. His father had been the tenant of several small Margam properties in Kenfig Lower as well as the owner of two (customary) acres on Paschal Hill. Amongst the items bequeathed HT under his father's will was a grate. From this time onwards Hopkin appears regularly for window, poll and land tax indicating that he lived in the borough. The Land Tax

seems to indicate that the amount of property he occupied was not great, and a document of 1714 states that it was actually a house and a rabbit warren valued together at £80. This seems rather high, but the reason may be that the house was actually The Angel Inn which adjoined a warren that extended down to the Cornelly/Margam road. HT was certainly a Kenfig licensee as he was twice reported for selling ale in short measure in 1731 at the same time as William Harry of The Corporation House (Prince of Wales). At this time these may have been the only two licensed premises in the lower borough. The property itself actually belonged to John Thomas of Marlas Farm, and was put up for sale by his son about 1730 following his death. In 1734 Hopkin was living at Pyle, but was buried back at Mawdlam where there is a memorial to him in the church. His wife was Maud Jenkin (d.1754) whom he married in 1703 and they had at least seven children of which one certainly died in infancy.

26. Thomas Davies (d. 1704). More commonly referred to as Thomas David, and one of two men of this name at Kenfig declared "too poor" to pay Poll Tax in 1689. The other died in 1692, but as an added complication there was a third TD living at Cornelly who died in 1702. I have, however been able to identify the material relating to this individual without too much difficulty. The earliest mention of him comes in 1673 when his wife is named as Elizabeth, and his son as William. There was also a daughter Ann who was married to Thomas the eldest son of **Rees Thomas** (No 14). He is also shown for small Land Tax payments that were presumably made in respect of a cottage and an acre of land in Kenfig. The Borough Minutes for 1752 indicate that he had been the owner of just such a property and that following the death of his children it became the subject of legal action by various claimants.

27. David Richard (d.1718) (signed) . I know very little about this individual. In 1698 Margaret Evan bequeathed a house to his daughter Catherine Richard who in 1721 is described as the step-daughter of Mary Richard who was presumably therefore David's' second wife. The identity of her own mother is not mentioned.

28. Nicholas Lewis (d. 1700). Nicholas is another about whom I have not been able to discover much information. In 1668 his father, Lewis Nicholas, and brother John sold a half acre of land they owned on Heol Las to the Margam Estate, at which time they were said to be of Margam. At the time of Nicholas's death he was said to be of the "parish of Pile in the burrow of Kenfig", and letters of administration were issued to his brother John and his sister Margaret who then lived at Pyle. He seems to have been quite a prosperous individual as his property was valued at over £55, though he had incurred debts in excess of £35.

29. Edward Rees (mark) . Another Higher Kenfig Farmer with no identified property in the Lower Borough. In 1693 he and his intended wife, Mary Wilkins of Llandyfodwg (now Glynogwr) secured a lease to two holdings. One, "The Cellar" (Ty'n Cellar in HK) amounted to nearly 40 acres; the other, Cae Glas in West Margam, to nearly fifty. Included with them was Edward's son (Edward Rees junior). By 1712 the trio had surrendered Cae Glas back to the estate "long since", and were apparently in arrears of rent. In consequence of their surrender of Cae Glas (here called Caeau Glayshon) they were however allowed to take out a fresh lease upon Ty'n Cellar. Edward died shortly after this, and the 1715 rental shows that the farm was then in the hands of his widow, Mary, who continued in possession until sometime after 1739. Although the implications of the original lease is that Edward junior was perhaps his father's son by a previous marriage, later documents quite clearly state that Mary Wilkins was in fact his mother. In signing documents Edmund used the mark "ER", but his son was able to sign his own name.

30. David Thomas Rees. So named to distinguish him from David Thomas William and David Thomas Bowen who lived at Kenfig at this time, but were not burgesses. The only other reference I have to this individual is that he is listed as a pauper on the Poll Tax return of 1689. His name, however, suggests that he may be an otherwise unknown uncle of **Rees Thomas** (No 14).

31. John Owen (d. 1721). He, his wife Ann (d. 1730?), and his father William Owen are listed for Poll Tax in 1689 as labourers. His father is shown for Land Tax in Kenfig Borough in 1695, but by 1699 had left to live in North Cornelly where he died in 1705. John presumably succeeded him as a burgess, and as occupant of this property. Later documents state that he was by trade a wheelwright, and he may be the man of this name who supplied oysters to Margam House in 1713. John and his wife baptised four children in the parish, but I have so far been unable to trace any descendants at Kenfig.

32. Rees Harry (d. 1720). Another I know very little about. He was the occupant of a small piece of land in the lower borough as there is a record of him paying tithes of barley, oats, rye and peas between 1712 and 1714. He may also have been a craftsman of some sort as he was paid for work done during the repairs to the fulling mill circa 1706. He was married to Ann, and they baptised a daughter Gwenllian in 1697.

33. William Harry (d 1741) (mark) . At an enquiry held by the Kenfig Corporation in 1758 he is mentioned as a previous tenant and licensee of The Corporation House (The Prince of Wales), though for what period is not stated. In 1731 he was twice reported for selling ale in short measure. In 1695 he married a woman named Gwenllian Lyddon, (d. 1722) but I have been unable to discover her connection with the main family. The couple had at least four children William may or may not be a WH connected with Ballas Bach and other properties in the manor of Horgrove during the early 18th century.

34. Jenkin Lyddon (d.1727) (mark) . Another member of the Lyddon family, and probably a cousin to **Joshua** (4) and **Noah** (24). He was the owner of some freehold land in the lower manor, and was twice tenant of Llanmihangel Corn mill between 1704 and 1712. Indeed, it was he who persuaded Mansel to close New Mill and keep this one running. In 1711 he is mentioned as the Margam bailiff for Kenfig which presumably indicates he was the Portreeve. He also rented some parcels of land from Margam, but by 1723 was in such arrears that he mortgaged his house and four acres to land to the estate in order to pay them off. After his death his widow Jennet Thomas (d. 1764) sold them the property. The couple had at least two children.

THE FREEHOLDERS.

David Edmund. Appears to have lived at Laleston, but may later have moved to Kenfig as he is listed as the Portreeve in 1713.

William Leyson. Apparently resident in North Cornelly, he died in 1703.

Hopkin William. Owned an acre of free land in Kenfig for which he is first listed in 1677.

Mary Savour, widow (d. 1704). Her husband was apparently the (unidentified) son of Thomas Jenkin of Ballas Uchaf farm on Stormy Down who owned about seven acres of freehold land at Kenfig in 1650. On his death between 1655 & 1658 the farm passed to his wife, Katherine Leyson, but Mary is mentioned living there in 1660 at which time she was a widow. Her father-in-law's Kenfig freehold seems to have been bequeathed to her, and when her eldest son Jenkin Thomas took over the farm in 1675 she apparently moved to Kenfig and supplemented her holding by renting a further 2½ acres at Marlas from the Margam estate. She however relinquished this prior to 1692. The Poll Tax of 1689 mentions that a Kate Thomas was then living with her.

Margaret Evan, widow (d. 1702). The widow of a burgess named Jenkin Griffith (d. 1673) who was the grandson of the Elizabethan Portreeve Evan Griffith. She herself was the daughter of an Evan John Evan of South Cornelly, and she lived in a cottage on Heol Kenfig. Although she is described as a labourer on the Poll Tax return of 1689 she in fact owned several cottages and acres of land at Kenfig. She and her husband apparently never had children, so she made her will in 1698 and several of those listed as burgesses above stood to benefit from her estate.

Mary Jenkin, widow. Nothing known, but presumably the widow of a burgess.

Eleanor John, widow (d.1714). Mentioned as a servant of Richard Waters in 1689 she is several times shown for 4d Land Tax which may relate to a cottage in the borough. Presumably the widow of a burgess.

Jennet Jenkin, widow (d. 1723). A daughter of Henry Jenkin (No 22), she is listed for Land Tax in the Borough in 1704, and will presumably have inherited this property from her former husband whom I have been unable to identify.

APPENDIX Money and Taxes

The Value of Money

We of the older generation frequently bewail the fact that money today is not worth what it used to be. My mother used to say the same to me, and I've no doubt whatsoever that she too heard it from her parents! In my younger days a hundred pounds was a lot of money, and a thousand a small fortune. Friends of mine bought a large, solid terraced house for £400! At the same time wages were also a lot smaller. At nineteen I was bringing home nearly ten pounds a week which was considered to be quite good money for a young chap of my age.

This highlights one of the main difficulties in appreciating the lives of our ancestors who lived hundreds of years ago. Even by the standards of my youth wages and the value placed upon goods is, taken at face value, ridiculously small, nor can we simply and conveniently use a single multiple to bring everything up to modern equivalents for the comparative value of some goods has changed so much. Take, for example, a chicken. A probate inventory of 1705 values two hens at 6d. which was the equivalent of a day's wage for a farm labourer! Chickens were kept for their eggs, and the only ones that normally found their way onto the food table were the tough old 'broilers' that were too old to lay. Back in my youth the only time we ate chicken was on Xmas Day. Turkey? That was only for rich people! At the same time we enjoyed a joint of lamb or beef most Sundays, as this was comparatively cheap.

As improvements in farming together with the introduction of the fridge and the freezer has turned the comparative value of our foodstuffs on its head, so too the industrial revolution and mass production has made manufactured goods considerably cheaper. In 1753 a French ship called *Le Vainqueur* was wrecked at Sker Point, and a witness to the subsequent pillaging of the vessel and its cargo was amazed to note that people were burning parts of the wreck to recover nails and bolts. When Henry Savours was carrying out repairs to Llanmihangel Fulling Mill in 1706 he was buying nails at the rate of fifteen for a penny. Again taking a farm labourer's wage as a standard, the latter would have to work half a day to buy just forty-five! The reason was, of course, that each nail would have been handmade by the local blacksmith. Savours, in fact, considered it money well spent to pay a man eight pence to recover and straighten nails from those parts of the building that were being demolished. The humble nail was therefore a valuable commodity, and those from the hull of *Le Vainqueur* even more so since they would have been made from copper which resisted corrosion far better than iron.

Furniture was also comparatively expensive. There are very few examples in Kenfig probate inventories where the value of such items are listed individually as normally they are all lumped together under the general heading of "household stuff". At Horgrove in 1665 however, the chairs in the home of a fairly prosperous local farmer are valued at a shilling each, and a "dining suite" consisting of table, chair and two stools in a labourer's cottage at Stormy in 1696 was worth 4s. 3d. These were 'second hand' prices, and in the case of the latter would have certainly been the 'bog standard' home-made article.

Craftsmen such as masons and carpenters employed on the same basis normally earned about a shilling a day, whilst the daily wage of sixpence for that of an agricultural labourer is a useful standard to gauge prices applied to items of this period. But it is still not a true reflection of the real value of earnings. These were 'day labourers' who took employment as and when they could get it. This was normally when local farms required extra temporary labour at times such as harvest or sheep-shearing. At other times, the labourer may have been able to find work assisting a craftsman engaged in repair or construction work or trimming hedges, repairing roads and suchlike. By its very nature therefore, his income would have been irregular and all wages carefully hoarded against an uncertain future. Consequently many contrived to acquire a small plot of land upon which to work during slack periods and raise food for their family. Labourers who were burgesses were in a slightly better position in that they could utilise their right as commoners to graze a cow and perhaps a few sheep

Larger farms in the district employed 'live-in' labourers employed on a yearly basis. A poll tax return (PM 5140) for the manor of Higher Kenfig in 1689 shows that their wages here were paid at £1. 6s. 0d. per annum for women, and between £2. 1s. 0d. and £.2 16s. 0d. for men. In addition their board and lodgings were all-found, and their working clothes were also usually provided. Their wage was therefore virtually pocket money. A 'day labourer' would have to work for 81 days to earn the equivalent of the lowest paid man, and still had to find rent for his cottage and food for his table.

Not listed on the tax return are the live-in labourers who actually received no wage but worked just for their keep. These were children, often as young as seven or eight years old, indentured to the farmer until the age of 21. Generally they came from large and poor families, often related to the farmer and his wife. It was an arrangement that usually seems to have worked quite well. The children were normally better fed and clothed than they would have been at home, and learnt various farming and household skills that would enable them to readily find employment once their apprenticeship was completed.

At the same time, human nature being what it is, there were often abuses and eventually the conscience of the nation was sufficiently moved by some of the more glaring examples so the practice was abolished. The evidence of abuses practised on these indentured labourers advanced during this period of agitation for its abolition has led to the practice being roundly condemned by historians, but in so doing they have, I feel, rather missed the point. Those seeking that it be removed advanced only the worst examples to support their case and made little or no mention of those where such child workers were properly cared for and perhaps even loved. I have come across several examples in local wills where the farmer made small bequests of money, a sheep, or a heifer to an indentured worker which surely shows that there was another side to the coin.

Rates & Taxes

Now on the face of it you may have thought that being an Aletaster was one of the plum jobs in the Borough of Kenfig. As their title implies those who held the office could turn up at one of the local hostelries and demand a pint of the Landlord's 'best'. Once served he would carefully pour the contents of the glass into a tankard supplied by the Corporation for the purpose to check that what was being served was indeed exactly one pint of the precious liquid. Then, of course, he tasted it to ensure that the ale was sufficiently good quality to be sold at Kenfig. The Borough possessed measures of various sizes to which those served by their publicans had to conform, and of course every and any alcoholic beverage they supplied had to be tested to ensure that it was good and wholesome. Quite a pleasant afternoon's work!

It was this aspect of the Aletaster's duties that gave rise to their name, but there were other duties that actually made this an office most burgesses sought to avoid! This is clearly apparent in the 18th century minute books where the office, together with the equally unpopular one of Constable, was one normally given to new burgesses as soon as possible after admission. Those who belonged to the petty gentry and wealthier farmers usually contrived to avoid their twelvemonth employed on these duties altogether!

The less attractive side of being an Aletaster was that their visits to alehouses was only one aspect of their duties as 'Weights & Measures' officers. Like the Constable therefore they were Law Enforcement officers, never the most popular members of even the most civilised societies! Furthermore the Aletasters had the added stigma that they were also the Borough's rate and tax collectors for Kenfig Lower!

Rates and Taxes enters my narrative at this point because the earliest taxation returns for both the higher and the lower borough date from the latter part of the 17th century, and are extremely helpful aids to the local historian. Details of local rates and suchlike only come to light in the following century, but this seems a good place to deal with both.

Kenfig Borough was a unit of local government. Locally and nationally this was based upon the shires each of which was subdivided into Hundreds (originally a group of a hundred homesteads). Both Higher Kenfig and the lower borough lay within the Hundred of Newcastle which in turn was subdivided into parishes. Here the two elements of the borough diverged since the first lay in the parish of Margam, and the latter in the parish of Pyle and Kenfig. Both were large parishes, so there was a further sub-division in which the 'hamlets' of Kenfig Higher and Lower were basic units within the overall administration.

When Parliament imposed a national tax these basic units were responsible for the actual collection and despatching their ac-

counts with the proceeds of the collection to the Hundred. From here these were transmitted onwards to Cardiff as the County town, and thence to London. At each unit responsibility for the actual collection rested with an 'assessor' and the 'collectors'. The first worked out who was to pay what; the latter went out and got it! At Kenfig we know from scattered references in the minute books that although overall responsibility would have rested with the Portreeve; the actual work was carried out by the Sergeant-at-Mace and the two Aletasters.

It is a fair bet that when in the early 1990s the British Government re-introduced the **Poll Tax** to replace the Council Rates they never consulted a historian, or if they did then they certainly did not listen to what he had to say! There had been three previous attempts to collect such a tax, one in the 14th century; another in 1641; and the third when it was re-introduced on the restoration of the monarchy in 1660. All three failed, and for the same reason as did our later venture. Even with the availability of the latest electronic gadgetry and computers it proved impossible to collect because it is very difficult to hit a moving target! It is an easy matter for people to avoid a monolithic system swathed in bureaucracy and red tape, and when they do it in large numbers, even tried and trusted methods designed to ensure enforcement become hopelessly bogged down.

Between 1660 and 1697 the tax was levied on eight occasions after which the government realised it was on a loser and gave up. Such widespread tax evasion also means that as an indication of population Poll Tax returns themselves are of little value. During the course of my project on Stormy and Horgrove, where I was able to check these returns against other information, I discovered (rather to my surprise) that an assessment made of Tythegston Higher in 1689 was apparently accurate in respect of my chosen area. Because of the lack of corroborative material at Kenfig I cannot say that this was the case there, but a comparison of the 1689 figures with those for a collection made in 1694 does show how unreliable a source these returns are. In 1689, 75 people in Kenfig Lower were listed for tax, with a further ten shown as paupers and too poor to pay it. The comparable figures for Higher Kenfig are 30 paying tax and five exempt through poverty. Five years later the return lists 46 people for tax in the lower borough and just 19 in Higher Kenfig. From a total of 105 taxpayers (which may actually have been very near the true number) the figure had slumped to an unbelievable low of 64!

Although therefore, the Poll Tax returns are of value for plotting the survival and continuation of individuals and families within local society, they are otherwise of limited value. The tax was only levied on persons aged 14 or over, and the term 'day labourers' can be misleading. These were casual workers taking work as and where they could get it, but included craftsmen as well as unskilled manual workers. For Kenfig we have the ones for 1689 and 1694, and also one for 1702, though my 'book of knowledge' appears to indicate that they had been discontinued by then! (Hey, 1996)

In an effort to improve their income the government attempted various means to combat the widespread evasion of the Poll Tax. One such, **The Hearth Tax**, was introduced in 1662 in the belief that it would be easy "to tell the number of hearths, which remove not as heads or polls do". Perhaps for this reason it proved highly unpopular and was discontinued in 1688. Although (taxwise) it was an improvement on the Poll Tax, the surviving returns are not completely accurate in that they merely indicate the number of hearths an individual was liable for and do not always include a list of those exempted by poverty. In the case of some people taxed on several hearths therefore one is never sure whether the figure relates just to those in their home or includes hearths in other cottages they also owned.

Two such returns survive in respect of Kenfig, but the second of these (1673) does not break the return down below parish level. The other, made three years earlier, lists 17 taxpayers in the lower borough with a further eight exempted, in respect of a total of 32 hearths. The Higher Kenfig return lists just ten people for 17 hearths, but the exemptions are not shown.

In 1697, with the Poll Tax still proving unsatisfactory, the government introduced a **Window Tax** which continued to be collected from time to time until 1851. Every house was taxed at a rate of two shillings, and those with more than 10 windows at six shillings. There were again exemptions for those too poor to pay the tax. Returns for the Lower Borough survive from 1699 (23 households) and 1700 (21 households), but no exemptions are included. Only Lewis and Lazarus Aylward were assessed at the six shilling rate, and John Thomas is listed for ten shillings which presumably included the higher rate for his home at Marlas Farm with two other payments for lesser properties.

These Government experiments finally resulted in the **Land Tax** first introduced in 1693 and only abolished 270 years later. Unfortunately the various returns are perhaps even less informative than those listed above. Following an amendment made in 1698 each county was given a set amount to raise through the tax, and in turn set its own quotas for the Hundreds. This continued down to the basic level, and assessment was made according to the estimated value of a property rather than its actual acreage. Ten acres of pasture "infested by the sands" was, for example assessed far lower than an equal amount of prime arable. The amounts shown against the names

of the occupants of properties are therefore no indication of the extent of their holding.

What I think we can take from these various returns is that within Higher Kenfig there were about ten major farmhouses with an uncertain number of cottages for labourers and farm workers. In Kenfig Lower the position is rather more complicated since many who lived here were craftsmen and labourers who owned and farmed smallholdings. The wealthier of these would have been included on these returns alongside the principal farmers, and the Hearth Tax (1670) suggests this number was as low as 17. The return for windows in 1699 puts it as high was 23 plus a further two for which John Thomas of Marlas was liable.

The above were taxes collected locally but paid to central government, but in addition there were the local taxes or rates. The **Poor Rate** was levied at parish level and was brought into being by Acts of Parliament made in 1597 and 1601 whereby Overseers of the Poor were appointed annually by the Parish Vestry and empowered to raise revenue for the relief of the poor of the parish. He normally served for just one year, and the office was unpaid, but nevertheless seems to have been accounted something of an honour.

It was also a very difficult task, on the one hand attempting to give sufficient assistance to those in need whilst all the time aware that his fellow parishioners were monitoring his every move to ensure that the Poor Rate he set was not hurting their own pockets too much! He needed to be constantly on the lookout for malingerers attempting to milk the system (some things never change in history!) as well as those who were genuine enough but had no claim on his parish since their origins (and hence their right to claim relief) lay elsewhere. In many instances these latter cases were only determined by the rival parishes after hearings at the County Quarter Sessions Court.

Like the Overseer of the Poor the Overseer of the Highways was a creation of the Elizabethan period (by virtue of an Act of 1555) and despite his grand title he also received no payment for his term of office. His principal task was to ensure that the main highways in his parish were kept in good repair, and although empowered to levy a **Highways Rate** upon the inhabitants for this purpose he mainly relied upon labour raised from amongst the inhabitants themselves. Under the terms of the Act every parishioner was expected to perform six days labour per year free of charge, and failure to perform this duty made them liable to a fine. As an added incentive the names of those who defaulted in their duty would be read out from the pulpit of the local church at Sunday service.

I have always felt that, human nature being what it is, this latter provision was rather self-defeating! One cannot imagine many of the more prosperous petty gentry sullying their hands filling in pot-holes on the local highways in all weathers, so they must simply have paid the fine and heard their 'offence' duly proclaimed. With one or two exceptions therefore the Sunday proclamations must have been something of a 'Who's Who' of local parishioners and anybody who had pretensions to a certain status in local society would have made darned sure their name was on it!

Information about the manner in which the Poor Rate and Highways Rate was imposed within Kenfig Borough is rather sketchy. With regards to the Poor Rate it seems that the inhabitants and burgesses of Higher Kenfig came under the umbrella of Margam parish. Those of Kenfig Lower however had their own vestry based upon the church at Mawdlam even though (in ecclesiastical terms) this was only a chapel-of-ease, and therefore subordinate to, the one at Pyle. A similar arrangement also seems to have covered the maintenance of the highways with Higher Kenfig being considered part of Margam and the Lower Borough having its own Overseer and organisation separate from that of the parish.

In addition to the above, Burgesses paid a **Borough Rate** which went towards such things as paying for the upkeep of their Town Hall, the salary of the Hayward etc. In truth we know very little about it, even how much each individual paid. Presumably their payments were graduated in some form like those for the Poor Rate where the yardstick was the annual rent due upon their holdings or (in the case of freeholders) the rent that could reasonably be demanded. The rate was then set at so much per pound rent.

As is mentioned elsewhere in this history once the Borough Rate had been collected the Portreeve paid a fixed sum of £2. 10s 0d. into the Treasury and pocketed the remainder which (or so the records infer) was probably a larger amount.

Nobody likes having to pay either rates or taxes but in the past the payment of **Tithes** was even more unpopular still. They were essentially a payment towards the provision of ecclesiastical facilities for the parish — a church to worship in; a priest to minister to its spiritual needs. A 'tithe' was a tenth of the increase of every living thing. A tenth of the yield of the crops in the field; or a tenth of the young born to all domestic livestock.

No doubt there had been grumbles about paying it even during the medieval period when (notionally at least) everyone was a member of the Roman Catholic Church. When Henry VIII broke with Rome, it was paid to the 'official' state church, which under his daughter Elizabeth became the Anglican religion. Tithes nevertheless continued to be demanded from residents whether they were dissenters or recusants, and as religious toleration gradually improved, so did their dissatisfaction

at having to pay towards the upkeep of a sect they neither supported nor agreed with.

Nor could it be said that tithes were imposed equally upon those who used the ecclesiastic facilities they provided. Whilst they were demanded from anyone with a few acres of land and a few head of sheep or pigs a shopkeeper or craftsman, however wealthy, provided he did not dabble in agriculture paid nothing. Payment as I have already said, was due only upon "the increase of every living thing".

Even many Anglicans were therefore unhappy with the system. Although technically the tithes were collected by the local parson, in many parishes (and Pyle & Kenfig was a case in point) collection was undertaken by a local landowner who, having sold the produce then used the proceeds towards meeting its spiritual needs. It was an agreement that was honoured in the breach rather than in the performance.

When the Mansels of Margam eventually acquired control of the tithes of Pyle and Kenfig they normally leased out the collection to local individuals together with the tithe barn (Scibor Degwm) on Heol Las and some adjoining fields. Until the very end of the 18th century however there is no record of there ever having been a parish priest. Instead the religious needs of the parishioners were supplied by the Vicar of Margam and his curate or curates.

The burgesses of Higher Kenfig were in rather a similar position. Their land lay in the parish of Margam where, in theory, all land was tithe-free, since the monks to whom it had originally belonged had been exempted from paying tithe by Papal Decree. When the Mansels acquired the property following the dissolution of the monastery they had also taken responsibility for providing for the spiritual needs of the inhabitants. They therefore imposed their own tithes on the inhabitants and collected them virtually as part of the rent!

Principal Sources & Abbreviations

Documentary Material

B/K	Borough of Kenfig MSS (Glamorgan Record Office, Cardiff)
B/K ALE	Kenfig Borough Minute Book 1817-1852. When seen by the author this was in private hands, but has now been deposited with Glamorgan Record Office, Cardiff (current reference not known)
BTT	Bishop's Transcripts, Tythegston Parish (National Library of Wales)
Bute MSS	Bute MSS (National Library of Wales)
CL Deeds	Cardiff Central Library MSS Collection
D/D Ty	Tythegston Estate MSS (Glamorgan Record Office, Cardiff)
Jones, David	David Jones of Wallington MSS (Cardiff Central Library)
Llandaff Wills	Llandaff Diocese MSS (National Library of Wales
PM	Penrice & Margam MSS (National Library of Wales)
PPR	Pyle & Kenfig Parish Registers (photocopy) (Glamorgan Record Office, Swansea)
PRO	Public Records Office, Kew (Formerly Chancery Lane, London)
Tithe Map	Tithe Map & Apportionment for Parish of Pyle & Kenfig, 1846 (Photocopy) (Bridgend Library)

Published Material

Whilst not a comprehensive list of the various publications consulted in the preparation of this history, the following are the ones that I seem to have consulted most concerning various aspects of Kenfig's past.

Birch, Walter De Gray (1897) *A history of Margam Abbey : derived from the origi nal documents in the British Museum, H.M. Record Office, the Margam muniments, etc* London, Bedford Press. Available at http://openlibrary.org/books/OL7235581M/A_history_of_Margam_Abbey

Clark, George Thomas (1910) *Cartae et Alia Munimenta quae ad Dominium de Glamorgan pertinent* 6 vols. Cardiff, William Lewis

Evans, A Leslie (1956) *Sker House;* Port Talbot (re-published 2008, with additional material relating to the restoration, Port Talbot Historical Society)

Evans, A Leslie (1964) *The Story of Kenfig;* Port Talbot

Glamorgan County History – see Williams, Glanmor

Granville, N, (1992) The Last Earl of Leicester, *Morgannwg* Vol XXXVI

Gray, Thomas (1909) *The Buried City of Kenfig;* London, T Fisher Unwin

Griffiths, Barrie (1990) *Sturmi's Land* Unpublished MSS available at Bridgend County Libraries.

Griffiths, Barrie (1996-1998) *Medieval Kenfig*, Parts I – V; The Kenfig Society

Griffiths, Barrie (2002) *The Five Mills of Kenfig*; The Kenfig Society

Griffiths, B & Lyons, J (1996) *Llyfnwy's History of Kenfig*; The Kenfig Society

Hay, David (ed.) (1996) *The Oxford companion to local and family history* London B C A

Higgins, L S (1968) *Newton Nottage and Porthcawl-from prehistoric times to 1950* Llandysul, Gomerian Press

Jones, D R L (1994) *Vicars of Llangynwyd* The Parochial Church Council of the Parish of Llangynwyd with Maesteg.

Lever, Tresham (1967) The Herberts of Wilton **London, John Murray**

Martin, Joanna (1981) Landed Estates in Glamorgan c.1660-1760, *Glamorgan Historian* Vol XII

Merrick, Rice (1578) *Morganiae Archaiographia (A Booke of Glamorganshire's An tiquities)*, Re-published 1983 by The South Wales Record Society, Barry Island (Brian Ll. James ed.)

Meyer A E (1915) *England and the Catholic Church under Queen Elizabeth* London, Kegan Paul.

Millward, Rosemary *A Glossary of Household and Farming Terms from 16th Cen tury Probate Inventories,* (Derbyshire Record Society), 1977

Mingay, G E (1977) *Agricultural Revolution: Changes in Agriculture, 1650-1880 (Documents in economic history)* A & C Black

Pugh, Frank H (1954), *Returns from Glamorgan Gaol Files and Glamorgan Sessions Calendar Rolls,1576-1602,* South Wales & Monmouth Record Society Publications No.3, pp 52-61

Riden, Philip (ed.) (1985) *Glamorgan Wills Proved in the Prerogative Court of Can terbury 1392-1571; An Interim Calendar.* 1985

RCAHMW (Royal Commission on Historical & Ancient Monuments Wales) *Glamorgan Vol IV; Part 1; The Greater Houses* (HMSO), 1981

RCAHMW, (Royal Commission on Historical & Ancient Monuments Wales) *Glamorgan Vol IV; Part 2; Farmhouses & Cottages* (HMSO), 1988

Rees, Thomas (1861) *History of Protestant Nonconformity in Wales* (John Snow),

Spencer, Marriane R *Annals of South Glamorgan* (1913) Reprint by Stewart Wil liams (1970

Williams, Glanmor (ed) (1974) *Glamorgan county history. vol. 4, Early modern Glamorgan ; from the Act of Union to the Industrial Revolution* Cardiff; Glamorgan County History Trust : Distributed by University of Wales Press

Family Historians

I am also extremely grateful to the following family historians that have kindly shared with me the results of their own research culled from family bibles and the memories of other family members.

Allan Bleddyn,
 Aberavon
Chris Ensor,
 Cheltenham
Jean Evans,
 Cowbridge
Anne James,
 Cardiff
Brian Ll James,
 Cardiff
Sharon Janousek,
 Vancouver, Canada
Chris Jenkins,
 Maesteg
Averil Jones,
 Bridgend
Caryl Jones,
 Brynamman
Howard & Sonia Lewis,
 Pontardawe

John Lyons,
 Narberth
Lynne Miller,
 USA
Mrs Terry Robbins,
 Porthcawl
Phillip Thomas,
 Cardiff
Margaret Williams,
 Neath
David Yorath,
 Laugharne
Mark Yorwerth-Middleton

INDEX

Over the years the Kenfig Society has published many booklets on the History and People of Kenfig including:

1994	Yvonne Carr	Shipwrecks around and about Kenfig (available as a re-print)
1999	Barrie Griffiths	A Spy for Wellington Sir John William Waters 1774 - 1842. (available as a re-print)
2000	Barrie Griffiths	The House at Sker Point (1e) 2002 (2e)
2001	Barrie Griffiths	The Inn at Pyle (available as a re-print)
2002	Barrie Griffiths	Welcome to Kenfig (in print)
2002	Terry Robbins	Digging Up Kenfig (in print)
2004	Dennis Jones	What the papers said Vol 7 Jan-Dec 1881 (in print)
2005	Barrie Griffiths	Once Upon a Time in Kenfig (in print)
2005	Dennis Jones	What the paper's said Vol 8 Jan-Dec 1882 (in print)
2007	Barrie Griffiths	Time Trekker (in print)
2008	John Blundell	From Kenfig to Ogmore: A personal history of the coast (available as a re-print)

For more details log on to our website:

www.kenfigsociety.org

ALSO BY BARRIE GRIFFITHS:

KENFIG FOLK PART I:
The FIRST BOROUGH of KENFIG
1147-1439

"..the topography of Kenfig is at the heart of the book and it is here that the author comes into his own. He proves himself to be an indefatigable researcher combining documentary sources - particularly the Margam Abbey charters published by Birch - and field archaeology. Indeed, the reader is left with the impression that every square inch of the local landscape has been tramped in the writer's cause. The results are presented with characteristic enthusiasm.

"The abiding value of this book is in its account of the abandonment of the 'old' town. This, the final chapter, shows the author at his best, telling with dramatic detail how the advancing sands constantly troubled the town's inhabitants and how they were unable to bring themselves to take the counteractive measures that would put an end to their livestock grazing.

"This attractive book is rounded off with a bibliography and a very useful index. It will be of value to anyone interested in the towns of Glamorgan, and as a topographical study is exemplary. The Kenfig Society has done Barrie Griffiths proud." (from the review by Tony Hopkins in *Morgannwg LV*, 2011)

Published May 2011. Available from the Kenfig Society

Still to come: Available in later in 2013, or early 2014.

KENFIG FOLK PART III:

This will take the story of Kenfig on into the 1700's when the very survival of the Borough looked unlikely, and constant disputes broke out with the local great landowners, the Mansels and the Talbots.